CHRIST THE MIRACLE WORKER IN EARLY CHRISTIAN ART

CHRIST THE MIRACLE WORKER IN EARLY CHRISTIAN ART

LEE M. JEFFERSON

Fortress Press
Minneapolis

CHRIST THE MIRACLE WORKER IN EARLY CHRISTIAN ART

Scripture quotations are from the New Revised Standard Version Bible, copyright © 1989 by the Division of Christian Education of the National Council of the Churches of Christ in the USA. Used by permission. All rights reserved.

Cover image: Vanni / Art Resource, NY

Cover design: Tory Herman

Library of Congress Cataloging-in-Publication Data

Jefferson, Lee M.

Christ the miracle worker in early Christian art / Lee Jefferson.

pages cm

Includes bibliographical references.

ISBN 978-1-4514-7793-1 (pbk. : alk. paper) — ISBN 978-1-4514-7984-3 (ebook)

1. Jesus Christ–Art. 2. Art, Early Christian–Themes, motives. 3. Jesus Christ–Miracles. I. Title.

N8051.J44 2014

700′.48232–dc23

2013034859

Manufactured in the U.S.A.

This book was produced using PressBooks.com, and PDF rendering was done by PrinceXML.

CONTENTS

Acknowledgements

This work would not have been possible without the support of many important people and institutions. The Graduate Department of Religion at Vanderbilt University and the administration of Centre College helped fund some of the research included in this study. Umberto Utro at the Vatican Museum was incredibly helpful in examining much of the primary evidence included in this volume. Amy Hirschfeld at the International Catacomb Society was also quite helpful in procuring images. I am especially indebted to J. Patout Burns, Barbara Tsakirgis, Bronwen Wickkiser, William Babcock, Annemarie Carr, and Ljubica Popovich. My colleagues at Centre College—namely, Tom McCollough, Beth Glazier-McDonald, David Hall, and Rick Axtell—were continually supportive of my work that is produced here.

I would like to especially thank my friend and mentor Robin M. Jensen. She has been a gracious instructor, editor, and guide since I was a novice in the field. She taught me the importance and benefit of examining the era of Late Antiquity through the lens of art and imagery. My sincere hope is to follow in her creative and pioneering footsteps. I would also like to thank Todd Green, who read through several parts of this book and whose friendship and advice I highly value. I am very indebted to Catherine Davis, Mike Gibson, Lisa Gruenisen, and the entire team at Fortress Press, who have been continually impressive with their help and guidance. Buran C. Phillips and Anna L. Ellis of Centre College compiled the index, helping this project in the final stages.

Finally, this endeavor could not have been possible without the support of my family, my children Grey and Ethan, and my wife, Leigh. Leigh was unfaltering in her encouragement and support, even when I wavered.

Abbreviations

ACW	Ancient Christian Writers
ANF	*Ante-Nicene Fathers*
ANRW	*Aufstieg und Niedergang der römischen Welt*
BAR	*Biblical Archaeology Review*
CCSL	Corpus Christianorum latinorum
CH	*Church History*
CSEL	Corpus scriptorum ecclesiasticorum latinorum
DOP	*Dumbarton Oaks Papers*
FC	Fathers of the Church
HTR	*Harvard Theological Review*
JAC	Jahrbuch für Antike und Christentum
JBL	*Journal of Biblical Literature*
JECS	*Journal of Early Christian Studies*
JEH	*Journal of Ecclesiastical History*
JJA	*Journal of Jewish Art*
JRS	*Journal of Roman Studies*
JTS	*Journal of Theological Studies*
LCL	Loeb Classical Library
LIMC	*Lexicon iconographicum mythologiae classicae*
NPNF	*Nicene and Post-Nicene Fathers*
PG	Patrologia graeca
PGM	Greek Magical Papyri
PL	Patrologia latina
RivAC	*Rivista di archaeologia cristiana*
SBLSP	Society of Biblical Literature Seminar Papers
SC	Sources chrétiennes
VChr	*Vigiliae christianae*

1

Introduction

Early Christians were drawn to using images in religious settings, revealing a very human desire to include visual aspects in devotional environments. Clement of Alexandria, like other early church authors, discovered in his fellow Christians a pervasive desire to create images, and this desire forced him to police the practice. Clement urged his audience to utilize certain types of symbols, such as doves, ships, and anchors, and to reject images he deemed negative, such as swords or prostitutes.[1] If Christians were going to use images, they should be cautious, and the nascent church should have some element of control over the practice.[2]

What stands out in Clement's text is that, early on, Christians found value in art and imagery. Early Christians were interested in visualizing their faith, with or without the endorsement of the clergy. Clement concedes to the whims of his congregation, after which early Christian art develops speedily, creating symbols such as an anchor or a fish or making images of Jesus. In doing so, early artistic examples of Jesus suggest that early Christians understood how the visual medium could convey deeper theological truths concerning their religion. They realized that art has the power to project difficult concepts while written texts and even sermons have some limitations. Thus, an image of Jesus performing miracles can neatly advertise Christianity while promoting important aspects of the nature of Christ.

The power art wields can be realized in our contemporary world. When I was in graduate school, the topic one day in our church history course was the christological controversies and the writings of Athanasius. *On the Incarnation* was dry material for the novice, and it was quite easy to get frustrated and confused concerning the nature and salvific action of Christ. At one point during the lecture, the instructor projected an image of a wooden icon of Christ

---

1. Clement of Alexandria, *Paedagogus* 3.11 (*ANF* 2.286).

2. Clement is not unaware of the dangers of art; in fact, at parts of his later writings, he is still adamantly against their use. See *Stromateis* 5.5.

1

from the sixth century (Figure 1).[3] He then discussed Athanasius's comparison, in his treatise, of an artistic image to the enduring necessity of Christ

While I had understood the basic comparison Athanasius was making, the deeper, more fundamental theological truth still eluded me until I saw the image. Given that I was in the dark regarding the tradition of early Christian art and iconography, my initial confusion was predictable. With the visual aid in class, Athanasius's reasoning was finally clear. The faded outlines yet lasting color of the portrait of Christ illuminate Athanasius's theology. The use of an early Christian artistic example served to illustrate patristic theology. And as I began to explore the numerous examples of fourth- and fifth-century images of Jesus performing miracles, my understanding of the early church was illuminated and deepened with the help of early Christian art.

For the student and scholar of early Christianity, the benefits of delving into early Christian art are quite tangible. Images from different eras of Christian history elucidate significant developments in the tradition, greatly enhancing the understanding of theological and historical movements. Christian art is a useful and effective medium to shed light on different aspects of Christian history, as students and observers can readily witness how images and architecture created centuries ago are connected to the relevant theological movements in the same period.

When examining the corpus of the earliest Christian art, one is initially entranced with repeated nonnarrative images and symbols, such as an anchor, a fish, or the Good Shepherd, or narrative scenes from Scripture, including figures such as Noah, Jonah, and Daniel. Of course, early Christians also began to create images of Jesus, involving narrative scenes from the gospels or nonnarrative images of Jesus depicted in the guise of rival gods. In early Christian images of Jesus, the images that show Christ performing healings and miracles stand out not only in their sheer number but also in their manner of depiction. For example, Christ healing the paralytic or raising the dead while wielding a wandlike instrument is a vivid and continuously repeated image in the early centuries. This book aims to examine why the theme of Christ performing healings and miracles was so popular for Late Antique Christians and to answer the question, What was the purpose of depicting Jesus as a healer and miracle worker?

Inevitably, careful attention to the chronology of images of Jesus will reveal that the image of Christ performing healings and miracles became ubiquitous in Late Antiquity, especially in the fourth century, and dissipated

---

3. Athanasius, *On the Incarnation* 14.8 (*NPNF* 2.4.44; PG 25, 120C-D).

after the fifth century, nearly disappearing altogether.[4] Scholars have attempted to interpret these images of Christ, concluding that the motif of Christ performing miracles portrayed Jesus as a philosopher or a magician. The pervasiveness of this image of Jesus can be partially explained by a rivalry with Christian opponents. The most reasonable interpretation of the theme's ubiquity addresses the context of the images and cognate texts of the early Christian writers. Early Christian images such as Christ performing miracles touted the superiority of Christ against all rivals in an effort to make Christianity the sole expression of true religion in the realm. Thus, the image of Jesus performing miracles was not isolated but signified a repeated theme for Late Antique Christians: Jesus is the miracle worker par excellence, superior to any rival deity.

The insistent theme of what can be called Christ the Miracle Worker occurred not only in art but in Christian texts as well, and the genres shared a common purpose: to promote the virtues and abilities of Jesus at the expense of competitors to Christianity. In the Synoptic Gospels as well as John's gospel, the miracles of Christ were given prominence. There are over thirty-five references to the healing power of Christ in the four gospels, the most belonging to Matthew. In early Christian texts, Jesus' superior healing ability was so emphasized that the statements reveal that Jesus' status as the greatest healer was disputed.[5] Augustine of Hippo preached that Jesus is "the complete Physician of our wounds" and emphatically stated that Christ "and no other" is the ultimate

4. For example, in G. Bovini and Hugo Brandenburg, *Reportorium der Christlich-Antiken Sarkophage*, Band I, *Rom und Ostia*, ed. F. W. Deichmann (Wiesbaden: F. Steiner, 1967), a catalog of Christian sarcophagi in Rome and Ostia, miracles and healings outnumber images of Christ enthroned in majesty (the *traditio legis*) by a considerable margin. The enthroned images of Christ make up a little more than half of the number of occurrences of Christ healing the blind. Specifically, in the Roman catalog there are over forty examples of the enthroned Jesus to seventy-one occurrences of the healing of the blind. See Deichmann, *Ikonographisches Register für das Repertorium der christlich-antiken Sarkophage* Band I, *Rom und Ostia* (Wiesbaden: F. Steiner, 1967), 122–24. As will be discussed later, the number of scenes of Christ's miracles in catacomb art and relief sculpture makes this theme the predominant one in early Christian art of the third and fourth centuries.

5. See Gerhard Fichtner, "Christus als Arzt: Ursprünge und Wirkungen eines Motivs," *Frühmittelalterliche Studien* 16 (1982): 8. Fichtner believes the early church authors are addressing the competition with Asclepius. As evidence, he cites Ignatius, *Eph.* 7.2; 20.2; Clement, *Exhortation to the Greeks* 2.30.1; Justin, *1 Apol.* 22.6; Tatian, *Address to the Greeks* 8.7; 21.3; Tertullian, *The Crown* 8.2; *Apology* 23.6; Lactantius, *Divine Institutes* 1.15.3; 1.15.23; Arnobius, *Against the Pagans* 1.48-49. See the following pages for more. On p. 8, "The direct confrontation between Asklepios and Christ occurs albeit rarely in the writings of the early church fathers.." He also notes the influence of Philo as well on p. 12: "Philo's influence on the theology of the Greek church fathers should not be underestimated."

healer.[6] These are words that provide comfort and succor but also suggest a degree of competition with other cults.

This book also offers a title for this theme of Jesus performing miracles: "Christ the Miracle Worker." *Christ* is, of course, a designation—a title, not a name. But in the fourth century, early Christians were drafting a Christology for their religion in text and art. Early Christians were interested in the Christ of faith rather than the Jesus of history, so the designation "Christ the Miracle Worker" appears apt.

Largely, the theme of Christ as the definitive healer and miracle worker was utilized to provide comfort for the living, often in a burial context. The images of Christ the Miracle Worker in Late Antiquity appear in a funerary context either in catacomb art or relief sculpture such as sarcophagi frontals. So the evidence that suggests the popularity of this theme is mostly funerary, and the context reveals the mind-set of the early Christian viewer. Christ the Miracle Worker was a handy template to provide consolation to Christians in more ways than one. The theme also reassured Christian audiences of the superiority of Jesus in a pluralistic religious environment and the security of the life beyond. Sermons and polemics were limited in their ability to convey these messages concerning Jesus. Art and imagery provided a medium to express Christ as a supreme miracle worker more vividly and in a more engaging manner than polemics or sermons. An examination into the prevalence of this theme underlines the utility of art as a means of community expresssion. The implementation of the image of Christ as a powerful healer and miracle worker illuminates what Christian life was like in Late Antiquity.

However, Christian art did not appear in the fourth century as fully developed. Early Christians created their visual language by observing and borrowing elements from the world around them. Early Christian art was marked by the commingling of Christian and non-Christian themes that clearly signal the remarkable experimentation that was under way in Christian art of the fourth century. This art was syncretistic, utilizing images, symbols, and themes from the Roman world to create a visual language. Some elements and motifs (such as the *traditio* legis, the giving of the law) during this period became deeply ingrained, while other features fell out of the visual canon (for example, the image of Christ utilizing a staff to perform a miracle largely disappeared after the fifth century).[7] Having examined catacomb paintings at

---

6. Augustine, *Tractates on the Gospel of John* 3.2 (CCSL 36.21; NPNF 1.7.19).

7. Grabar discusses the innovation of early Christian art in *Christian Iconography: A Study of its Origins* (Princeton, NJ: Princeton University Press, 1968). Three articles that discuss enigmatic themes and features reflecting such experimentation are Robin M. Jensen, "The Economy of the Trinity at the

Domitilla or Via Latina, we may conclude that Christian viewers in Rome likely had little difficulty with non-Christian images such as Ceres, Hercules, or even depictions of Christ in the semblance of other gods. Jás Elsner has argued that Christians viewed pagan scenes allegorically, and the audience at Roman catacombs or other funerary environments could recognize Christian themes such as resurrection in non-Christian images such as Hercules rescuing Alcestis from Hades.[8]

In early Christian art, there is a strong corpus of images of Jesus dressed in the guise of competing gods. Christ was represented as Helios in the third-century mosaic of Tomb M in the Vatican necropolis beneath St. Peter's, as Orpheus in the catacombs of Rome, and (if the art historian Thomas Mathews is to be believed) as Jupiter in the mosaic of Sta. Pudeniziana.[9] Such portrayals of Jesus in the guise of a rival god exudes a message of superiority and supersession, and the theme of Christ the Miracle Worker exhibits Jesus subsuming perceived religious threats—a visual "clash of gods," as Mathews so memorably described it.

After viewing the manifold images of Christ performing miracles, one might ask why the Christian populace was so determined to portray Jesus as a miracle worker. In fact, early Christians naturally emphasized the importance of healings and miracles, given the prominence they enjoyed in the Greco-Roman world. Healings and miracles were important in the cultic life of non-Christians, as evident in the cult of Asclepius. The most common evidence of healings and miracles is found in ancient texts. Often the documentation of a successful healing was left at the temples of Asclepius engraved in stone, clay, or wood tablets known as *stelai*, praising the effectiveness of the god's therapeutic power. Healings and miracles were captured in narratives demonstrating some type of divine intervention that can only be described as supernatural. These narratives were cataloged in diverse Greco-Roman works attributed to Diodorus Siculus, Cicero, Pliny the Elder, Aelius Aristides, and Julian the

Creation of Adam and Eve," *JECS* 7, no. 4 (1999): 527–46; Lee M. Jefferson, "The Staff of Jesus in Early Christian Art," *Religion and the Arts* 14, no. 3 (2010): 221–51; and Jefferson, "Superstition and the Significance of the Image of Christ Performing Miracles in Early Christian Art," *Studia Patristica: Proceedings from the Fifteenth International Conference on Patristic Studies*, vol. 44 (Leuven: Peeters, 2010), 15–20.

8. Jás Elsner, *Art and the Roman Viewer* (Cambridge: Cambridge University Press, 1995), 271–72. Elsner continues his discussion of syncretism by using the Hercules Via Latina cycle to suggest the non-Christian influence on Christian visual language. See also his *Imperial Rome and Christian Triumph: The Art of the Roman Empire AD 100–450* (New York: Oxford University Press, 1998).

9. For a Jupiter-Pudenziana discussion, see Thomas Mathews, *The Clash of Gods* (Princeton, NJ: Princeton University Press, 1993), 97–109.

Apostate. They are also found in Jewish and Christian scripture, most notably in the canonical gospels. Recognizing that healings and miracles were not isolated in their importance to early Christianity, one can begin to understand why early Christians were so fascinated with miracles. But by examining the textual emphasis on miracles, one can also understand why early Christians produced so many images of Christ's miracles. The healing and miracle stories of Asclepius and Asclepius iconography can reveal such an understanding of the image of Christ the Miracle Worker. Any interpretation of the art must take into account Christian and non-Christian textual accounts of healings and miracles, the Asclepius cult, and its relevance in Late Antiquity—something not often done in existing approaches to religious studies.

The ubiquity of miracles and miracle imagery in early Christian texts and art has prompted attempts to answer why the theme was so prominent. Yet "miracle stories," Greco-Roman or otherwise, were not thoughtfully considered until the late nineteenth and early twentieth centuries. With the advent of biblical form criticism, scholars such as Martin Dibelius and Rudolf Bultmann began to take notice of the miracle stories. The stories, though, were often dismissed as evidence of Christianizing of pagan narratives and were considered non-Christian material, and thus not relevant for any useful gospel study.[10] Miracle stories narrowly featured Jesus performing tasks as the Miracle Worker, not Jesus the "herald of the Kingdom of God."[11] In any subsequent Christian inquiry, the stories of the miracles of Jesus were intentionally neglected as not containing any real value.[12]

This pattern of interpreting Christian tradition was deeply affected by the seminal work of Adolf von Harnack, one of the first social historians of the early church. One can easily recognize the influence of his *The Mission and Expansion of Christianity in the First Three Centuries* on most church historians and biblical scholars. Harnack argued that early Christians were preoccupied with sickness and intentionally couched their faith as a religion of "salvation or healing."[13] Nonetheless, the study of the miracle stories declined, in part due to Harnack's persuasive theory of the Hellenization of Christianity. Harnack's

---

10. Dibelius labels Jesus' miracle stories with the patronizing label "tales" in his *From Tradition to Gospel*, trans. Bertram Lee Wolf (New York: Scribner, 1965), 70. Also see Rudolf Bultmann, *The History of the Synoptic Tradition*, trans. John Marsh, rev. ed. (New York: Harper and Row, 1968).

11. Dibelius, *From Tradition*, 80.

12. Ibid., 79.

13. Adolf von Harnack, *The Mission and Expansion of Christianity in the First Three Centuries*, trans. and ed. James Moffatt (New York: Harper, 1962), 108. The phrase quoted is emphasized in italics in the original.

position proposed "an almost complete isolation of primitive Christianity from its historical environment."[14] As a result, miracle stories in Christianity were not compared with similar instances in Greco-Roman religion.[15] The miracle stories could not be properly considered without placing them in historical context.[16]

Later scholars consider this move unfortunate and rather too simplistic. Ramsay MacMullen notes that Harnack's work *The Mission and Expansion of Christianity in the First Three Centuries* included thousands of source references but not a single non-Christian source, implying that the Christian mission was created *ex nihilo*. Robert Wilken has recently offered a counterargument to Harnack's established theory that Christianity was thoroughly Hellenized in the first centuries. Instead, Wilken argues that the obverse appears to be true: Hellenism was thoroughly Christianized by the early Christian writers from Origen to John of Damascus.[17] This is not to say that early Christians were *not* influenced by Hellenistic or Jewish writings. Rather, the early Christians were so influenced by them that the culture was transformed by Christianity into something unique.

Wilken's theory obviously applies to early Christian thought. His theory is also applicable to early Christian art. Christians appropriated the artistic corpora that were available to them, including the visual imagery of their non-Christian neighbors. Pagan artistic elements were effectively Christianized. Christ often appears quite like rival gods Jupiter, Dionysius, Sarapis, or Asclepius. Stylistic traits of rival gods such as Jupiter, Sarapis or Asclepius were incorporated into the depictions of Christ, with the intention of characterizing Christ as the most powerful god. Scriptural episodes that involved Christ were featured in early Christian art following 200 CE, and among these, the miracle stories were the most popular.

Still, Harnack planted the seed of inquiry in his analysis of healing and miracle in early Christianity, particularly the question of the similarities between Jesus and rival gods. He cited several ancient sources as evidence of

14. W. G. Kümmel, *The New Testament: The History of Investigation of Its Problems*, trans. S. McLean Gilmour and Howard Clark Kee (London: SCM, 1973), 206.

15. Arguably, Harnack's position weakened his ability to compare the early images of Jesus to Asclepius, as witnessed in the opening quotation. However his position was not primarily concerned with imagery.

16. Howard Clark Kee criticizes Dibelius for this move quite eloquently in his *Medicine, Miracle, and Magic in New Testament Times* (New York: Cambridge University Press, 1986), 76–77.

17. Robert Louis Wilken, *The Spirit of Early Christian Thought* (New Haven, CT: Yale University Press, 2003), xvi–xvii.

this phenomenon, but he claimed that the greatest testimony is found in the popularity of the cult of Asclepius. The god of healing, Asclepius, enjoyed great prominence in Late Antiquity, largely due to the fervent belief that the cult could cure bodily ills and provide comfort. As Christianity began to grow, Christians encountered several non-Christian deities that influenced their perception of Jesus and were conceivable threats. One of these figures was Asclepius, and as a result, Christians further emphasized Christ's abilities as a healer and physician. As I will show, the evidence for the Christ-Asclepius conflict is apparent in the writings of the early church.[18] The early church authors were aware of the Asclepius cult and were hostile to its existence.

Art and imagery of Late Antiquity is an underestimated body of evidence that reflects the dispute with the competing cult of Asclepius. Images of Christ performing healings and miracles were quite abundant in the second, third, and fourth centuries and rapidly proliferated toward the end of this time period.[19] Harnack hints at such a visual competition, or at least an influence, in his landmark text:

> No one has yet been able to show that the figure of Christ which emerges in the fifth century, probably as early as the fourth, and which subsequently became the prevailing type in all pictorial representations, was modeled upon the figure of Asclepius. The two types are certainly similar; the qualities predicated of both are identical in part; and no one has hitherto explained satisfactorily why the original image of the youthful Christ was replaced by the

18. For an alternative view, Thomas Heyne suggests that the case for a Christ-Asclepius conflict stretches the patristic evidence, and that early Christians were neither preoccupied nor interested in physical healing and the Asclepius cult. See Thomas Heyne, "Were Second-Century Christians 'Preoccupied' with Physical Healing and the Asclepian Cult?" *Studia Patristica: Proceedings from the Fifteenth International Conference on Patristic Studies* (Leuven: Peeters, 2010), 44:63–69. Although he focuses on the apostolic fathers, Freyne does not adequately treat the evidence from Justin Martyr that suggests a rivalry with Asclepius.

19. In terms of periodization, "Late Antiquity" is slightly ill defined and is often used as a catchall phrase for the transition from classical antiquity to the Middle Ages. However, for the purposes of this study, it is used throughout to refer to the period of the mid-second century through the fifth century. Even in this usage, it is not a perfect term. It cannot be said that "Late Antiquity" began in the second century, although features of the religious and cultural developments that arose in the fourth century began to appear in the second century. The images central to this book emerge in the fourth century, and while the term Late Antiquity is perhaps overburdened in its usage here, its limitations are noted from the outset of this book. There is much quibbling about when Late Antiquity began. See Peter Brown, *The Making of Late Antiquity* (Cambridge, MA: Harvard University Press, 1978), 1–4; and Brown, *The World of Late Antiquity, AD 150–750* (New York: Harcourt Brace Jovanovich, 1971).

later. Nevertheless, we have no means of deriving the origin of the Callixtine Christ from Asclepius as a prototype, so that in the meantime we must regard such a derivation as a hypothesis, which, however interesting, is based upon inadequate evidence.[20]

Harnack suggests that a parallel between Christ and Asclepius existed. Christians in Late Antiquity were heavily interested in healing. Bishops including Polycarp were instructed to take care of the sick as an embodiment of the ministry of Jesus, and to visit them directly.[footnote]Polycarp, *To the Philippians 6*; Amanda Porterfield, *Healing in the History of Christianity* (New York: Oxford University Press, 2005), 47. Recently, studies have demonstrated the existence of a competition between healing cults such as the cult of Asclepius and Christianity, even asserting as Hector Avalos does that Christianity was a low-cost, less cumbersome health care option than any other cult.[21] Scholars such as Avalos, Amanda Porterfield, and R. J. S. Barrett-Lennard have argued that attention to healing was a major factor in the growth of Christianity.[22] This book will assess the parallel in text and art of Jesus and his healing rival, Asclepius.

The image of Christ the Miracle Worker cultivated a strong sense of self-definition among early Christians. By incorporating elements of prominent healing cults, as well as the influence of magic and miracles in Late Antiquity, the image of Christ the Miracle Worker served as a unifying and supplanting figure. Early Christians selected suitable elements from pagan and Jewish culture and incorporated them for their benefit into narrative and art, and thus provided a Christian understanding to Hellenistic motifs. Just as Robert Wilken argues that early Christians transformed Greco-Roman culture into something new, I contend that the same can be said for early Christian art. The art and

20. Harnack, *Mission and Expansion*, 118–19. The predominant image of Christ that Harnack was referring to was the bearded Christ.

21. See Amanda Porterfield, *Healing in the History of Christianity* (New York: Oxford University Press, 2005), and Erich Dinkler, *Christus und Asklepios* (Heidelberg: Carl Winter, 1980); Hector Avalos, *Health Care and the Rise of Christianity* (Peabody, MA: Hendrickson, 1999), 93; R. J. S. Barrett-Lennard, *Christian Healing after the New Testament: Some Approaches to Illness in the Second, Third and Fourth Centuries* (Lanham, MD: University Press of America, 1994). Avalos's conclusions will be discussed in the following chapter. While the Asclepius cult was not precisely "free," it too offered a low-cost and ubiquitous option to the sick.

22. Also see Morton Kelsey, *Healing and Christianity* (Minneapolis: Fortress Press, 1995); and Evelyn Frost, *Christian Healing* (London: A.R. Mowbray, 1940); also the volumes of Ludwig Edelstein and Emma Edelstein, *Asclepius: A Collection and Interpretation of the Testimonies* (Baltimore: Johns Hopkins Press, 1945).

imagery of Christ the Miracle Worker appropriated artistic elements of Late Antique culture and transformed those elements into representations that were similar to their antecedents, but uniquely Christian.

While Christian art was syncretistic, any blanket claim that all figures in Christian art were derivative is problematic. For example, the images in the Christian catacombs were influenced by Roman prototypes. In the Callistus catacomb and beyond, Endymion became Jonah, a Roman stevedore became the paralytic, Osiris became Lazarus, and a Greco-Roman magus, philosopher, or physician was possibly the prototype for Jesus. The images in the catacomb of Callistus certainly reveal pagan influences, but any conclusions that early Christians were purely imitative are specious. Such an argument is shortsighted without viewing the immediate context of the image under discussion, the accompanying scenes, and the narrative purpose.[23]

Since Christian art borrowed elements from the visual resources available in Late Antiquity, it was up to the viewers to use their belief system to fill the image with meaning.[24] The burden of interpretation was placed upon the viewer. Patrons, sculptors, and viewers were not indifferent as to how their subjects were depicted in imagery. Images that contain features such as Jonah's resemblance to Endymion and the appearance of Hercules and Orpheus in the catacombs can be explained: Christians were influenced by the pagan imagery surrounding them. Christian patrons ordered a specific image, and sculptors crafted it using the accustomed mode of depiction, which is the resulting appearance of early Christian images.[25] Without adequate evidence detailing the intent of the artist, it is impossible to determine the exact authorial intentions for these early images of Christ. However, with the multiple examples of Christ performing healings and miracles, it is easier and perhaps more illuminating to assess how viewers responded to these artworks. And in the absence of any reliable reports gauging audience reaction of these images, the best possible measure of an early Christian response can be gleaned from patristic texts. The early Christian viewers understood Christ as a healer and

---

23. P. C. Finney, *The Invisible God: The Earliest Christians on Art* (New York: Oxford University Press, 1994), 186. To be clear, Finney believes that the early Christians were creating something unique; however, his statements regarding image prototypes can be misinterpreted. Finney defends the early dating of Callistus convincingly, although this dating should still be considered uncertain.

24. This is the view of Jás Elsner, *Imperial Rome and Christian Triumph*, 153, and more recently, James Francis in his paper "Biblical Not Scriptural: Perspectives on Early Christian Art from Contemporary Classical Scholarship," *Studia Patristica: Proceedings from the Fifteenth International Conference on Patristic Studies*, vol. 44 (Leuven: Peeters, 2010), 3–8.

25. See Elsner, *Imperial Rome and Christian Triumph*, 153ff.

miracle worker, greater than any other in an environment that included more than a few.

The images of a miracle-working Christ under discussion did not appear *ex nihilo*. The images of Christ healing and performing miracles were similar to images of heroes and Olympian gods, but they were created in a context of antagonism between Christians and pagans. Christians likely received the images of a miracle-working Christ with the echo of invectives from Christian leaders in the background.[26] A Christian observing an image of Christ in the act of healing may be reminded of the perils of entering a temple of the cult of Asclepius. The healing Christ cured one's body and soul, while going into the Asclepieion for a remedy put one's soul in peril. Moreover, these images largely occurred in a funerary environment, reminding observers of the future resurrection and life through Christ. Early images of Christ provided a sense of understanding and identity to early Christians. Viewers could witness their chosen healer and miracle worker as greater than any rival, for not only was Christ's brief tenure as an earthly healer efficacious, he continually provided for the future life.

By the late fourth century, the image of Christ healing and performing miracles had not only persisted but increased. In a post-Constantinian age, when Christians were more or less secure from persecution, the image of Christ the Miracle Worker was more popular than in the earlier age of Christian persecution. This fact challenges the long-held understanding of twentieth-century art historians who argue that post-Constantinian art largely reflected the imperial cult by featuring an enthroned Jesus. Post-Constantinian Christians were secure from persecution but not from illness, and the data this book offers reveal a greater interest in healing and miracle-working imagery. The influence of the imperial cult upon early Christianity, including its impact on Christian art, has been well established in twentieth-century scholarship by figures such as Ernst Kitzinger, André Grabar, and Hans Belting.[27] Arguing from the perspective of imperial worship, these scholars suggested that Christian

---

26. For example, consider Tertullian's attack against Christians attending the games or partaking in pagan festivals in *On the Shows* 13, ordering them to keep their gullets free from any contagion of idol food, (Translated by T. R. Glover. Loeb Classical Library. Cambridge, MA, 1931. Also see Minucius Felix, *Octavius* 38.1. More recently, see Daniel Boyarin, *Borderlines: The Partition of Judaeo-Christianity* (Philadelphia: University of Pennsylvania Press, 2004).

27. André Grabar, *The Beginnings of Christian Art, 200–395* (London: Thames and Hudson, 1966); also see Ernst Kitzinger, "The Cult of Images before Iconoclasm," in *Dumbarton Oaks Papers*, no. 8 (1954), 89; Hans Belting, *Likeness and Presence: A History of the Image before the Era of Art* (Chicago: University of Chicago Press, 1994), 106.

images involving Jesus radically shifted following Constantine. Images of Jesus as the Good Shepherd or as a benevolent philosopher or miracle man evolved into an image of an enthroned king, mirroring the emperor. Mathews notably challenged this position in his work *The Clash of Gods*, calling the imperial argument the "Emperor Mystique." While Mathews is not totally wrong, nor completely right, his work claims that fourth- and fifth-century images of Jesus need to be reevaluated without resorting to a myopic focus related to imperial worship that creates a visual "game of thrones."[28] That reevaluation is the driving purpose of this book.

Miracle imagery likely proliferated in post-Constantinian Christianity partially because church leaders did not desire their congregations be fractured in their observance. Sermons and treatises of early Christian figures such as Ambrose and Augustine reveal the utility of preaching Christ as the supreme physician and miracle worker. Congregants were likely tempted to participate in myriad pagan festivals and rituals that included the healing cult. To curtail what may have been a losing battle, church leaders preached sermons of Christ the physician and miracle worker, reminding their hearers of the ultimate Christian "healing" in baptism, the perils of idolatry, and the final resurrection made apparent by the miracle-working Christ. The homiletic theme of Christ the Miracle Worker corresponds to the popularity of the visual image; they both send their audiences a similar message of Christian superiority.

In an era when Christ had less threatening opponents, the image of Christ performing healings and miracles was used by early Christians to promote a distinct and powerful image of Jesus to the ears and the eyes of the populace. This study will focus on the rise and eventual predominance of the image of Christ the Miracle Worker in the early Christian era, examine the contributions of early Christian writers, and demonstrate that this early Christian image appropriated elements of various religious traditions. These traditions included the healing cult of Asclepius as well as the person of Moses in order to create an unrivaled religious figure, a supreme god.

OVERVIEW OF THE BOOK

Much of this book treats the art of Christ the Miracle Worker. But the initial chapters assess the textual references to miracles and healings in order to lay an adequate foundation for the discussion of the art and imagery. The initial chapter examines the role of healing and miracles in non-Christian sources.

---

28. For example, I contend with Mathews' interpretation of the wand of Jesus as a mark of a magician. See my "The Staff of Jesus in Early Christian Art," *Religion and the Arts* 14, no. 3 (2010): 221–51.

After providing some background on physicians and magicians in Late Antiquity, it assesses primary evidence of the role of healing and miracles, beginning with Celsus. This is followed by a treatment of magic and a discussion of Apollonius of Tyana, a figure whose hagiography promoted him as a Christ-like being.

The second chapter assesses the Christian references to miracles and healings, focusing on the early Christian writers of the second and third centuries, such as Justin, Clement, and Origen. It also treats the mentions of miracles and healings in fourth- and fifth-century authors such as Ambrose and Augustine. In early Christian texts, one can witness a keen interest in promoting Jesus as not only a healer, but the preeminent healer, hinting at a competition with healing cults like the cult of Asclepius.[29] Furthermore, early Christians cite the title of Christ the Physician consistently in their polemics. In Greek and Latin authors such as Arnobius of Sicca, the message is clear: earthly physicians and the healing gods rely on terrestrial means to procure healings, while Christ relies only on his divine power to effect cures. Christ heals with his physical presence through touch and voice, and does not prescribe treatments, potions, or medicines to administer healings, as in the cult of Asclepius.

The subsequent chapters treat the theme of Christ the Miracle Worker in early Christian art, beginning with images of Christ performing specific healings that are mentioned in the gospels: the healing of the paralytic, the woman with the issue of blood, and the healing of the blind. The image of Christ performing healings and miracles conveys the theme of divine relief and resurrection. The artworks also appear in different artistic genres. This book analyzes the evidence of Christ the Miracle Worker on the walls of the catacombs and the carvings on sarcophagi frontals. While there is room for distinction between catacomb images and sarcophagi images, the funerary context of each illuminates the value of the image for early Christian audiences.

The final chapter addresses the most vexing stylistic element of the image of Christ the Miracle Worker. More often than not, the depiction of Christ performing healings and miracles includes a curious implement wielded by Jesus. The figure of Jesus holds what can be construed as a staff or a wand. The staff of Jesus is a puzzling accessory, and initially it is mysterious to see Christ depicted in such a way. Art historians such as Thomas Mathews have notably argued that the wand indicates that Jesus is in fact intentionally portrayed as a magician.[30] However, the wand in Christian art of the third and fourth

---

29. The term persists into the scholastic period. Bonaventure will continue the tradition of identifying Jesus as *Christus medicus,* demonstrating that the depiction of Christ as a physician did not lose its import over time, *Sermones dominicales* 50.2.

centuries is not necessarily evocative of magic, philosophy, or any other non-Christian influence and is not really a wand at all, but a staff. The instrument is possibly meant to recall the miracle worker Moses and depict Jesus and Peter as the "New Moses" of the Christian faith.

While Mathews may overstate the association between Jesus and magic, he correctly insinuates the competition between Jesus and rivals that is addressed in Christian iconography. The image of Christ the Miracle Worker was polyvalent; a Christian viewer could recognize Jesus as the New Moses bearing the staff as well as recognize Christ as greater deity than a healing rival like Asclepius. There are no handy museum placards by these images that reveal what an early Christian context thought of them. With the images involving the staff, particularly in the scenes of the striking of the rock, the sacrament of baptism appears to be emphasized as well. Moses, healing, and baptism were all possible interpretations that were congruent with a fourth-century context that stressed the authority of the church. The miracle images, especially the ones featuring the staff, exhibit the development of Christian iconography and also illustrate that there is not one solitary interpretation. Miracles were the currency of the faithful in Late Antiquity. The third-century Alexandrian author Origen highlights this trait by noting the great esteem granted Moses for his miracle-working ability, claiming that Jesus followed in his wake.[31]

For early Christians, Jesus was the singular figure who could supplant the abilities of any rival. While authors of the early church make the superior attributes of Jesus clear in sermons and texts to the faithful, Christian art preached a sermon to their audience in paint and stone. To suggest there is only one interpretation of these images of Jesus for either early Christian or contemporary audiences is a mistake and neglects the complexity and syncretistic function of Christian art as well as the importance of the images themselves. More significantly, such a solitary interpretation neglects the polyvalence of Christian art. The overall theme of Christ as a dominant miracle worker was crucial enough to early Christians that it dominates the landscape of their burgeoning artistic language. This book will explain why it was so important and apparent in the visual record of early Christian art, and why Christ the Miracle Worker was so popular for the early Christian audience.

30. See Mathews's chapter "The Magician" in *Clash of Gods*, 54–91.

31. Origen, *Against Celsus* 1.45; 3.24 (PG 11, 947A–C; Chadwick).

2

Healing, Miracle, and Magic in Non-Christian Sources

After the beginning of the third century, early Christians were increasingly insistent on portraying Christ as a miracle worker. In the catacombs and on funerary monuments such as sarcophagi, Christ heals and performs miracles as mentioned in the Gospels. However, any viewer will begin to notice the unique features in the artworks depicting Christ. The implement that Christ wields as he performs his divine office has been the subject of some debate. While it appears to be a wand, this determination is far from conclusive. The art historian Thomas Mathews has memorably suggested that this iconographic inclusion suggests that Jesus was considered a magician.[1]

However, the "wand" of Jesus does not indicate that he was necessarily understood as a magician. While the specific issue of the so-called wand will be treated in the final chapter, the next two chapters provide a valuable summary of the non-Christian and Christian evidence concerning healing, miracle, and magic in Late Antiquity. The eminent art historian Erwin Panofsky states that any true interpretation of an image must acknowledge a strong familiarity with cognate literary sources.[2] This truly makes the interpreter's task an interdisciplinary one. Only by examining the context of the image of Christ the Miracle Worker can we discover a cogent interpretation.

In Late Antiquity, individuals were greatly concerned about their health and well-being. The fragile nature of existence became only too apparent when illness or injury struck. Remedies were sought with fervor that bordered on fanaticism. With limited options in the health care system of Late Antiquity, the belief in miraculous cures was very pervasive. Medicine and miracle would naturally be linked together, since healing was so closely associated with

---

1. See Thomas Mathews, *The Clash of Gods* (Princeton, NJ: Princeton University Press, 1993), 54–89.

2. E. Panofsky, *Studies on Iconology: Humanistic Themes in the Art of the Renaissance* (New York: Harper and Row, 1972), 15.

religion. Generally speaking, the belief in supernatural cures naturally rose from belief in the unbelievable.

Health care in Late Antiquity was not completely dissimilar from our contemporary system. Care was difficult to procure, not always effective, and occasionally expensive. In general, a sick person seeking treatment in antiquity had four options. The person could (1) go to a physician, (2) use homeopathic self-administered remedies, (3) seek the aid of a magician or employ magical incantations, or (4) visit a temple of the local healing cult. All of the health care options except homeopathic remedies required some type of payment. While all four options never lacked practitioners, I will claim that the healing cult was the most popular in the first four centuries. Moreover, physicians acknowledged the healing cult, since the cult treated chronic illnesses such as paralysis or blindness. The divine healing option often provided more individual attention to such chronic ailments. Even if the effect was "care" more than actual "cure," the treatment of the healing cult was touted as successful more often than not.[3] Although greatly ridiculed in some quarters, magic was widely practiced. However, the realm of magic and the excessive expression of devotion (*superstitio*) were viewed by intellectuals as improper, manipulative, and abhorrent. As the rivalry between non–Christians and Christians elevated in the second and third centuries, magic and the magical arts were terms of slander for the parties to use against each other.

The images of Christ the Miracle Worker were possibly influenced by all four options, but they were particularly affected by healing cults that served as competitors in the realms of religion. Images of Christ healing could visualize Jesus effecting cures and securing eternal life, showing Christianity as superior to any competing healing cult. In Late Antiquity, the line separating the category of healing and miracle working from that of religion was often quite fine. Figures such as the healing god Asclepius or the magician Apollonius of Tyana were parallels as well as potent adversaries of the emerging Christian religion and its chosen deity of Jesus Christ.[4]

Late Antique religion had certain rubrics of acceptable and unacceptable behavior. Excessive frivolity or superstition was maligned on one side, while nonbelief or atheism was ridiculed at the opposite end. Healing and miracle working often crossed the borderline separating true *religio* and *superstitio*.

3. See Vivian Nutton, "Healers in the Medical Market Place: Towards a Social History of Greco-Roman Medicine," in *Medicine in Society* (Cambridge: Cambridge University Press, 1992), 33.

4. Gary B. Ferngren, *Medicine and Health Care in Early Christianity* (Baltimore, MD: Johns Hopkins University Press, 2009). Ferngren devotes some significant space to the influence of the cult of Asclepius upon early Christianity.

Cicero affirmed that true *religio* was a positive expression of the preservation of ritual and tradition in relation to the gods, while he branded *superstitio* as excessive and antiquated.[5] A healing or a miracle may fall somewhere in between these two polarities. However, non-Christian and Christian writers appear to be in agreement in their thoughts on superstition and opposition to magic, although this similarity did not stop one group from lobbing verbal epithets at the other.

This chapter will discuss the historical context of Late Antiquity that is so critical to understanding the images of Christ performing healings and miracles. First, the background and understanding of miracle and magic in Late Antiquity will be examined. By considering how non-Christian groups viewed miracles and magic, one can perceive similarities with the Christian understanding of miracles. The understanding of magic is relevant to any study of healing and miracle working, since they share some significant overlap. The critic Celsus, the references in Greek Magical Papyri, and the hagiography of Apollonius of Tyana by the author Philostratus provide ample evidence of this. Finally, the popularity and tradition of the healing cult of Asclepius will be detailed, showing the impact Asclepius had on Late Antiquity. By the third century, the Late Antique culture was a receptive atmosphere for the images of Christ the Miracle Worker that became the motif of choice in early Christian art.

BACKGROUNDS: MAGICIANS AND MIRACLE MEN IN LATE ANTIQUITY

The belief in divine healing maintained a powerful place in ancient medicine, whether doctors liked it or not. Physicians attempted to minimize the role of the divine—what we will (with some trepidation) generally call "religion"—in medical treatment. They claimed that any successful healing treatment of a patient was due to the prescription they themselves provided, not an incantation or the will of gods, and more importantly, that the cause of the malady also was not due to the gods.[6] Still, people of all walks of life placed a high value on religiously associated healings. Faced with the choice of heeding the advice

---

5. Cicero, *On the Nature of the Gods* 2.28. Translation by H. Rackham, Loeb Classical Library (New York: G. P. Putnam, 1933).

6. The writings of the Hippocratic Corpus argue that disease has less to do with philosophy and more to do with medical explanations dealing with the physical body. The author of the treatise *Sacred Disease* attacked any notion that disease is caused by the gods and that any proper treatment can be performed by magical incantations and the like. See *The Sacred Disease* 1.2; and Nutton, *Ancient Medicine* (New York: Routledge, 2004), 65.

of his physician or the cult of the healing god Asclepius, the second-century orator Aelius Aristides favored the divine prescriptions.[7] Methods of healing in antiquity encompassed medicine, miracle, and magic, and religion seeps through all three areas. Medicine was a category that included practicing physicians in the empire. Late Antique physicians usually treated patients for a fee, and prescribed any number of healing methods. These prescriptions might include the drinking of wine or gentle exercise as prescribed by Asclepiades, or the balance of humors and attention to anatomy as expounded by Galen. Medicine was not without its severe critics. It also was not opposed to religion. Galen, perhaps the best-known and most influential Late Antique physician, dedicated his first essay on anatomy to Asclepius and exalted the divine cures of the god as a reality.[8]

"Miracle" is perhaps a more difficult term to define in the context of Late Antiquity. Miracles in paganism and Christianity were a result of a direct appeal to the gods and were acts of divine benevolence bestowed upon believers in response to their faith. The miracles of Jesus in the gospel accounts in the New Testament loosely follow this definition. In the early twentieth century, Rudolf Bultmann deconstructed the formula of a miracle story, claiming it was a three-part sequence with a problem, the resulting miracle, and a demonstration of the efficacy of the miracle, occasionally followed by praise for its effectiveness.[9] The healing of the paralytic in Matthew 9 follows this sequence. A paralytic is brought to Jesus; Jesus orders the man to take up his mat and walk (9:6); the paralytic walks home, and the awe-struck crowd praises God.

Miracle stories had an evangelistic dimension. The end result of healing accounts in the gospels was often faith in God on the part of onlookers or one-time opponents of Christianity. Many accounts end with the crowd's "amazement" at Jesus' miracle. In Acts 13:4-12, belief was brought about through miraculous punishment, not healing. Summoned by the governor in Cyprus, Paul and Barnabas encountered a magician, whom Paul rebuked and struck blind in the name of God. The story's dénouement is the belief that was instilled in the witnessing governor.[10]

---

7. Aristides, *Orations* 49.8-15 (Behr). Even to the apparent detriment of his health.

8. Nutton, *Ancient Medicine*, 279; Howard Clark Kee, *Medicine, Miracle, and Magic in New Testament Times* (New York: Cambridge University Press, 1986), 61.

9. Rudolf Bultmann, *The History of the Synoptic*, trans. John Marsh, rev. ed. (New York: Harper and Row, 1968), 210.

10. A. D. Nock, *Conversion: The Old and the New in Religion from Alexander the Great to Augustine of Hippo* (Oxford: Clarendon, 1933), 14.

The evangelistic element of miracle accounts was not unique to Christianity. Philostratus reported that the miracles of Apollonius were followed by recognition and belief, such as the imprisoned Apollonius removing his leg from the fetters, astonishing and instilling belief in his follower Damis.[11] Apuleius' *Metamorphoses* described Lucius' transformation from an ass to a human as evidence enough for Lucius' conversion to the Isiac mysteries.[12]

Both non-Christian and Christian miracle stories followed a similar formula of describing a successful action by the god. One difference between the two sets of stories concerns the miracle of raising the dead, particularly the episode of Zeus killing Asclepius for performing a resurrection. This aspect of Asclepius' story enjoyed some prominence in antiquity, given the mentions by Plato, Cicero, Justin, Clement, and Tertullian.[13] Servius claimed Asclepius was killed for the resurrection of Hippolytus, drawing the ire of Hades and forcing the divine retribution of Zeus.[14] On the other hand, Diodorus Siculus maintained Asclepius raised a great many people from the dead, and Apollodorus in the first century specifically reported six people resurrected by Asclepius.[15] Whether Asclepius was guilty of performing one resurrection or many, the result of his action was death by the thunderbolt of Zeus.

Christ is credited with several resurrections in the four gospels, most notably the raising of Lazarus in John 11:1-10. Although resurrection stories can be described as "miracles," it is still debatable whether healings should be considered as such. In John, the Lazarus story is not necessarily a healing, but it is restorative. Lazarus is not resurrected to eternal life just yet. He is restored to a human condition; he is vulnerable to disease and will die again. A resurrection may not appear to be a typical healing. However, in the Bible and art, resurrections and healings appear to operate similarly. They exhibit and promote the healer's power in order to instill awe and gain the belief of onlookers.

Reports of Asclepius or Apollonius of Tyana resurrecting men could have the same effect as reports of Jesus raising Lazarus. Like a miraculous healing,

---

11. Philostratus, *Life* 7.38. Damis retells this story and how he came to recognize Apollonius as divine in 8.13.

12. Apuleius, *Metamorphoses* 11.5.

13. See the testimonies collected in Emma and Ludwig Edelstein's *Asclepius: Collection and Interpretation of the Testimonies*, vols. 1 and 2 (Baltimore: Johns Hopkins Press, 1945), 48–57.

14. Servius's *Commentary on the Aeneid*, 6.398 in Edelstein, T. 111. The resurrection of Hippolytus is often mentioned. See Pausanias, *Description of Greece* 1.27.4-5; and Sextus Empiricus in *Against the Professors* 1.260-262.

15. Diodorus Siculus, *The Library of History* 4.71.1-3; Apollodorus, *The Library* 3.10.3-4.

a resurrection would gain support for the healer from the watching crowds. Miracle and healing stories achieved the desired result by amplifying the dramatic tone of the narrative. Miracle accounts were excellent marketing and public relations tools for religion. The nature of the healing that occurred guaranteed that the tale would be remembered, and the success and popularity of the healing deity involved would be subsequently spread. Several accounts of healings by Asclepius also embodied an ineffable sense of drama. Prior to the era of Late Antiquity, in the work of Aristophanes from 380 BCE, two snakes purportedly licked the patient Plutus's eyes, and his vision was subsequently restored.[16]

Although miraculous healing accounts existed in Late Antiquity, bountiful evidence also exists of patients healed by means of ancient medicine or by the cult of Asclepius. These healings can be described as fairly mundane. Even without the "miraculous" element as exhibited in the snakes of Plutus, and even if they lacked the drama of miracle stories, healings procured by divine aid were still credited to the divine. Howard Clark Kee argues that the number of ordinary healings in the early centuries indicates the difference between this era and earlier Hellenistic medicine.[17] It would be a mistake to claim that miracles and healings were becoming separate entities in Late Antiquity. In fact, the development of Greco-Roman medicine beginning in the Common Era exhibited a close relationship between healings and miracles. Beginning in 160 CE with Julius Apellas's report of his healing at Epidauros, Asclepius was seen not only as a divine friend and helper, but also as a savior. Asclepius' treatment altered the course of his life, and Apellas sincerely believed his life was now under the care and protection of the god.[18]

Apellas' belief marked a new direction in Asclepius devotion in Late Antiquity. Efficacious healings by Asclepius were followed by a broader transformation of the patient's life. Aelius Aristides indicated that Asclepius was not only a healer of the body, but a healer of the soul as well. Asclepius healed the patient externally and internally. This characterization of healing recalls the healings of Christ in the gospels. Jesus healed both body and soul. The man born blind in John 9 was healed and cleansed of sin. Thus, a working definition of "miracle" in a Christian context could be any healing through a divine channel that involves an inward and outward transformation.[19]

---

16. Aristophanes, *Plutus* 633-747.

17. Howard Clark Kee, *Miracle in the Early Christian World* (New Haven, CT: Yale University Press, 1983), 89.

18. Ibid., 88.

While healings and miracles can be described as intertwined in Late Antiquity, the same cannot be said of miracles and magic. Miracles were products of divine agents, while magic involved the human manipulation of the divine for personal means. Magic involved repetition of a spell in order to produce a desired end. Like *superstitio*, the term *magic* and the practice of magic were maligned. Respected by some but despised by many in Late Antiquity, magic is most often described as originating in Persia, as Pliny the Elder describes the migration of magic from Persia to Greece in his *Natural History*.[20] Book 30 of Pliny's *Natural History* largely ridicules the practice of magic.[21] In republican Rome, the practice of magic usually involved love spells. Any negativity toward magic in Rome usually arose from concern that it could be used to threaten established property rights.[22]

In imperial Rome, magic began to take on a negative connotation, in part due to the heightened sensitivity toward non-Roman influences, as recorded in Pliny the Elder's *Natural History*. Up to the present, the term *magic* has surely been interpreted quite negatively.[23] Disputes concerning magic often addressed the issue of authority. Plutarch, who lived from 50 to 120 CE, described the divergent roles of superstition and atheism in his essay "On Superstition."[24] Plutarch was not against religion. He believed that for a citizen, "the pleasantest things that men enjoy are festal days and banquets at the temples, initiations and mystic rites, and prayer and adoration of the gods."[25] The superstitious person won favor with the gods with spurious rites and rituals. For Plutarch, *deisidaimonia* (the Greek term used for "superstition") included magic and incantations.[26] His descriptions of the misguided rituals of the superstitious

19. This definition is also what critics call the marks of a magician. Morton Smith, *Jesus the Magician* (San Francisco, CA: Harper and Row, 1978), 81. For evidence of Christian healings as superior, see Smith, chapter 3, 92 and the apocryphal *Acts of Peter and the Twelve*, 11.

20. Pliny, *Natural History* 30.3-13.

21. Ibid. 28.10.47; 28.12.49; 28.4.21; 28.5.28.

22. Fritz Graf, "Excluding the Charming: The Development of the Greek Concept of Magic," in *Ancient Magic and Ritual Power*, ed. Marvin W. Meyer and Paul Mirecki (Boston: Brill Academic, 2001), 41. Sulla in 81 BCE dictated edicts against the use of sorcery, although this was an edict against those who used poisons or magic for murder.

23. Jonathan Z. Smith, "Trading Places," in Meyer and Mirecki, *Ancient Magic and Ritual Power*, 16. Smith argues that magic is an evaluative term, used to characterize "the other."

24. Plutarch, *On Superstition* 170A. While the essay has usually been ascribed to Plutarch, it is questionable whether he is its true author or not. For further reading, see Smith, "De Superstitione," in *Plutarch's Theological Writings and Early Christian Literature*, ed. Hans Dieter Betz (Leiden: Brill, 1975), 6-7.

25. Plutarch, *Superst.* 169D (Babbitt, LCL).

person depicted the workings of a magician in antiquity. Plutarch described the strict attention to detail and correctness of the superstitious sacrifice—for example, praying to the gods in a normal cadence and not resorting to fitful, "barbarous" phrases.[27] Superstition made demands of the gods, instead of supplicating and honoring the gods.[28] In his depiction of people plagued with superstitious fear, Plutarch claimed their fatal flaw was their susceptibility to magic. While atheism was the polar opposite of superstition, Plutarch understood why one would choose ignorance over depraved magic.[29] His task was not to condemn superstition and atheism equally, but to show how both ways of thinking avoided the waters of "true religion" that lay between the opposing realms.[30]

Atheism and despicable magic dwell outside Plutarch's understanding of true religion. Within true religion, there was indeed room for miracles and liturgical drama. Plutarch's understanding was echoed by Marcus Aurelius in 170 CE. Marcus Aurelius credited Diognetus for advising him "not to busy myself about trifling things, and not to give credit to what was said by miracle-workers and jugglers about incantations and the driving away of demons and such things."[31] For Marcus Aurelius, the practice of magic was a distracting nuisance.

Superstition was not the path to true religion, and any element of Christianity would bear the stain of superstition if it persisted in outwardly displaying signs of a magical nature. The philosopher Celsus attacked Christianity with a similar understanding of superstition. His attack, however, focused on the person and work of Christ, as he chose to malign the Jesus with the term *magician*.

---

26. See Introduction for a treatment of the terms *superstitio* and *deisidaimonia*. The terms are better described as loosely related rather than a Greek and Latin word for the same thing. *Deisidaimonia* can refer to "religion" in general, but could also indicate a negative aspect of religion, superstition. Plutarch's treatise, *deisidaimonia* is synonymous with *superstitio*.

27. Plutarch, *Superst.* 166B.

28. See H. Armin Moellering, *Plutarch on Superstition* (Boston: Christopher, 1962), 78.

29. Plutarch was more concerned that those who are superstitious are not similarly condemned as the atheists. See *Superst.* 169F. Also see Robert L. Wilken, *The Christians As the Romans Saw Them* (New Haven: Yale University Press, 2003), 61. Plutarch wondered why atheists then are accused of impiety while superstitious people are not. He cited *The Odyssey*, in which Anaxagoras called the sun a stone and was brought to trial, while the Cimmerians who never believed in the sun were never accused of impiety. See Moellering, *Plutarch on Superstition*, 78–79.

30. Plutarch, *Superst.* 171F.

31. Marcus Aurelius, *Meditations* 1.6 (Long). See Marcus's praise of divine healing at 1.17, and see the Introduction.

CELSUS ON MAGIC AND MIRACLES

Celsus was a pagan philosopher who around 177 CE wrote an influential work against the Christians, entitled *The Great Doctrine*.[32] Much of what we know about Celsus can be gathered in Origen's *Against Celsus*, written about eighty years later, and in a statement in Eusebius's history. Eusebius wrote in his history that when Origen was over sixty years old, he wrote the eight treatises in reply to the work of "Celsus the Epicurean," branding Celsus with a questionable label handily provided by Origen.[33] Origen's response to Celsus reveals the fact that Celsus's work was fairly well known, since it prompted him to construct a rebuttal. Origen was obviously worried that Christians "may be shaken and disturbed by the writings of Celsus," indicating that this was a serious matter indeed.[34]

Celsus decried Christianity as a superstition from the outset, citing the secret rites of the religion: "Christians perform their rites and teach their doctrines in secret."[35] Celsus was vicious in tearing down any association between Christianity and philosophy.[36] He attempted to devalue Christianity by insisting that it reeked of superstition. Celsus described Christians as similar

32. The date of Celsus's work depends on the identity of the "Celsus" in question. Origen, *Against Celsus*, pref. 4, and 1.8; PG 11, 669B. For example, this is not the same Celsus as the author responsible for the books *On Medicine*. The Celsus from Nero's time was likely the author of *On Medicine*, Aulus Cornelius Celsus. The latter Celsus from Hadrian's time was probably the philosopher in question, but his identity as an Epicurean is problematic, for if anything, the Celsus portrayed in Origen's response is a Middle Platonist. For further reading, see Lucian, *Alexander the False Prophet*, 25, 47, 61; Chadwick in his introduction to his translation of *Contra Celsum* (Cambridge: Cambridge University Press, 1953), xxv; Michael Frede, "Origen's Treatise *Against Celsus*," in *Apologetics in the Roman Empire: Pagans, Jews and Christians*, ed. Mark Edwards, Martin Goodman, and Simon Price (Oxford: Oxford University Press, 1999), 148; Theodor Keim, *Celsus Wahres Wort* (Zurich: Fussli, 1873), 276; R. Joseph Hoffman, *On True Doctrine* (New York: Oxford University Press, 1987), 30–33.

33. Eusebius, *Ecc. History* 6.36.2 (PG 20, 596C).

34. Origen, *Cels.* pref. 4 (PG 11, 647A). For a more recent Greek text, see M. Borret, *Contre Celse*, SC 4 vols. 132, 136, 147, 150 (Paris: Éditions du Cerf, 1967–76). The English translation cited of *Against Celsus* derives from Henry Chadwick, *Contra Celsum* (Cambridge: Cambridge University Press, 1953).

35. Origen, *Cels.* 1.3-4 (PG 11, 657–664; Chadwick).

36. Galen's role in this discussion is worthy of note. See Richard Walzer, *Galen on Jews and Christians* (London: Oxford University Press, 1949); and Robert Wilken, "Collegia, Philosophical Schools, and Theology," in *The Catacombs and the Colosseum: The Roman Empire as the Setting of Primitive Christianity*, ed. Stephen Benko and John J. O'Rourke (Valley Forge, PA: Judson, 1971), 277; and Wilken, *The Christians*, 74. Galen aligned Judaism and Christianity under the subject heading of philosophy. He further ridiculed both groups' systems of inquiry: "If I had in mind people who taught their pupils in the same way as the followers of Moses and Christ teach theirs—for they order them to accept everything on faith—I should not have given you a definition." Walzer, *Galen on Jews*, 15.

to "worshippers of Mithras and Sabazius, and whatever else one might meet, apparitions of Hecates or of some other daemon or daemons."[37] In Celsus's mind, Christians prey on the gullible, just as superstition does. The Christians are thus guilty of duping people into belief by preying upon their irrational fear; the same fear Plutarch identified in his laments *On Superstition*. According to Celsus, Christianity bears the stain of superstition. The philosopher spoke of Christianity as a precarious foreign cult, and therefore Christianity was an invalid road to true piety.

One of Celsus's primary tactics was to accuse Christianity of magical practice. Celsus claimed that "Christians get the power which they seem to possess by pronouncing the names of certain daemons and incantations," insinuating that Christians use magical chants and charms to garner power.[38] Celsus maintained that magic is not the mark of a true philosophy.[39] By placing Christianity in the realm of magic, Celsus could argue that Christianity cannot be a philosophy. The practice of magic is wholly outside the realm of philosophy. Magicians cannot be philosophers.[40] Celsus was not disputing that Christians have power; he was merely criticizing the source and use of that power. Celsus accomplished this by focusing on the person of Jesus. According to him, the miracles of Jesus were the true calling card of a magician. In an attempt to prove that Jesus used magic, Celsus asserted that there was no divine hand involved in the miracles. Jesus might have worked miracles, but Celsus disputed the Christian claim that he was the Son of God.

Much of Celsus's attack on Christianity was based on his characterization of the miracles of Jesus as the marks of a magician. Celsus claimed, "It was by magic that he was able to do the miracles which he appeared to have done; and because he foresaw that others too would get to know the same formulas and do the same thing, and boast that they did so by God's power, Jesus expelled them from his society."[41] Celsus argued that the miracles performed by Jesus were the work of a magician, since he used magical incantations. Jesus naturally had to protect his status as a magician. He had to prevent anyone from learning his

37. Origen, *Cels.* 1.9 (PG 11,676B; Chadwick).

38. Origen, *Cels.* 1.6 (PG 11, 665ᵃ; Chadwick). Also see Robert M. Grant, *Greek Apologists of the Second Century* (Philadelphia: Westminster, 1988), 136–39.

39. Origen, *Cels.* 1.69 (PG 11, 789). Origen questioned whether this Celsus is the same Celsus as Lucian's, who wrote several books against magic, indicating that his opponent is possibly amenable to magic.

40. Eugene Gallagher, *Divine Man or Magician? Celsus and Origen on Jesus* (Chico, CA: Scholars, 1980), 46; also see Wilken, *The Christians*, 94.

41. Origen, *Cels.* 1.6 (Chadwick).

spells, the secrets of his tradecraft; thus, he was forced to expel some people from his circle. By associating Christ's miracles with the practice of magic, Celsus was able to besmirch Christ's divine reputation. Christ's miracles could have been just magic tricks:

> Let us believe that these miracles were really done by you . . . the works of sorcerers who profess to do wonderful miracles, and the accomplishments of those who are taught by Egyptians, who for a few obols make known their sacred lore in the middle of the market-place and drive daemons out of men and blow away diseases and invoke the souls of heroes, displaying expensive banquets and dining-tables and cakes and dishes which are non-existent, and who make things move as though they were alive although they are not really so, but only appear as such in the imagination. . . . Since these men do these wonders, ought we to think them sons of God? Or ought we to say that they are the practices of wicked men possessed by an evil daemon?[42]

In his response to Celsus's slander against Christianity, Origen refuted any characterization of Jesus as a marketplace magician. While agreeing that the miracles of Jesus could not be explained, Origen said calling them magical spells was erroneous. He pointed out that Christians make no use of spells; the disciples performed miracles only in the name of Jesus, not by using incantations.[43] Jesus did not perform tricks to show off his own powers; he used his power to call observers to moral reformation.[44] Furthermore, Origen claimed he knew of no sorcerers who used tricks to educate people about God or to persuade people to live lives as men of God. Magicians were in the business of producing love charms or health remedies, not transforming the lives of humanity. Jesus was unique in the fact that his strong moral life served as an example to his followers, a quality that no sorcerer exhibited, since sorcerers were swallowed up by their own greed.

The force of Origen's defense shows that Celsus's accusations against Jesus were considered serious.[45] Origen countered them by focusing not on Jesus' methods, but on his end results—namely, moral transformation and the

42. Origen, *Cels.* 1.68 (Chadwick).

43. Ibid.

44. Ibid.

45. See Harold Remus, *Pagan-Christian Conflict over Miracle in the Second Century* (Cambridge, MA: Philadelphia Patristic Foundation, 1983), 58.

call to live a life under God. For Origen, the source of Jesus' power was unquestionably divine, since it was selfless and for human benefit. The label of "magic" was a powerful one in Late Antiquity. Origen and other church fathers often had to maneuver around such a charge instead of combating it head-on. In their polemic, Celsus and Origen both maintained that magic was disreputable. For us to measure the weight of their disdain, we must examine the negative conception of magic in Late Antiquity.

THE GREEK MAGICAL PAPYRI (PGM)

The use and practice of magic was fairly widespread from the sixth century BCE through Late Antiquity. While magic had faithful practitioners, there were critics who feared its influence or envisioned it as a threat to religion. Just as the terms *deisidaimonia* and *superstitio* may have been positive at one point but slowly came to be considered negative, the same can be said for the terms *goes* or *magos* (terms used to signify a "magician"). Plato connected the term *goes* with *magos*, designating religious figures as corrupt seers.[46] Plato believed that the magician threatened the relationship between humans and the gods; the use of magical practices aimed at manipulating the gods corrupted the ideal relationship of human submission to the gods' will.

Just as Alexandria was renowned as a center for medicine in the ancient world, its sister Egyptian city of Memphis was noted as the center for magic. The early church father Jerome and the Late Antique satirist Lucian among others, cited Memphis as the capital of magic.[47] In Jerome's *Life of Hilarion*, a boy engraves a spell upon a copper sheet and buries it beneath the house of the object of his desire. Hilarion restores the girl to health and orders the copper sheet bearing the incantation to be removed. Jerome's story offers several insights into the use of magic in the ancient world. First, magic is obviously a learned art and cannot be successfully performed by just anyone. In the *Life of Hilarion*, the boy from Gaza had to travel to Memphis to procure his charm. Jerome's text also illustrates a customary use of magic: love spells. In the ancient world, it was fairly common for men to employ magic in order to gain the affection of a woman. Love spells and incantations were not used

---

46. *Goes* and *goeteia* were terms associated with ritual mourning, the practice of healing and divination. After Plato, *magos* and *goes* were similarly defined and understood. See Fritz Graf, *Magic in the Ancient World*, trans. Franklin Philip (Cambridge, MA: Harvard University Press, 1997), 24–25.

47. Jerome, *Life of Hilarion* 21; Lucian, *Lover of Lies* 34-36. See Graf, "How to Cope with a Difficult Life: A View of Ancient Magic," in *Envisioning Magic: A Princeton Seminar and Symposium*, ed. Peter Schäfer, Hans G. Kippenberg (Leiden: Brill, 1997), 93–94.

for wanton sexual gratification, but rather to obtain a wife, usually as a last resort. A wife was often an economic asset; through marriage, a man could gain access to a family's fortune.[48] This should not give magic a veneer of nobility, however; love spells to procure an unwilling wife were precisely what led to legal restrictions against magic in the empire.[49] In the first century, the book of Acts of the Apostles reports the burning of books of spells in Ephesus. And according to Suetonius, Augustus ordered that all books of the occult—books that would have included love spells—be burned upon their discovery.[50]

The Greek Magical Papyri (PGM), a collection of spells and formulae from Egypt spanning the second century BCE to the fifth century CE, record hundreds of magical incantations.[51] The PGM provides insight into the use of magic for divination. Many recorded spells are for oracles and encounters with the gods, usually by dreams.[52] Their efficacy depended on reciting the spell in the correct manner and never deviating from its prescription. The PGM indicates such an emphasis by insisting that the formula be said properly. In a proper magical rite, it was essential to speak the name of the deity and the name of the supplicant: "Wherefore, O Lady (Aphrodite) act, I beg, attract (name) whom (name) bore, to come with rapid step to my door."[53] If one wants to quench fire, kill a snake, send dreams, or ensure a wife's fidelity, the spell must be said properly to the letter.[54]

Many spells are love charms, while others are for healings and remedies. The PGM describes many rites and incantations for the purposes of healing. Saying, "the wrath of Apollo, far-darting Lord," will cure bloody flux, and carrying around the inscription "Would that you be fated to be unborn and to die unmarried" serves as a contraceptive.[55] There are numerous spells for

---

48. Graf, "How to Cope," 104. In Rome, akin to the propagation of Greek medicine, magic's foreign nature likely did not engender it favorably to the elite. Cicero is ambivalent, as he associates the magi with Persia, saying they interpreted the dreams of Cyrus and are a group of "wise men and scholars among the Persians." See Cicero, *On Divination* 1.46.91. The poet Catullus, a contemporary of Cicero's, also associated the magi with Persia, noting that the magi are a product of incest, and thus impious. See Catullus, *Carmen* 90.

49. Magic used to falsely marry a widow and accrue at least a portion of her property (or at the very least higher status) is precisely what Apuleius is accused of nearly two hundred years later. See Apuleius, *Apologia* 90.

50. Acts 19:19; Suetonius, *Life of Augustus* 31.

51. Hans Dieter Betz, ed. and trans., *The Greek Magical Papyri in Translation, Including the Demotic Spells* (Chicago: University of Chicago Press, 1986).

52. *PGM* VII 664–85 (Betz).

53. *PGM* IV 2907 (Betz).

54. *PGM* XIII 264–325 (Betz)

restoring sight and aiding sleep. Whether for divination or for healing, spells were popular because humans wished to take actions into their own hands to obtain divine or miraculous aid. Magic required only careful attention, repetition, and of course, a fee or sacrifice to the magician or source who provided the formula.

The spells contained in the PGM mandated secrecy. Commands to secrecy were essential to prevent knowledge of the magic from spreading, and also to protect the interests of the magician.[56] If everyone knew the spell, the magician would be useless and unimportant.

Late Antique authors often followed the precedent of earlier authors such as Catullus or Pliny in casting magicians as disreputable characters. The satirist Lucian criticized the life and death of the Cynic philosopher Peregrinus, once a Christian, who manipulated crowds into believing in his magical ability. Lucian argued, "He manufactures myths and repeats certain oracles . . . to the purport that he is to become a guardian spirit of the night; it is plain, too, that he already covets altars and expects to be imaged in gold . . . it would be nothing unnatural if, among all the dolts that there are, some should be found to assert that they were relieved of quartan fevers by him, and that in the dark they had encountered the guardian spirit of the night!"[57] Lucian decried Peregrinus as acting in a vainglorious manner, all the way up to his self-immolation. But even after his death, his followers still believed in his resurrection and reported seeing his risen body dressed in white raiment.[58] Lucian's account indicates people's need and desire to believe in the ineffable, even when the circumstances of the story are quite ridiculous and beyond logic. The figure of the magical man such as Peregrinus fulfills such a desire. Lucian provided an insight into the ability of magicians to attract a vast following in Late Antiquity.

APOLLONIUS OF TYANA

According to his hagiographer Flavius Philostratus, Apollonius of Tyana would be misplaced in any discussion of magic. Even while describing Apollonius's wondrous acts, Philostratus never called him a magician and appeared to hate magic as much as Celsus and the early Christians. Philostratus's work, published around 217 CE, was a defense of Apollonius, not as a magician but as a miracle worker with a divine nature. Apollonius performed healings, exorcisms, and

---

55. *PGM* XXIIa 2-14 (Betz).

56. Gerd Theissen, *The Miracle Stories of the Early Christian Tradition*, trans. Francis McDonagh (Philadelphia: Fortress Press, 1974), 68.

57. Lucian, *Passing of Peregrinus* 27-28 (Harmon, LCL).

58. Lucian, *Passing of Peregrinus*, 40.

even resurrections, but according to Philostratus, he was not a magician, since he never accepted remuneration or used any spells or sacrifices; he accomplished miracles through his divine nature.[59] Given Apollonius's background, Philostratus's task of defending Apollonius against charges of magic was clearly difficult. Philostratus admitted that Apollonius had purportedly lived with magi in Persia and India, had the gift of foresight, and exorcized demons. His primary defense against charges that Apollonius was a magician was to present him as a worker of wonders that were beyond the power of any ordinary magician.

Apollonius was a landmark neo-Pythagorean figure, and as a neo-Pythagorean himself, Philostratus was motivated to defend Apollonius against charges of magic. However, his motives to write such a biography were also political in nature. The philosopher started the project at the behest of the empress Julia Domna, the wife of Septimius Severus, at the beginning of the third century, at least a hundred years after Apollonius's death. The empress commissioned him not only to defend Apollonius and refute any slanderous accusations that he was merely a magician, but also to construct a pagan response to the Christians and to author a pagan gospel, highlighting a Christ-like figure.[60] It seems quite plausible, then, that Philostratus had Jesus firmly in mind while he was constructing the vita of Apollonius.[61] Following the passion narratives in the gospels, Philostratus asserted that Apollonius, like Christ, was arrested, imprisoned, and awaited execution. But unlike Christ, Apollonius escaped from his fetters and, in overcoming his penalty, proved that he was the superior miracle worker.[62]

Philostratus claimed to have based many of his findings on some recollections of the life of Apollonius written by a disciple of his named Damis. According to Philostratus's text, a relative of Damis approached the empress Julia and gave her the memoirs.[63] However many stories he borrowed from this supposed memoir is questionable. Some of Philostratus's stories may have had a basis in the actual writings of Damis,[64] but Philostratus likely credited Damis to give his biography a sense of legitimacy, providing eyewitness testimony to the life of the man from Tyana.

---

59. Philostratus, *Life*. 7.38. This text describes the moment when Apollonius removes his fetters in prison.

60. Kee, *Miracle in the Early Christian World*, 260.

61. Ibid.

62. See Philostratus, *Life* 7.38.

63. Philostratus, *Life* 1.3.

64. See Conybeare's introduction to the LCL edition of the *Life*, ix.

In Philostratus's *Life of Apollonius*, Apollonius was a neo-Pythagorean holy man and miracle worker who lived from 69 to 98 CE. He purportedly learned his trade from groups of magi in Persia and Brahmin priests in India.[65] Philostratus emphasized that Apollonius was, in fact, divine and was conversant with gods and goddesses such as Apollo and Athena.[66] Apollonius resided at one of the Asclepieia in Aegae and gained a reputation as a healer. Philostratus credited Apollonius with performing at least 107 miracles.[67] In Philostratus's work, Apollonius treated everyone without discrimination and made no requirement of faith. Apollonius did not make any demands of his supplicants, which set him apart from healing gods such as Asclepius.[68]

Philostratus found it beneficial to associate Apollonius with Asclepius. According to Philostratus, Apollonius lived at the temple at Aegae as a child. During this time, Apollonius was trained as a healer and was so successful that Asclepius purportedly told a priest that he was glad to have Apollonius there as a witness.[69] At one point, a man dying of dropsy who took solace in drink came to the temple seeking a cure, and the god refused. The man went to Apollonius, who berated him for his foolishness but still provided a treatment. Philostratus mentioned this incident to associate Apollonius with Asclepius and to demonstrate Apollonius providing wisdom to the ignorant.

Some of the healing accounts that Philostratus preserved were rather mundane, such as a story of Apollonius healing a man with a paralyzed hand: "Another man had his hand paralyzed, but left their presence in full possession of his limb."[70] These accounts have little to do with magic, and in Philostratus's opinion, were more evidence of Apollonius's attunement to nature, since the author went on to describe Apollonius's special insight into the flight of sparrows.[71] What gave Apollonius special insight into the divine and allowed

---

65. Philostratus, *Life* 1.18.

66. Philostratus, *Life* 1.11. Christopher P. Jones has contributed a recent LCL translation of the *Life*; however, F. C. Conybeare's translation has been the standard for just under a century (and has a still very useful introduction).

67. Most of these miracles, by Morton Smith's admission, were not healings but exorcisms. See Smith, *Jesus the Magician*, 109. Also see Simon Swain, "Defending Hellenism: Philostratus, In Honour of Apollonius," in Edwards et al., *Apologetics in the Roman Empire*, 157.

68. Cleimenes of Argus related how he dreamed that Asclepius ordered him to take a cold bath to cure his affliction. When he refused, the god proclaimed he would not treat the cowardly. See *Inscriptiones Graecae*, 4.1.121-122, Stele 2.37 (Edelstein T. 423); and Johannes Wolmarans, "Asclepius of Epidaurus and Jesus of Nazareth," in *Acta Patristica et Byzantina* 7 (1996): 122.

69. Philostratus, *Life* 1.9.

70. Philostratus, *Life* 3.39.

71. Philostratus, *Life* 4.3.

him to effect cures was his unique discipline. Philostratus had Apollonius describe his own theology, in which he claimed that while some worshipped him as a god, he had never ordered them to do so; his only concern was the betterment of man.[72] Other miracles of Apollonius were more embellished and more magical, as in the healing of a boy bitten by a mad dog:

> Apollonius reflected a moment and said, 'O Damis, the dog is a white shaggy sheep-dog, as big as an Amphilochian hound, and he is standing at a certain fountain trembling all over, for he is longing to drink the water, but at the same time is afraid of it. Bring him to me to the bank of the river, where there are the wrestling grounds, merely telling him that it is I who call him.' So Damis dragged the dog along, and it crouched at the feet of Apollonius. . . . He bade the dog lick the wound all round where he had bitten the boy, so that the agent of the wound might in turn be its physician and healer.[73]

Philostratus also emphasized the great similarity between Apollonius and Christ. He claimed that Apollonius was chaste like Christ and never fell prey to sexual passion.[74] Apollonius and Jesus were both unjustly imprisoned by the authorities. Apollonius refused to eat meat, wear shoes, shave, or cut his hair, all in accordance with followers of the Pythagorean cult, and traits that bear a similarity to Jesus. Magicians such as Apollonius were not normally considered healers; rather, they were revered for their ascetic lifestyle and not for their actions of theurgy.[75] He embodied the ideal of perfection, and Philostratus effectively mined the legends surrounding the life of Apollonius to portray him as a miracle worker similar to Christ.

In Philostratus's text, Apollonius was not like an ordinary human.[76] Philostratus describes Apollonius's release from his shackles in prison as a moment when an onlooker realized that "Apollonius' nature (was) godlike and more than human. Without sacrifice, or prayer, or a single word, he made light of his chains, and then put his leg back into them and acted like a prisoner."[77]

72. Philostratus, *Life* 8.7.

73. Philostratus, *Life* 6.43 (Conybeare, LCL).

74. Philostratus, *Life* 1.13.

75. Robin M. Jensen, *Understanding Early Christian Art* (New York: Routledge, 2000), 123; and see René Josef Rüttimann, *Asclepius and Jesus: The Form, Character and Status of the Asclepius Cult in the Second Century CE and Its Influence on Early Christianity* (Ann Arbor, MI: UMI Dissertation Services, 1987), 191. For an examination of the term *theurgy* and its distinction from magic, see chapter 7.

76. Philostratus, *Life* 1.28.

77. Philostratus, *Life* 7.38 (Conybeare, LCL); also see 1.31-32.

Philostratus portrayed Apollonius as a Christ-like figure who did not need to rely on any sort of incantation to produce divine works. After his death, he appeared before his disciples, proving his own immortal nature and the immortality of the soul. A doubter much like the apostle Thomas in John 20:24 did not believe that Apollonius was immortal. While he was sleeping, the holy man approached him in a dream, convincing him of his divine status and the truthfulness of his teachings.[78] Thus, with the doubting Thomas figure and the dream revelation, Philostratus's Apollonius resembled Christ and Asclepius, appearing superior to both.

Philostratus took great care to emphasize Apollonius's abilities as a healer and miracle worker as similar to Christ. Like Jesus, Apollonius was depicted as performing resurrections, one involving a person on a bier, recalling Luke 7:11-17: "A girl had died just in the hour of her marriage, and the bridegroom was following her bier lamenting . . . . Apollonius then witnessing their grief, said 'Put down the bier, for I will stay the tears that you are shedding for this maiden' . . . but merely touching her and whispering in secret some spell over her, at once woke up the maiden from her seeming death; and the girl spoke out loud, and returned to her father's house, just as Alcestis did when she was brought back to life by Hercules."[79] In this account, Philostratus could not resist solidifying the pagan claim to miracle working by inserting a reference to the myth of Hercules resurrecting Alcestis. By rooting Apollonius's miracles in the pagan tradition, Philostratus emphasized superiority over the Christians in their claim to resurrection miracles.

Morton Smith famously made the connection between Apollonius and Jesus by claiming that both were miracle workers, were persecuted for their use of magic, and taught an inner circle of disciples.[80] Smith's argument was distinctive since he was a modern author discovering a theme in ancient writings, and made an more definitive comparison than Philostratus. As Smith pointed out, both Jesus and Apollonius ascended to heaven upon their death and continued to appear to their followers. Both figures had followers who believed they were descendants of gods and had enemies who impugned them as magicians. Smith believed Philostratus intended to create an Apollonian gospel to circumvent any association between Apollonius and magic.[81] Smith claimed that Philostratus's and the gospel writers' defense of Apollonius and Jesus of the charge of magic actually implicates them as magicians. In other

78. Philostratus, *Life* 8.31.
79. Philostratus, *Life* 4.45 (Conybeare, LCL).
80. Smith, *Jesus the Magician*, 85.
81. Ibid., 87.

words, their vicious rebuke of magic reveals a widely held understanding of the life and ministry of Apollonius and Jesus. By including miracles and exorcisms, Philostratus leaves his hero open to suspicion as a magician.

Smith, however, is a problematic source to consider. He has been accused of manipulating gospel citations to his advantage. Further, he disregards the rather central issue that magic was universally maligned by pagans and Christians alike in Late Antiquity.[82] Smith believed that the gospel writers attempted to minimize any magical traits in the person of Jesus, although the miracles were the marks of a magician.[83] According to Smith, the importance of magic in the first century is found in the Gospel of Matthew with the appearance of the magi in the infancy narrative. Smith contended that the visit of the magi to honor Jesus' birth identifies Jesus as possibly the supreme magus.[84] This particular argument appears unlikely, given the symbolism attached to the magi by Matthew. The gifts given to Christ were symbolic of different aspects of his future life. For example, the gift of myrrh, used to embalm the dead, reveals the sacrificial role the infant Jesus would later play.

Smith's identification of Jesus as a magician also has been rebutted on the grounds that the Christians would never intentionally characterize their savior as a type of figure that was much maligned in Late Antiquity. Since the patristic authors were committed to advancing the perception of Christianity in the Roman world, it does not appear that Christianity was a magical sect devoted to Jesus as the supreme magus. Origen's response to Celsus, reminding him that Jesus did not use incantations, could work just as well against Smith.[85] Paul Corby Finney argues that surely by the fourth century, Christians had

---

82. Graham Twelftree, *Jesus the Exorcist* (Tübingen: Mohr Siebeck, 1993), 153. Howard Clark Kee, *Medicine, Miracle, and Magic in New Testament Times* (New York: Cambridge University Press, 1986), 114. Bernd Kollmann catalogs the various viewpoints on *Jesus the Magician* in his *Jesus und die Christen als Wundertäter: Studien zu Magie, Medizin und Schamanismus in Antike und Christentum* (Göttingen: Vandenhoeck and Ruprecht, 1996), 36–38.

83. Smith, *Jesus the Magician*, 87–93.

84. Ibid., 86; and also *Life* 1.31, in which Philostratus depicts an interesting scene where Apollonius sacrifices using the element of frankincense. If the magi were understood as magicians, the notion that they were paying homage to the supreme magus of Christ is dubious. This implies that there was a hierarchy among Late Antique magicians.

85. Origen, *Cels.* 1.68; Twelftree, *Jesus the Exorcist*, 153. Kee points out Smith's inconsistent use of the gospel accounts, such as leaving out the eschatological implications, and ridicules his argument as based upon his "eclectic personal preferences." Kee, *Medicine, Miracle, and Magic in New Testament Times*, 114. Spells were usually spoken softly and guarded securely in order to prevent theft. See Theissen, *The Miracle Stories*, 64.

been programmed to reject all comparisons of Christ to a "smarmy magician."[86] Identifying Jesus as a magician is far from assured.

Smith saw the gospel writers' portrait of Jesus as resembling Philostratus's objective in describing Apollonius. Philostratus denounced magic as a fraudulent art that was used primarily for love charms.[87] In contrast to magic, which according to Philostratus relied upon proper technique, Apollonius's power to bring about miracles relied upon divine wisdom and monastic discipline.[88]

To achieve his main goal of rehabilitating Apollonius's reputation, Philostratus not only associated Apollonius with Christ, but also depicted him as a preeminent philosopher. Philostratus attached the label of philosopher to Apollonius by reporting that Emperor Vespasian had sought Apollonius's advice during a trip to Egypt: "If all men, Apollonius, were disposed to be philosophers in the same spirit as yourself, then the lot not less of philosophy than of poverty would be an extremely happy one; for your philosophy is pure and disinterested, and your poverty is voluntary. Farewell."[89] Philostratus not only provided an imperial endorsement, he also portrayed Apollonius as a philosopher and not a purveyor of depraved superstition. He further distanced Apollonius from charges of magic by depicting Vespasian's meeting with Apollonius as taking place in a temple, a venue that is not the realm of sorcerers. Noting that Apollonius's poverty was voluntary also cast him in a favorable light. It characterized him as a man of the people who paid attention to the poor.

The response Apollonius evoked from Lucian and the Roman historian Dio Cassius indicated that Apollonius's notoriety was fairly widespread. Just as Philostratus characterized Apollonius as a divine miracle worker, other writers such as Lucian and Dio Cassius characterized him as a magus in the full negative sense the word may imply, insinuating that he had a stained reputation.[90] Accordingly, Lucian ridiculed Alexander of Abonoteichus as a follower of Asclepius and of Apollonius:

---

86. Paul Corby Finney, "Do You Think God Is a Magician?," in *Akten des Symposiums früchristliche Sarkophage*, (Marburg: Deutches Archäologisches Institut, 1999), 106.

87. Philostratus, *Life* 7.39.

88. Philostratus, *Life* 8.7. Apollonius credited his light diet for enabling him to foresee the plague of Ephesus: "This diet, my king, guards my senses in a kind of indescribable ether or clear air, and forbids them to contract any foul or turbid matter, and allows me to discern, as in the sheen of a looking-glass, everything that is happening or is to be" (Conybeare, LCL).

89. Philostratus, *Life* 8.7 (Conybeare, LCL).

90. Smith, *Jesus the Magician*, 88.

Among others, he had an admirer who was a quack, one of those who advertise enchantments, miraculous incantations, charms for your love-affairs, "sendings" for your enemies, disclosures of buried treasure, and successions to estates. As this man saw that he was an apt lad, more than ready to assist him in his affairs, and that the boy was quite as much enamored with his roguery as he with the boy's beauty, he gave him a thorough education and constantly made use of him as helper, servant, and acolyte. He himself was professedly a public physician . . . this teacher and admirer of his was a man of Tyana by birth, one of those who had been followers of the notorious Apollonius, and who knew his whole bag of tricks. You see what sort of school the man that I am describing comes from![91]

In a few lines, Lucian succeeded in depicting Apollonius as a medical quack, a prescriber of love-charms, and a nefarious sorcerer who used spells on people to transfer estates (a most dire crime in the eyes of Romans). He also managed to depict Apollonius as a boy-lover and a false physician, and he hinted at Apollonius's poor reputation by reminding Celsus of his most profane school of followers.

Dio Cassius in the third century recalled the emperor Caracalla, who "was so fond of magicians and *goetes* [seers and healers, see note 46] that he even praised and honored Apollonius the Cappadocian, who flourished in Domitian's time and was a *goes* and *magos* in the strict sense of the words. Yet Caracalla built a temple for (those who worshipped Apollonius as a hero)."[92]

These criticisms were a logical consequence of the renewed attention paid to Apollonius following Philostratus's great efforts following Philostratus's great efforts to resurrect the name of Apollonius. Hierocles, a governor under Emperor Diocletian, noted that Apollonius was as famous a miracle worker as Christ.[93] The emperor Alexander Severus, who ruled during the years 20-5–235 CE, was devoted to the image of Apollonius. In a biography of his life

91. Lucian, *Alexander the False Prophet* 5 (Harmon, LCL).

92. Dio Cassius, *Roman History* 78.18 (Carey, LCL). See Smith, *Jesus the Magician*, 88. Carey interestingly translates *goes* as "juggler." Apollonius was never considered a performer or court jester, so this translation is perplexing. See Smith, *Jesus the Magician*, 189, noting that κρίβής can be, and has been, translated as "thorough" (as Carey does), but Smith is right to endorse a more negative connotation with "in the strict sense of the words." Dio's discussion of Caracalla's enjoyment of magicians is not a positive reflection; rather, *goes* and *magos* are dirty words here and elsewhere in antiquity.

93. Reconstructed from Eusebius's response in his treatise against Philostratus's work and Hierocles. See *Against Hierocles* 5 (Conybeare, LCL)

preserved in the *Historia Augusta*, the author described Alexander's morning routine: "If he had not lain with his wife in the early morning hours, he would worship in the sanctuary of his lares, in which he kept statues of the deified emperors—of whom, however, only the best had been selected—and also of certain holy souls, among them Apollonius, and . . . Christ, Abraham, Orpheus, and others of this same character, and besides the portraits of his ancestors."[94] Alexander was not a Christian, although his mother, Julia Mamaea (niece of Philostratus's patroness Julia Domna), was a devoted Christian who had been taught by Origen.[95] He was undoubtedly well versed in Christianity, making the elevation of Apollonius to the same level of Christ all the more intriguing. Apollonius was included in the emperor's inner sanctum, alongside the images of Christ, Abraham, and Orpheus, since he exhibited the same characteristics. Apollonius's status was equal to that of the prominent deities of the Jews, Christians, and pagans.

Unsurprisingly, Philostratus's work drew a response from Christians. Eusebius provided the strongest rebuttal to any of Philostratus's characterizations of Apollonius as anything other than a magician. Eusebius was motivated to respond to Philostratus' work by Hierocles's parallel between Apollonius and Christ: Hierocles was as guilty as Philostratus in attempting to draw comparisons between the Christian savior and the man from Tyana. Eusebius argued that Apollonius was a charlatan, if a magician at all, and if he had any magical powers, they were due to the evil demons within him. He refuted any claim that Apollonius was a philosopher, saying Philostratus hid behind the "mask of Pythagorean discipline."[96] If Apollonius were divine, Eusebius asked, then why had he needed training at the Asclepieion or in Persia and India, as Philostratus reported?[97] According to Eusebius, Apollonius's acts were a learned technique and therefore magic. Christ, in contrast, did not

---

94. Historia Augusta, *Life of Severus Alexander* 29 (Magie, LCL). The work is often attributed to Lampridius, but its authorship remains in doubt. It should be noted that the Historia Augusta is a very problematic source and perhaps not very accurate concerning the actual life of Severus. See Thomas A. J. McGinn's discussion of its reliability in *Prostitution, Sexuality, and the Law in Ancient Rome* (New York: Oxford University Press, 1998), 272–73. However, in spite of its problems, the mere mention of an image of Apollonius in proximity to an image of Jesus warrants a mention.

95. *Life of Severus Alexander* 22. As emperor, Alexander was very favorable to the Christians. He allowed Jews and Christians to practice their faith unmolested.

96. Eusebius, *Against Hierocles* 5 (Conybeare, LCL). The title alone alludes to the content: "The Treatise of Eusebius, the Son of Pamphilus, against the Life of Tyana Written by Philostratus, Occasioned by the Parallel Drawn by Hierocles between Him and Christ." This text is preserved in the works of Philostratus edited by C. L. Kayser, *Flavii Philostrati Opera* 1 (Leipzig: Teubner, 1870) and in Migne (PG 22, 796–868).

require any training or extensive travel to various lands to acquire his power as a miracle worker. Eusebius claimed that Apollonius performed exorcisms and healings due to his association with demons. He discredited the resurrection story of Apollonius involving a young girl in Rome, claiming, "Anyhow [Philostratus] hesitates, and doubts, whether after all a spark of life might have not lingered on in the girl unnoticed by her attendants."[98] If the event had occurred in Rome, as Philostratus reported, then it would have been noticed by the philosopher Euphrates, who later directly accused Apollonius of wizardry.[99] Eusebius argued along the same lines as Origen in his response to Celsus. He did not dispute that Apollonius performed miracles, but he pointed to the source of the power. For early Christians, the source of Jesus' power was divine; Apollonius was in league with demons and thus a fraud.[100]

It is noteworthy that Eusebius was attacking Philostratus's work directly. If Philostratus intended to create a pagan gospel rivaling the Christian gospels, then Eusebius had to respond. Opponents may accuse Apollonius or Jesus of being a magician, but their core of believers saw them as unique miracle men and universally treated magic with disdain and suspicion.

JESUS AND ASCLEPIUS

Homer first mentions Asclepius in the eighth century BCE in the *Iliad* as the mortal father of two heroes, but there is no indication of Asclepius worship until around the sixth century BCE.[101] The Homeric references described Asclepius as a physician without peers, and his son Machaon was referred to as "the blameless physician."[102] Other heroes such as Achilles typically dressed wounds on the field of battle, but Machaon was summoned specifically to treat Menelaus; his actions are those of a physician, not a warrior.

The poet Pindar was the first to introduce the notion that Asclepius was the product of a divine father, Apollo, and a human mother.[103] Apollo came down from Olympus and had an affair with a mortal woman, Coronis, who was married. At the moment of her death, Apollo came down and rescued the child

97. See Philostratus, *Life* 1.1, where Philostratus established the Pythagorean notion of divinity; also see 1.9; 1.18; Eusebius, *Against Hierocles* 9.

98. Eusebius, *Against Hierocles* 26 (Conybeare, LCL).

99. Ibid.

100. Kee, *Miracle in the Early Christian World*, 273.

101. Homer, *The Iliad* 11.518; also see Carl Roebuck, "The Asklepieion and Lerna," *Corinth*, vol. 14 (Princeton, NJ: American School of Classical Studies at Athens, 1951), 25.

102. Homer, *The Iliad* 4.194.

103. Pindar, *Pythian Odes* III.59 (See Edelstein, T. 1).

that was the fruit of their illicit union. Apollo gave the child, Asclepius, to the centaur Chiron for safekeeping, and Chiron taught Asclepius the art of healing.

There were variations of the genesis myth of Asclepius, but the mention of the city of Epidauros was one common feature in most versions. It was told that Coronis gave birth to the child in the vicinity of Epidauros, a city known as a healing center.[104] Epidauros was considered the city of Apollo, a god also known for his healing power; thus Asclepius became a healer due to his lineage and his geographical environment. The myth presented an interesting pattern. Asclepius replaced a popular deity known and worshipped for his fame as a healer.

Asclepius, like Christ, has a popular history attached to him. Testimonies recorded that Asclepius lived and worked as a healer in Epidauros and raised a family. His most notable family member was his daughter Hygieia (occasionally referred to as his wife), who represented Health and overshadowed all the other siblings. Asclepius was a preeminent physician who cared for the healthy and cured the sick. According to mythology, Asclepius drew the ire of Zeus when he raised a person from the dead. Zeus threw down a thunderbolt, killing Asclepius and the patient. After his death, Asclepius was raised to Olympus, achieving full divinity.[105]

There are several different accounts of Asclepius's transgression that resulted in his death at the hands of Zeus. Diodorus Siculus reported around 60–50 BCE that Asclepius resurrected "many," upsetting Hades, since the number of dead was diminishing.[106] In the first century, Apollodorus claimed that Asclepius raised six people from the dead, prompting Zeus to respond.[107] Pliny and Lucian both stated that Asclepius was killed for bringing Tyndareus back to life.[108] Sextus Empiricus recorded the many references to Asclepius's daring act, noting the popularity of the legend and the different ways in which

104. Johannes Wolmarans, "Asclepius of Epidaurus and Jesus of Nazareth," in *Acta Patristica et Byzantina* 7 (1996), 118.

105. It is fairly common for the product of an immortal father and mortal mother to be raised to divine status after death. Along with Asclepius, Hercules is a primary example; their myths speak of their dual nature. They are "heroes" during their mortal life and then gods upon their deaths. Still, Asclepius holds rank over Hercules. In a constructed dialogue, Lucian makes this distinction clear, as Zeus settles the dispute, claiming that Asclepius is superior due to the fact that he died earlier. Lucian, *Dialogues of the Gods* 15(13).

106. Diodorus Siculus, *Library of History* 4.71.1–3.

107. Apollodorus, *The Library* 3.10.3–4.

108. Pliny, *Natural History* 29.1.3; Lucian, *The Dance* 45.

it had been transmitted.[109] As Sextus noted, Asclepius's legend continued to resonate in Late Antiquity.

Asclepius healed through a process known as incubation, namely, attending to his patients in dreams. The typical patient would first bathe in the waters of the temple and then make an offering at the altar, before being led to a room called the *abaton*, where he would sleep. As Aristophanes recounted the procedure to Plutus, the patient was told by the priests not to wake up if he heard strange noises.[110] Asclepius gave the prescription for treatment in the patient's dream. As soon as the patient was healed, he had to make an offering to the temple, the obligatory "payment" for the medical cure. The offering would take place in the immediate area surrounding the image of Asclepius and would be in the spiritual form of prayer, an animal sacrifice, or the physical form of a votive offering. Votive offerings were left outside the Asclepieion at Corinth, dating from the fourth century BCE, depicting the afflicted body parts that were healed, including legs, arms, ears, feet, fingers, and representations of breasts and genitals.[111]

Recovered from the Asclepieion in Epidauros were numerous *stelai*, slabs of stone or wood that bear inscriptions that rest outside the temple and are carved with curative accounts from patients at the Asclepieion. The testimonies of Asclepius's cures range from the mundane to the obscure. Among the most vivid is the case of a man complaining of a blockage in his urinary tract. After he dreamed of "lying with a fair boy" in the *abaton*, the patient woke up feeling refreshed, holding the kidney stone in his hands.[112] The *stelai* were surely encouraged by the priests at Epidauros in order to advertise to the community and beyond the city's status as the preeminent Asclepieion.

---

109. Sextus Empiricus, *Against the Professors* 260-262.

110. Aristophanes, *Plutus* 633-747 (In Edelstein, T. 421).

111. Carl Roebuck in his analysis of Corinth concludes that the Corinthian Asclepieion is similar to the Asclepieia at Troizen and Athens, which contain two main structural parts with one serving a cultic function while the other is reserved for social use. The fountain in Corinth is separate from the cultic area of the Asclepieion, a conclusion also based upon the ancient description of the area by Pausanias. See Roebuck, "The Asklepieion and Lerna," 25; and Pausanias, *Description of Greece* 2.4.5. Andrew Hill has written on Paul's "body language" in "The Temple of Asclepius: An Alternative Source for Paul's Body Theology," in *JBL* 99 (Spring 1980): 437–39. F. T. van Straten treats the practice of votive offerings extensively in his chapter "Gifts for the Gods," in *Faith, Hope and Worship: Aspects of Religious Mentality in the Ancient World*, ed. H.S. Versnel (Leiden: Brill, 1981), 65–151.

112. *Inscriptiones Graecae* 4.1.121-124 (Edelstein, T. 423). Another collection more recent than Edelstein that includes a translation of the inscriptions is Lynn R. LiDonnici, *The Epidaurian Miracle Inscriptions: Text, Translation, and Commentary* (Atlanta: Scholars, 1995), 85–131.

Early on in the development of ancient medicine, its practitioners understood that there were limits to what they could treat, and it was not shameful to turn away patients. With Asclepius, patients could seek treatment in a centralized and reputable healing center. Furthermore, while physicians were adamant in their disapproval of charlatans and magicians, they were hardly critical of Asclepius or other healing cults.[113] Such an endorsement certainly helped the public embrace healing gods like Asclepius, and it also created a sort of partnership between physicians and healing cults, rather than a competition. Physicians were not always effusive in their praise for divine healing, but they did not have a problem with healing cults administering to chronically ill patients.[114]

Cases such as paralysis or blindness would be deemed untreatable by physicians, and these constituted a good portion of documented cures by Asclepius. Infertility, kidney stones, and gout were among other illnesses that the Asclepieia would treat, while doctors would not. Gout was mentioned in the Hippocratic Corpus specifically as an ailment a doctor should refuse to treat, "As for patients with gout . . . (they) are all incurable by the human art, as far as I know."[115] The accounts of the cult's effective treatments recorded its ability to treat the untreatable.[116]

The treatment of untreatable ailments contributed to the popularity of the cult of Asclepius, but it was not the only factor. It was rather the style of healing

113. In a commentary ascribed to the second-century physician Galen, the author argued that cures derived from dreams of Sarapis, Asclepius, or Isis are just as effective as any treatment existing. It should be noted that the fragments of this commentary were preserved in Arabic and may not have been penned by Galen. See Galen, *Commentary on the Hippocratic Oath* fr. 1; also see Franz Rosenthal, "An Ancient Commentary on the Hippocratic Oath," *Bulletin of the History of Medicine* 30 (1956): 52–87.

114. Epilepsy was seen to have a point beyond the capabilities of a physician; see Hippocrates, *The Sacred Disease* 2.1-7. At Pergamum, Asclepius was praised as a healer of epilepsy. See Oribasius, *Medical Collections* 45, 30, 10-14 (Edelstein, T. 425), reported by Rufus of Ephesus in the first century. See Bronwen Wickkiser, *The Appeal of Asklepios and the Politics of Healing in the Greco-Roman World* (Ann Arbor, MI: UMI Dissertation Services, 2003), 53. Doctors often sacrificed to Asclepius as a patron deity. Ancient medicine and the healing cult were not diametrically opposed as "rational" and "irrational" entities. See Nutton, *Ancient Medicine*, 409 n. 63.

115. Stele 2.43 from Epidauros mentions the healing of gout, *Inscriptiones Graecae* 4.1.21-22 (Edelstein, T. 423), while Hippocrates, *Prorrhetic* 2.2.8.1-4, lists gout as something physicians should avoid treating. *Prorrhetic*, which consists of treatises dealing with prognoses, is divided into two books. The first is possibly genuinely Hippocratic, while the second is considered spurious, although Galen mined the work for useful information. Wickkiser notes this in *The Appeal of Asklepios*, 109.

116. As in Stele 2.43; Oribasius, *Medical Collections* 45, 30, 10-14 (Edelstein, T. 425); Aelianus, *Fragment* 100 (Edelstein, T. 405). Pausanius, in *Description of Greece* 2.27.3, noted the *stelai* recording the names of cured patients.

that ultimately won the populace over. The healing cult would give patients personal attention that served to bring them comfort. The somnolent cures of the cult soothed away anxiety.

Unsurprisingly, the cult grew in popularity in the wake of widespread plagues, and the Romans established the cult of Asclepius in Rome during the event of a plague dating around 295–292 BCE.[117] Civic leaders apparently found that Asclepius's presence in the plague-stricken city had some value, as the arrival of the cult may have calmed a heightened level of anxiety, even though the Romans were surely aware that Asclepius cured individuals and had never been known as a god that cured plagues.[118] To put it quite simply, a healing cult provided what a physician could not. A doctor could not cure blindness, but a god certainly could.

Medical care was expensive in antiquity. Only the rich could afford the private care offered by physicians. Treatments at the Asclepieia were less expensive. Indeed, before the Common Era, Aristophanes noted that at such clinics "there are no fees."[119] Accounts testify to the philanthropic nature of the god, and the offerings in lieu of a monetary fee: "Accept the aftercourse of this cock whom I sacrifice, heard of the walls of my house. For we draw no bounteous nor ready spring; else might we, perchance, with an ox or stuffed pig of much fatness and no humble cock, be paying the price of cure from diseases thou didst wipe away, Lord, by laying on of gentle hands."[120] As a result of being a welcoming and widely accessible medical alternative, Asclepius gained a reputation as a god who took care of the poor: "Asclepius may heal Pauson and Iros and any other of the poor people."[121] As a terrestrial god, Asclepius

---

117. Livy, *History of Rome* 7.27; 4.20-25. Livy was actually the first to record this and dates the plague around 295 BCE. The Roman plague is also mentioned in Ovid, *Metamorphoses* 15.621-752; and Valerius Maximus, *Memorable Doings and Sayings* 1.8.2. Also see Wickkiser, *The Appeal of Asklepios*, 193. Since these sources are late, the "plague" in the case of Rome may have been conflated with other threats to the city.

118. The Roman arrival of the Epidaurian Asclepius is notable for several reasons, as previously mentioned. One result of the importation of the god is the Latinized spelling of his name, changing it from Asklepios to Aesculapius or, as some scholars have utilized (and what this dissertation follows), Asclepius. However, there is a slight difference between the Greek god Asklepios and the Roman god Asclepius. Roman Asclepius followed the pattern of the Roman adoption of their gods; the arrival of a foreign god shows favor toward Mother Rome. And as the importation stories such as Ovid's illustrate, Asclepius willingly came to Rome to be a citizen. Therefore, Roman Asclepius shows favor toward Rome and not toward any enemies of Rome. For a brief history of the Latinized spelling of the god, see Wickkiser, *The Appeal of Asklepios*, 206–207.

119. Aristophanes, *Plutus* 407.

120. Herondas, *Mimiambi* IV, 1-95 (Edelstein, T. 482).

was thought to pay greater attention to the poor than Olympian gods such as Zeus: "the Olympians are helpful to the great . . . when appearing to them, the celestials to the middle classes, the terrestrials to the poor."[122] While Asclepieia were not exactly free clinics, their munificence was exploited on occasion. In Rome, Suetonius reported that under the emperor Claudius during an outbreak of sickness, slave owners dumped their slaves at the temple on Tiber Island.[123] The emperor rebuked the slave owners for manipulating the philanthropy of the temple and granted freedom to any slave who fully recovered.

The temples of Asclepius made up for any monetary loss through generous offerings from rich benefactors. Evidence of how these charitable contributions came about can be found in the second-century writings of Aelius Aristides, who told of the god visiting him and imploring him to offer animals and distribute money to pilgrims: "And I believe he gave some other instructions in addition to these. Afterwards, I should go to the holy shrine and offer perfect sacrificial animals to Asclepius and set up holy craters and distribute holy portions to all the fellow pilgrims."[124] The spirit of benevolence and care of the poor did exist in pagan religion in antiquity, although it was minor compared with the attention paid by the Christians. Still, the evidence maintains that Asclepius was regarded as the most "man-loving" of the gods and the most interested in the well-being of all humankind, including the poor.[125]

AELIUS ARISTIDES'S SACRED TALES

The locus for Asclepius worship would eventually shift from Epidauros. The Asclepieion at Pergamum distanced itself from other temples and enjoyed a renaissance during Hadrian's reign. After several reported healings, Hadrian capitalized on an ever-growing resurgence of the Asclepieion and began to rebuild the temple.[126] Antoninus Pius continued the work of his predecessor, completing the "greatest" Asclepieion in the empire.[127] Pergamum was the city

---

121. Aelianus, *Fragmenta* 100 (Edelstein, T. 405).

122. Artemidorus, *Onirocritica* II, 34 (Edelstein, T. 259).

123. Suetonius, *Life of Claudius* 25.2. Ludwig Edelstein claimed that Asclepieia resembled Christian charitable hospitals. *Asclepius*, vol. 2, 176. That is not really the case. While Asclepius was obviously beloved and the cult moderately cared for the poor, treatment was not free for everyone. See the section on Julian later in this chapter. If Julian had believed the pagans were doing such a good job of attending to the poor, he would not have rebuked them for allowing the Christians to do a better job.

124. Aristides, *Sacred Tales* 48.27 (Behr).

125. Aristides, *Oratio* 39.5.

126. Adolf Hoffmann, "The Roman Remodeling of the Asklepieion," in *Pergamon: Citadel of the Gods* (Harrisburg, PA: Trinity Press International, 1998), 42.

of Galen, and the physician practiced in that city before his arrival in Rome. The cult and temple of Asclepius in Pergamum became the preeminent cultic center for healing in Late Antiquity. Its renown was augmented by the first-person accounts of the healing power of the god in the *Sacred Tales* of Aelius Aristides, written around 149 CE.

Aristides was a prominent rhetorician from Smyrna who became incapacitated by illness. Galen examined him in Pergamum and commented that he had never come across such a strong mind in such a frail body.[128] At one point, Aristides was afflicted by a plague. His symptoms included fever, a "bilious mixture," headaches, coughing, and difficulty in eating or walking.[129] Aristides's vivid details of his ailments and how they were cured suggest that he might have been chronically ill. Aristides championed the unique effectiveness of divine cures, but many of the divine treatments Aristides described are not out of line with what a physician would prescribe. Using water and restoring balance to the humors were textbook methods for Late Antique physicians. In several instances, he recorded the divine prescription of blood-letting. Aristides claimed that the god "commanded that I have blood drawn from my elbow, and he added, as far as I remember, sixty pints . . . . Two days later, he commanded me again to draw blood from my forehead."[130] Mostly Aristides described the curative properties of water and its proximity to the temples of Asclepius.[131] His descriptions provide some revealing detail about the cult of Asclepius and the relationship between healing and religion. Aristides described the visitation of Asclepius in his dreams and his prescriptions, including one that ordered him to bathe in an icy river during winter, the efficacy of which prompted Aristides to proclaim, "Great is Asclepius!"[132]

Aristides was not against medicine or physicians. In fact, he consulted physicians as well as the cult of Asclepius. Galen's teacher, Satyrus, was summoned to examine Aristides, and the patient heeded his advice, as long as it did not conflict with the divine prescription. Satyrus advised that the bloodletting cease and a plaster be applied to treat his abdomen. Aristides replied that he "did not have the authority to do one thing or the other," but "while the god commanded the letting of my blood, I would obey whether willing or

127. Otfried Deubner reports this in *Das Asklepeion von Pergamon* (Berlin: Verlag für Kunstwissenschaft, 1938), 19. Also see Kollmann, *Jesus und die Christen als Wundertäter* 80–82.

128. Nutton, *Ancient Medicine*, 277.

129. Aristides, *Sacred Tales* 48.37-45.

130. Aristides, *Sacred Tales* 48.47-48 (Behr).

131. Aristides, *Oratio* 39.12.

132. Aristides, *Sacred Tales* 48.21 (Behr).

not, or rather never unwilling. Still I did not ignore Satyrus' prescription, but took and kept it. It was no cornucopia."[133] In his dissatisfaction with Satyrus's treatment, Aristides implied that the divine treatment was always preferable and one he heavily endorsed. It also did not appear that Aristides was untreatable. Although he may have been afflicted with some chronic illnesses, doctors such as Satyrus, Heracleon, and his foster father Zosimus, who was "skilled in medicine," were ready and willing to treat him.[134] Aristides found more value in divine healing, and while he primarily describes the cult of Asclepius, he also described appearances by the familiar healing deities from Egypt, Sarapis and Isis.[135] The second-century orator recounted his personal experience with the healing power of Asclepius in almost embarrassing detail, calling the god a "great magician."[136] This is not meant as an accusation, but rather as a testament to the miraculous results effected by the god. For Aristides, Asclepius was the "gentlest and most generous of gods."[137]

Aristides's praise of Asclepius was certainly effusive; it also extended beyond mere praise for services rendered. Asclepius healed Aristides when human doctors could not. Aristides's fierce devotion stemmed not only from the incidents of divine healing, but from the conviction that Asclepius now guarded over his life. Aristides called Asclepius a beacon of light in his daily affairs. The god was praised for revealing a shipwreck to Aristides on the day he was due to embark on a voyage, thus saving him from certain death.[138]

These were not the qualities of an unbiased physician treating a patient. They were the qualities of a benevolent god caring for one of his supplicants. Asclepius was not only a healer of the body, but a savior. Aristides' accounts reflected the sincere devotion that the act of healing can instill. For Aristides, Asclepius was akin to a patron saint or guardian angel on his shoulder, constantly protecting him.[139]

The notion of Asclepius as a savior to all continued after the time of Aristides. Beginning in 160 CE with Julius Apellas's report of his healing at Epidauros, Asclepius was seen as more than just a divine friend and helper. Apellas's treatment altered the course of his life, and he sincerely believed his

133. Aristides, *Sacred Tales* 49.8-10 (Behr).

134. See Aristides, *Sacred Tales* 48.21; 47.75.

135. Aristides, *Sacred Tales* 48.45.

136. Aristides, *Sacred Tales* 39.14.

137. Aristides, *Oratio* 39.5 (Behr).

138. Aristides, *Sacred Tales* 48.13.

139. See Steven C. Muir, "Touched by a God: Aelius Aristides, Religious Healings, and Asclepius Cults," in SBLSP 34 (Atlanta: Scholars, 1995), 362–79.

life had come under the care and protection of the god.[140] The compassion of Asclepius compelled many to feel such sentiments. In Late Antiquity, pagans and Christians lived together and mingled. In Corinth, the Christians were intermixed with their pagan neighbors, sometimes engaging in activities Paul found abhorrent, such as eating idol food, forcing Paul to admonish his brothers in his first letter to the Corinthians (particularly chs. 8–10).[141] Christian apologists painted Asclepius as an adversary of Christ in order to protect the community against idolatry. However, it was rare for a devotee of pagan religion to point to Christ as a competing threat. The brief reign of Julian offered an opportunity to witness such a moment.

JULIAN THE APOSTATE

Asclepius devotion continued in popularity in Late Antiquity from the second century well into the third and fourth centuries. The influence of the cult is evident in the mid-fourth century. Known as "the apostate," Julian was raised as a Christian. Upon his ascent to power, Julian viewed Christianity as a betrayal of the Greco-Roman tradition and desired a return to traditional forms of worship. Julian's attention to the cult of Asclepius must be understood in the context of his own apostasy. Julian was not alone in returning to the fold. A recovered poem from third-century North Africa addressed a senator who was once a Christian, ridiculing his transgression: "Yet, since you have crossed the threshold of the true Law and come to know God for a few years, why do you cling to what should be abandoned or why do you give up what should be retained?"[142] For Julian and others, the traditional observance of the gods was not to be discarded and replaced by Christianity.

After a brief conflict with his cousin Constantius, Julian entered Constantinople in 361 and publicly affirmed his new faith: "Know that I worship the gods, I worship the gods publicly, and all the soldiers returning with me do the same. I sacrifice oxen in view of all; I offer tons of thanks offerings. And why? Because the gods have revealed that it is their will that I

---

140. See Edelstein, T. 432; Kee, *Miracle in the Early Christian World*, 88.

141. See G. D. R. Sanders's piece "Archeological Evidence for Early Christianity and the End of Hellenic Religion in Corinth," in *Urban Religion in Roman Corinth* (Cambridge, MA: Harvard University Press, 2005), 419–42. Sanders notes that observance at the Asclepieion in Corinth continued until the end of the fourth century; it was likely low-key, and continued use is difficult to demonstrate archaeologically. Also see my "The Pagan Feast and the Sacramental Feast: The Implication of Idol Food Consumption in Paul's Corinth," in *Sewanee Theological Review* (Christmas 2007): 22–47.

142. Pseudo-Cyprian, *Carmen ad Senatorem* 35–46.

should restore their worship in its original purity. I obey them, with absolutely no reservations."[143]

Julian believed his ascent to the throne was due to his silent devotion to Greco-Roman religion, the true faith.[144] He immediately restored public sacrifices, an aspect of pagan religion that Julian had always enjoyed and Constantius had thwarted: "It was this that shook him to the core, as he saw their temples in ruins, their ritual banned, their altars overturned, their sacrifices suppressed, their priests sent packing and their property divided up between a crew of rascals."[145] He initially established a pagan "church" of sorts with Helios as its prime deity, influenced no doubt by Aurelian and possibly Constantine's interest in the sun god of the Roman empire, Sol Invictus.[146] Julian also believed the Christians were appropriating Greek literature at the expense of pagan religion. He instituted boundaries for Christians, insisting that they could not teach anything from the Greek literary tradition. Julian had witnessed these Christian "border crossings" as a schoolmate of the Cappadocian Basil the Great and friend of Gregory Nazianzus, and the incidents obviously festered.[147] He ordered that all teachers be trained to represent Greco-Roman religious values. If Christians were so disdainful of pagan religion, then Julian believed they should not partake in an educational system that was grounded in traditional values that were in part constructed by adherents of pagan religion.

Julian viewed the *paideia*, the classical style of education in the Greco-Roman world, as the foundation of a philosophic life and found that it was hypocritical to include the Christians. It was normal for Christians to obtain a classical education in philosophy and rhetoric. Basil and Gregory of Nazianzus were classically educated, and John Chrysostom was a pupil of Libanius as well. During his rule, however, Julian made it more difficult for Christians to obtain that education, as he made religion part of the requirements.[148] His actions drew protests from Christian leaders such as Gregory, but Julian was very aware of what he was doing. As Bowersock notes, Julian expected that all of the educated elite in the empire would be pagan within a generation.[149]

---

143. Julian, *Letter to Maximus* 8.415C. More recently, R. Joseph Hoffmann has offered a collection and translation, *Julian's* Against the Galileans (Amherst, NY: Prometheus, 2004). The above text derives from Hoffmann's translation, and unless otherwise noted, the LCL edition is cited.

144. G.W. Bowersock, *Julian the Apostate* (Cambridge, MA: Harvard University Press, 1978), 61.

145. Libanius, *Orations* 18.23 (Norman, LCL).

146. Jeffrey Hargis, *Against the Christians: The Rise of Early Anti-Christian Polemic* (New York: Peter Lang, 1999), 100.

147. Ibid., 101.

148. Wilken, *The Christians*, 175.

Julian echoed a general antagonism of imperial traditionalists toward Christianity. The concept that a religion demanded uncompromising, uniform faith was abhorrent to traditional non-Christians. The pagan religionists of Late Antiquity loved local and naturalized traditions. Nock claimed that most pagans found great value in the worship of the household and of the state, as well as the reverence of the dead. Moreover, they deeply feared the loss of their rituals. Worship for pagan religionists was different from philosophy; "it rested on emotion and not on conscious theory and thinking; it had deeper roots in their natures, and was not easily refuted by reason."[150]

Julian advocated for change among his pagan brethren. He identified several Christian traits that he believed pagan religion must adopt, or else die. Julian was aggressively championing Hellenic reform; he desired a return to the virtuous ways of Greco-Roman religion. He wrote to Arsacius, the high priest of Galatia that "the Hellenic religion does not yet prosper as I desire."[151] Julian understood that pagan religion must adapt, and he found elements in Christianity that were useful to appropriate: "Why, then do we think that this is enough, why do we not observe that it is their benevolence to strangers, their care for the graves of the dead and the pretended holiness of their lives that have done most to increase atheism?"[152] It was too easy to argue, as Plutarch did in *On Superstition,* that the baseless superstitions of the Christians were responsible for turning people into atheists. Rather, Jewish and Christian funerary practices and their philanthropy were worthy of emulation. Julian found it unconscionable that Jews and Christians took better care of the poor than the pagans. He encouraged his fellow religionists to emulate the Christians and the Jews in their devotion to charity and active consideration of pervasive social problems. In his letter to Arsacius, Julian ordered that one-fifth of the money he sent be distributed among the poor, for "it is disgraceful that, when no Jew ever has to beg, and the impious Galileans [Christians] support not only their own poor but ours as well, all men see that our people lack aid from us."[153] It was embarrassing for Julian that Christians provided better care for pagans than the pagan cults did.

---

149. Bowersock, *Julian the Apostate,* 84.

150. Nock, *Conversion,* 163.

151. Julian, *Letter to Arsacius* 429C (Wright, LCL).

152. Ibid. 430A (Wright, LCL).

153. Ibid. 430D (Wright, LCL). Julian consistently belittled the Christians with the term *Galileans.* To identify them as Christians would grant credence and recognition to their religion. Also see Vivian Nutton, "From Galen to Alexander," 7.

Libanius urged Julian to "refute those writings which make a god and a son of a god of the man from Palestine."[154] Julian discovered that in order to successfully counter the rising Christian threat, he needed to a single, powerful figurehead to stand in opposition to Jesus. Helios, or *Sol Invictus*, could not mount a fierce campaign against such a powerful figure as Jesus was for the Christians, although Julian made an unconvincing attempt in a letter to the Alexandrians.[155] In this letter, Julian argued that the Christians did not even acknowledge the present good that the gods provide. Instead, the Christians were wasting their time on the memory of a dead man and living in the past.

Julian needed to find a suitable opponent to Christ, and in his hymn, he attempted to offer Helios. Julian countered the apologetic argument that Christ was existent before creation by citing that Helios had existed from time immemorial. However, Helios was not a figure that could win hearts and minds for Julian. In his campaign against Christ, Helios would not do. In his paean to Constantius written during his campaign in Gaul around 359, Julian described the role of emperor as a "savior," and an emperor was "like a good physician" who makes every effort to cure his people's ills.[156] In likening himself to a physician, he may not have intentionally recalled Asclepius. However, in his invective against the Christians, Julian was more specific in his praise of the god. Julian's low popularity meant that he could not effectively present himself as a healing savior to rival Christ.[157] Asclepius, a benevolent, universally loved healing figure in the pagan pantheon, fit this role perfectly. In Asclepius, Julian found a suitable opponent to Christ; he was a physician whom Julian would trumpet as "savior."

Just as Asclepius had provided Celsus with a figure to maintain Greco-Roman tradition, the healing god would serve a similar function for Julian. Julian's polemic against the Christians was anticipated by Celsus. Like Celsus, Julian believed the Christian religion destroyed the foundation of Greco-Roman tradition and culture. Julian argued against the Christians on similar philosophical grounds that Christ's miracles were inferior and the work of a low-class magician. Julian ridiculed Christians for being duped into a false faith

---

154. Libanius, *Orations* 18.178 (Harmon, LCL).

155. Julian, *Ep.* 47.434B-D (Hoffmann).

156. Julian, *The Heroic Deeds of Constantius* 89B.

157. See Rowland Smith, *Julian's Gods: Religion and Philosophy in the Thought and Action of Julian the Apostate* (London: Routledge, 1995), 6, 169. Julian was largely ridiculed in Antioch by Christians and pagans alike. His attempts at restoration of the gods around 362 was attacked by Christians and tepidly noticed by pagans. Julian's results in Antioch arguably established his reputation; however, his experience there did have a deep effect on him.

by a charlatan healer. Julian placed even more emphasis on the inferiority of Christ and superiority of Asclepius.[158] He appeared to believe that Asclepius was the superior god, and he endorsed Asclepius's superiority.

Julian called Christians "Galileans," refusing to acknowledge their name, and he belittled Christianity as merely a localized, regional cult. Much of his *Against the Galileans* was recovered by Cyril of Alexandria, who, like Origen, felt it was necessary to refute the views of the apostate emperor years later in his fifth-century *Against Julian*.[159] Cyril believed that Julian's work was disturbing and filled with many unsubstantiated attacks upon Christianity.[160] Due to Julian's privileged knowledge of Scripture and Christian tradition, his books were particularly dangerous in the eyes of the early church fathers. Julian argued that Jesus was less worthy than the gods, since he had been known for only three hundred years, "and during his lifetime he accomplished nothing worth hearing of, unless anyone thinks that to heal crooked and blind men and to exorcise those who were possessed by evil demons in the villages of Bethsaida and Bethany can be classed as a mighty achievement."[161] The Christians were hypocrites and, moreover, power-hungry. Julian argued that Christians corrupted their own Scripture: "Nowhere did either Jesus or Paul hand down to you such commands."[162] Echoing Porphyry, Julian claimed that the Christians were guilty of misrepresenting the meager words of Jesus, who never desired Christians to attain such power.[163] Julian intended to paint Jesus as a minor village healer who spawned an aberrant faith that threatened the traditional religion and values of the imperial realm.

The similarities between Asclepius and Christ allowed Julian to uphold Asclepius at Christ's expense. And there are obvious similarities between Asclepius and Christ. Asclepius was the product of a divine father and mortal mother, as was Jesus.[164] Both figures walked the earth as mortals. Both figures gained a reputation as preeminent healers. Furthermore, both Jesus and

158. Smith, *Julian's Gods*, 203. See notes 172 and 173 below for evidence.

159. See William J. Malley, *Hellenism and Christianity: The Conflict between Hellenic and Christian Wisdom in the* Contra Galileos *of Julian the Apostate and the* Contra Julianum *of St. Cyril of Alexandria* (Rome: Università Gregoriana Editrice, 1978).

160. Cyril, *Against Julian* Book 1.3. See the French translation by Paul Burguière and Pierre Évieux in *Contre Julien*, SC (Paris: Éditions du Cerf, 1985).

161. Julian, *Against the Galileans* 1.191E (Wright, LCL).

162. Julian, *Against the Galileans* 1.206A. (Wright, LCL).

163. Porphyry notably points out hypocrisy concerning Jesus' sayings and Paul's hypocrisy concerning idol food in *Apocriticus* 3.7-18 and 3.30-36. Also see Wilken, *The Christians*, 126.

164. The poet Pindar is the first to introduce the notion that Asclepius is the product of a divine father, Apollo, and a human mother, Coronis, in *Pythian Odes* III.59.

Asclepius were killed and resurrected to divine status, although Asclepius's death was directly inflicted by a divine hand, not by a group of humans. Jesus and Asclepius were similarly proclaimed by their followers as "savior of the world." To combat Christianity, Julian had to diminish the person of Christ. In Christ, the Christians had a very personal deity who lived and walked on earth, performing miracles and exuding care and concern for the poor.

Tertullian derided the pagan worship of Asclepius, saying he was deserving of his death at the hands of Jupiter.[165] Asclepius was as intimidating to Christians as Christ was to the pagans. Thus, Julian emphasized the god Asclepius as the heart of all pagan worship. At moments during his reign, he claimed, "Asclepius is savior of the whole world." Julian went on to proclaim, "I mean to say that Zeus engendered Asclepius from himself among the intelligible gods, and through the life of generative Helios he revealed him to earth. Asclepius, having made his visitation to earth from the sky . . . is present everywhere on land and sea. He visits no one of us separately, and yet he raises souls up that are sinful and bodies that are sick."[166] In a hymn to King Helios, Julian asked, "Shall I now go on to tell you how Helios took thought for the health and safety of all men by begetting Asclepius to be the savior of the whole world?"[167] This portrayal of Asclepius as begotten by Zeus and engendered by Helios is no accident and may have been a direct juxtaposition with Christ. Early Christians including Justin Martyr understood Jesus as the divine Logos sitting at God's side at the creation event.[168] Thus, so was Asclepius, accompanying Helios even before creation.

Julian's mockery of Christ's miracles followed the typical playbook of pagan–Christian polemical debates. As Morton Smith points out, such claims were valuable to Julian.[169] In the reflections of Apellas or Aristides, the work of Asclepius indicated a present reality and interaction in the here and now.[170] Julian emphasized the role of Asclepius and the gods as omnipresent helpers, a stance supported by his own experience. Julian faulted Christians for upholding the salvific work of Jesus to a point that any tangible and present divine interaction was irrelevant. In Julian's eyes, the great failure of the Christians was that they refused to acknowledge the active blessings of the gods in daily life. This failure was all the more manifest in their particular abhorrence toward

---

165. Tertullian, *To the Heathen* 2.14.42 (CSEL 20.127; *ANF* 3.144).

166. Julian, *Against the Galileans* 1.200B (Wright, LCL). Also see *Oration* 4.144B, where Julian juxtaposes Asclepius to Christ; and 153B for his claim of Asclepius as "the savior."

167. Julian, *Hymn to King Helios* 153B (Wright, LCL).

168. Justin, *1 Apol.* 63.

169. Smith, *Jesus the Magician*, 203.

170. Kee, *Miracle in the Early Christian World*, 88.

pagan images and temples: "It is our duty to adore not only the images of the gods but also their temples and sacred precincts and altars."[171] In turn, Julian acknowledged his deep disgust for Christian veneration of sacred spaces in their persistent devotion to the tombs and sepulchers of local martyrs. He denigrated the Christians' ritual observance as abominable while ridiculing their lack of proper ritual observance of the pagan cult. Julian believed the funerary practices of the Christians to be "the work of sorcery and foulness."[172] His animosity toward the Christians was motivated by his belief in the present reality of the gods.

Julian's choice of Asclepius had political implications as well.[173] As already mentioned, the emperor attempted to associate his name with Asclepius at a time when Julian's own popularity was rather low.[174] Libanius noted Julian's motivations in one of Libanius's orations, claiming that Julian's actions to restore pagan religion embodied the resurrecting power of Asclepius.[175] Julian credited Asclepius's training in a type of *paideia*, his education under Chiron, as contributing to the majesty of the god. Julian was manipulating the Asclepius legend by asserting that Asclepius was not a mortal hero raised up to divinity upon his death. Rather, he was sent down, "engendered by Zeus," and was fully divine upon his arrival on earth. The emperor attributed powers to Asclepius that borrowed from the understanding of Christ as "savior of the world." Julian stated that Asclepius "raises souls up that are sinful."[176] With this phrase, Julian paints Asclepius as a healer of the soul as well as the body. Julian also proclaimed a personal relationship with Asclepius: "At any rate, when I have been sick, Asclepius has often cured me by prescribing remedies."[177] The emperor advanced his agenda of excluding Christians from classical education by emphasizing the role that education played in demonstrating the existence of the true "savior of the world."

Julian's descriptions of Asclepius's attributes were not unique: Aristides recalled his personal relationship with Asclepius, and Julius Apellas depicted Asclepius as a healer of the soul.[178] What made Julian's descriptions significant

171. Julian, *Fragment of a Letter to a Priest* 296B-C (Wright, LCL).

172. Julian, *Against the Galileans* 335B (Wright, LCL). See Smith, *Jesus the Magician*, 204, as Smith noted this may be the first charge specifically against the cult of the saints.

173. Polymnia Athanassiadi-Fowden, *Julian and Hellenism: An Intellectual Biography* (Oxford: Clarendon, 1981), 165–69.

174. Julian, *Against the Galileans* 1.200B (Wright, LCL). Also see *Oration* 4.144B

175. Libanius, *Orations* 13.42.

176. Julian, *Against the Galileans* 1.200B (Wright, LCL). Also see *Oration* 4.144B.

177. Julian, *Against the Galileans* 1.235D (Wright, LCL).

was that he was speaking as a former Christian. Competition with Christ was foremost in his mind when he constructed his polemic and called Asclepius the savior of the world. "Savior" assumed a new meaning in Julian. In Aristides' works, the term was used fairly innocently, and in Julian's writings, it denoted war with Christianity. Julian understood the growing pluralism of the religious landscape and the hurdles traditional pagan religion faced. The Asclepius cult was philanthropic by Roman standards, but the Jews and Christians were more advanced in caring for the poor. The emperor was seeking a unifying face for his pagan reestablishment, and he found it in Asclepius. Just as Philostratus appropriated Christ by focusing attention on Apollonius, Julian accomplished the same result with Asclepius. Asclepius became the "savior" in response to claims of Christ as savior. The words and actions of Julian reflected the intense competition for cultic survival and, perhaps for Julian, the survival of Roman identity.

In his appropriation of Christian elements, Julian offered an obscure and unique characterization of Asclepius in the fourth century. Whenever the word *appropriation* is employed in reference to pagan-Christian contact, it most often refers to Christian appropriation of non-Christian elements. As we will see in Christian art, Christians possibly appropriated elements of the Asclepius cult to enlarge magnify and heighten the qualities of Jesus. Julian provides a rare case of a reverse appropriation—the pagan appropriation of Christianity. He desired pagans to emulate certain traits of the Christians: their attention to the poor, their charity, and their care of the dead. He also needed Asclepius to possess all of the qualities the Christians claimed for Jesus.

In the figure of Asclepius, Julian had already won the battle of longevity, as Asclepius worship reaches back to the sixth century bce. Julian's reign was very short, mitigating any lasting influence. However, Julian's writings were read well into the fifth century, and Cyril believed them dangerous enough to require a rebuttal. Julian was familiar with Christian scriptures, rites, and traditions, and could use them against the religion.[179] His juxtaposition of Asclepius and Christ was informed by his Christian background. Any outsider

---

178. See Edelstein, T. 432; Kee, *Miracle in the Early Christian World*, 88; and Aristides, *Oratio* 39.5.

179. Julian, *Against the Galileans* 335B (Wright, LCL). Porphyry was a similar threat, since he was so knowledgeable in Christian scripture. However, Porphyry was never a Christian; Julian was. The fact that Porphyry wrote against the Christians is undisputed, given the numerous refutations directed against Porphyry. Fragments of his lost work *Against the Christians* indicate that Porphyry directed his polemic against Jewish and Christian scriptures. See R. Joseph Hoffmann's *Porphyry's* Against the Christians*: The Literary Remains* (Amherst, NY: Prometheus, 1994) for a good collection of these fragments in translation.

could observe similarities between Asclepius and Christ, but Julian amplified them to directly counter any claims of the Christian Jesus. His descriptions of Asclepius had a strong tradition in Late Antiquity, and the cult already enjoyed prominence. Julian modeled Asclepius after Christ and made Asclepius into the greater opponent. Julian's writings exacerbated the conflict between the two rival gods, and his writings and policies did nothing to dissuade Christians from desecrating pagan temples and images.

CONCLUSION

Within this context, we can begin to realize the importance of healing and miracle as they relate to religion. Asclepius and his cult held a strong currency in Late Antiquity. Pagan opponents to Christianity utilized the god's popularity to situate him as the principal challenger to Christ. Christian authors recognized Asclepius's threat and similarly appropriated traits of the god to promote the peerless nature of Jesus. The appropriation of Asclepius can be witnessed in the visual art of Christ the Miracle Worker. The favorable portrayal of such figures as Apollonius and Asclepius found in the writings of Philostratus, Aristides, and Julian help explain the Christian motivation to appropriate traits and features of these religious rivals.

3

Healing and Miracles in Early Christian Writings

Despite their religious differences, Christians and their non-Christian neighbors were united in the belief that religion could cure their physical maladies. The notion that a figure like Asclepius or Christ could restore one's health was appealing. In healing cults and in Christianity, the image of the divine physician became a comfort to people in need. Medical imagery was commonly intertwined with theology.[1] In Ignatius of Antioch's letter to the Ephesians, he reminds his listeners that "there is only one Physician" and that the Eucharist is the true medicine of immortality.[2]

In Late Antiquity, the Asclepius cult was a popular source of religious healing. According to Adolf von Harnack, "A further testimony of much greater weight is afforded by the revival which attended the cult of Asclepius during the Imperial age."[3] For many non-Christians, the divine physician of choice was Asclepius. The previous chapter discussed the tendency of pagan culture to devote attention to the cult of Asclepius. This chapter will focus on Christian sources that emphasized the portrayal of Christ as an unrivaled physician and miracle worker. The textual references to Christ's superiority as a healer and miracle worker, especially during a time of Christian peace in the fourth century, are mirrored in visual art in the persistent image of Christ the Miracle Worker.

As opposed to the cult of Asclepius, what exactly did "Christian" healing look like in Late Antiquity? If the early church authors were so vehemently

---

1. See Gerhard Fichtner, "Christus als Arzt: Ursprünge und Wirkungen eines Motivs," *Frühmittelalterliche Studien* 16 (1982): 7. Fichtner asserts that in the first centuries, "Christ the savior is Christ the physician." Fichtner notes Ignatius's letter to the Ephesians, as well as Tatian, Athenagoras, and Lactantius on his 8–9.

2. Ignatius, *Letter to the Ephesians* 7.2; 20.2 (Staniforth).

3. Harnack, *The Mission and Expansion of the Christians in the First Three Centuries*, trans. and ed. James Moffatt (New York: G.P. Putnam, 1908), 105.

set against the cult of Asclepius, could their alternative in Christ really be a viable figure, since he was an earthly healer for only three years? In their espousal of Christ as the divine physician to rival Asclepius, unlike the healing cult, early church writers did not have the backing of a centuries-old support structure. A Late Antique Christian could not walk into a church and expect to be cured of a chronic illness. As the fourth century ended, Christian churches began to replace the temples of Asclepius, and these churches were often constructed upon the foundations of the razed buildings. A Christian basilica was built at the Asclepieion at Epidauros. The Asclepieion at Pergamum was virtually whitewashed of its pagan imagery by the Christians. The builders of the Christian church at Pergamum appropriated the healing spring of the Asclepieion as its baptismal font.[4] The Asclepieion at Rome on Tiber Island is now the Church of San Bartolomeo, and for interested tourists, a commentary of Asclepius's arrival in Rome can be heard there.

The early church authors in Late Antiquity could not offer the services of a Christian hospital as an alternative to the temples of Asclepius, as a structural system of hospitals did not yet exist. Instead, they promoted the notion of Christ as the unrivaled physician, healer of soul and body, and performer of the final resurrection. Christians might look upon an image of Christ in the act of healing and be reminded of their own "healing" by Christ: the ritual baptismal washing that cleansed them of sin and marked them out as Christ's own. In Late Antiquity, Christ the Miracle Worker could not effectively rival the cult of Asclepius as a viable healing alternative, and Christians could easily call upon the cult if they so desired. Instead, early church authors utilized the image of Christ healing and working miracles in the gospels to remind their audience of the perils of idolatry, the salvation secured by Christ, and their participation as baptized members in the ecclesia.

SECOND- AND THIRD-CENTURY WRITINGS

Second-century Christian documents contain numerous depictions of Jesus as a physician. They also acknowledge the popularity of the cult of Asclepius. Latin and Greek early church writers consistently attacked Asclepius, as they did the other gods of the pantheon, by insisting that they were not gods at all. However, they treated Asclepius slightly differently than other pagan gods,

---

4. Vivian Nutton, "From Galen to Alexander, Aspects of Medicine and Medical Practice in Late Antiquity," in *Dumbarton Oaks Papers* 38 (Washington, DC: Dumbarton Oaks Research Library and Collection, 1985), 38:7. Baptism and the curative powers of water are certainly related, and the use of a healing spring for the "spiritual healing" of baptism is indicative of an early understanding of the rite as an action of purity and healing.

since his reputation as a healer was firmly entrenched and he had a large number of followers. Asclepieia throughout the Mediterranean healed the rich and poor alike.

Denying Asclepius's divinity on the basis that he was only an apotheosized man was not a strong enough argument for the early church authors. Christian writers offered an alternative to the healing power of Asclepius by depicting Christ as a viable competitor and practitioner with superior methods. For the patristic authors, Christ was greater than Asclepius in every way. They promoted Christ as the supreme physician who heals the soul as well as the body. The early church writers emphasized the cleansing of the soul and the life to come, and associated physical healing with communal interaction in a Christian setting.

APOCRYPHAL TEXTS

The apocryphal texts generally depicted miracles of healing, exorcism, or punishment. The frequent appearance of curative miracles was meant to highlight Christ as the preeminent healer.[5] In the *Acts of John*, a late-second-century text, John prays to Christ the "physician who heals freely."[6] The author of the *Acts of John* appeared to understand that Christ's competitor Asclepius also healed the poor and subsequently stressed that Christ was a physician who did not require payment.[7] François Bovon notes the numerous instances of the image of the physician in the *Acts of Philip*, as the apocryphal author insisted that Christ was the physician of soul and body.[8] Even in the instances of the

---

5. See François Bovon, "Miracles, magie, et guérison dans les Actes apocryphes des apôtres," in *JECS* 3 (1995): 245–59. Bovon agrees on 248, "The miracles are the visible signs of a superior physician "

6. *Acts of John* 22-4 and 108; Also see 69, where he compares miraculous works to the work of a physician. French and Greek text in *Acta Iohannis*, Corpus Christianorum Series Apocryphorum 1-2, E. Junod and J. D. Kaestli (Turnhout: Brepols, 1983). Later apocryphal texts use the term ἰατρός. For example, see *Gospel of Thomas* 10; 37; 95; 143 from the third century and the *Acts of Philip* from the fourth to fifth centuries (40). See *Acta Philippi*, CCSA 11, ed. François Bovon, Bertrand Bouvier, and Frédéric Amsler (Turnhout: Brepols, 1999).

7. Gervais Dumeige, "Le Christ Médecin," in *RAC*, nos. 1–4 (Rome: Pontificio Istituto di Archeologia Cristiana, 1972), 123–24. Dumeige thinks that Asclepius can be witnessed in the *Acts of John*, and the author of *Acts of John* has Asclepius firmly in mind. While the competition between Asclepius and Christ is explicit in these texts, I find that conclusion likely, given that the phrase "physician who heals freely" occurs in the longer version of the *Acts*, read on John's feast day (108) as well as in section 22. This designation is not limited to the *Acts of John* in the apocryphal genre; in the *Acts of Thomas*, 156, Christ is the "physician that heals without payment," another reference to Christ's competitor in Asclepius.

8. *Acts of Philip* 40. Nicanora's husband believed she was healed by magicians, while she rebuked her husband, telling him of the inner cleaning of the Physician. Bovon, "Miracles, magie et guérison," 251.

apostles performing cures, their goal was the deeper healing of the soul.[9] The early-third-century *Acts of Peter and the Twelve* recorded Jesus ordering his disciples to go out into the world and heal. John questioned Jesus, asking how they could possibly act as true physicians. Jesus answered that the physicians of the world healed only the body, while the disciples had the power to act as physicians of the soul, healing the heart.[10] The third-century *Acts of Thomas* repeatedly referred to Christ as the "physician of the souls," even offering a distinction between earthly physicians and Christ: "Yes, he is the physician, and he is different from all other physicians, for all other physicians heal these bodies which shall be dissolved, but this physician heals the bodies with the souls, which shall never more be dissolved."[11] In the third-century *Acts of Pilate*, a spurious account describes the Roman governor's interaction with Jesus. In this text, Christ is directly associated with Asclepius, a unique event in apocryphal literature. Pilate claimed Jesus' acts of healing were not the "casting out of demons by an unclean spirit, but by the god Asclepius."[12] With this association between Jesus and Asclepius, Pilate attempted to subordinate Jesus' power to the healing power of the god and stated that Asclepius was the higher authority.[13] While the apocryphal examples were more implicit in their comparison of Christ and Asclepius, the *Acts of Pilate* offered a very direct juxtaposition, as Pilate reflected a position that early Christians may possibly have faced in Late Antiquity: Asclepius was considered greater than Christ.

JUSTIN AND CLEMENT OF ALEXANDRIA

The patristic texts encapsulated the general threat posed by the cult of Asclepius. Just as the gospel and apocryphal writers made sure to portray Christ and his followers as healing both body and soul, many of the early church writers also emphasized Christ as a physician and savior.[14] The emphasis on "savior" may recall some characterizations of Christian opponents as "savior," including but not limited to Asclepius. Whether explicit or implicit, in the Greek and Latin

9. Ibid.

10. *Acts of Peter and the Twelve* 11. See Schneemelcher, *New Testament Apocrypha* II, 423.

11. *Acts of Thomas* 95; also see 143, 156 and 37. See text and commentary in A. F. J. Klijn, *The Acts of Thomas* (Leiden: Brill, 2003). Thomas was also called "sorcerer" or "wonder worker," not in a derogatory sense, but intentionally connected him with the wonder works of Jesus.

12. *Acts of Pilate*, or *Gospel of Nicodemus*, 1.1 (Musurillo).

13. Dumeige, "Le Christ Médecin," 121. Dumeige claims that the text is affirmation of the subordination of Jesus to Asclepius.

14. Dumeige, "Le Christ Médecin," 116: The physician title is invoked just as the title of Jesus the savior of the soul.

patristic texts, Christ was depicted as a physician within a context of uneasy competition.

In some examples, Jesus was depicted as the great physician without equal; in other examples, the competition with Asclepius and other threats to his superiority as a healer are apparent.[15] In the early second century, the bishop Ignatius of Antioch wrote a letter to the Ephesians in which he warned them not to heed the poisonous words of heretics: "You need to be on your guard against their bites, because they are by no means easy to heal. There is only one Physician."[16] For Ignatius, "their bites" referred to outside threats that possibly included the Asclepius cult. In the *Letter to Diognetus*, the author called Jesus "Nourisher, Father, Teacher, Counselor, Healer," among other names.[17] In a fragment of Pseudo-Justin, the author states, "But if our physician Christ, God, having rescued us from our desires, regulates our flesh with his own wise and temperate rule, it is evident that he guards it from sins because it possesses a hope of salvation, as physicians do not suffer men whom they hope to save to indulge in what pleasures they please."[18] Occasionally, it is God rather than Jesus who is referred to as the physician, as in the mid-second-century homily attributed to Clement: "While we have time to be healed, let us place ourselves in the hands of God the physician, giving him recompense."[19] In the majority of cases, it is Jesus who is the agent of healing. This designation becomes standard following the second century; it is Jesus who performs the divine act of healing.

Writing in the mid-second century, Justin Martyr provided some detailed evidence comparing Christ to a physician as well as directly noting a rivalry with the cult of Asclepius. In his *First Apology*, Justin intentionally cast Jesus in the mold of Asclepius: "And when we say that He [Christ] healed the lame, the paralytic, and those born blind, and raised the dead, we appear to say things similar to those said to have been done by Asclepius."[20] Just as Asclepius healed,

15. See Fichtner, "Christus als Arzt," 8. Fichtner believes the early church authors are addressing the competition with Asclepius. As evidence, he cites Ignatius, *Eph.* 7.2; 20.2; Clement, *Exhortation to the Greeks* 2.30.1; Justin, *1 Apol.* 22.6; Tatian, *Address to the Greeks* 8.7; 21.3; Tertullian, *The Crown* 8.2; *Apology* 23.6; Lactantius, *Divine Institutes* 1.15.3; 1.15.23; Arnobius, *Against the Pagans* 1.48–49.

16. Ignatius, *Eph.* 7. See Dumeige, "Le Christ Médecin," 118–19, where he notes the vigorous employment of the invective by Ignatius and introduces Aristides's understanding of Asclepius as a healer of body and soul, exhibiting the competitive arena where *Le Christ Médecin* was born.

17. *Letter to Diognetus* 9.6. (PG 2, 1181A; trans. author).

18. Pseudo-Justin, *On the Resurrection* 10 (ANF 2.299; PG 6, 1591A). It is debatable whether the original author is Athenagoras or Hippolytus, although Dods in the *ANF* believes this section is genuinely Justin. Most recently, Wheatley argues for Hippolytus in "Pseudo-Justin's *De Resurrectione*: Athenagoras or Hippolytus?" *VChr* 60, no. 4, (2006): 420–30.

19. *Second Clement* 9.7–10 (Lightfoot; also see *ANF* 9.253).

so did Christ, and Justin further elaborated on their similarity by pointing out, "We propound nothing new beyond what you believe concerning those whom you call sons of Zeus . . . Asclepius, who though he was a great healer, after being struck by a thunderbolt ascended to heaven."[21] Justin alluded to the similarities between the two healing gods to show that Christian beliefs were not completely unlike those of the pagans. With these comments, one might think that Justin was characterizing Christ as an imitator of Asclepius.[22] However, Justin was merely portraying both figures as physicians, and these remarks in his *Apology* are balanced with his later argument that the healing cults were the imitators, not Christ.

The crux of Justin's polemic against the non-Christians was that Christ predated the gods of non-Christian myths and was predicted by the Old Testament prophets. Thus, Christ could not be a follower of Asclepius, since he existed before Asclepius. The Divine Logos existed before creation and was therefore "older" and superior to any divinity the non-Christians touted. Justin asserted, "The Father of the Universe has a Son; who being the Logos and first-begotten is also God. And formerly he appeared in the form of fire and in the image of a bodiless being to Moses and to the other prophets; but now in the times of your rule, as we said before, he became man of a virgin according to the will of the Father for the salvation of those who believe in him."[23] For Justin, the Jews were guilty of not interpreting the prophets correctly by not acknowledging the incarnation of Christ, and the non-Christians had used the prophets to offer alternatives to Christ.

Accordingly, Hercules, Dionysius, Hermes, and others were imitators of Christ. Therefore, Justin can argue that "when they [the pagans] knew what was said, as has been cited before, in the ancient prophecies, 'Strong as a giant to run his course,' they said that Heracles was strong and traveled over all the earth. And, again, when they learned that it had been predicted that He would heal every disease and raise the dead, they brought forward Asclepius."[24] Justin claimed that the pagans pointed to Hercules in response to this prophecy. He asserted that the Old Testament prophecies predicted Jesus, which explained the

20. Justin, *1 Apol.* 22 (Marcovich, 63:2–6), trans. Leslie William Barnard, ACW (New York: Paulist, 1997), 39.

21. Justin, *1 Apol.* 21 (Marcovich, 63:2–6; Barnard, 37).

22. See Dumeige, "Le Christ Médecin," 120. These mentions of Justin exhibits a possible intention to integrate or at least copy the healing cult into Christian theology.

23. Justin, *1 Apol.* 63 (Marcovich 121–23; Barnard, 69).

24. Justin, *1 Apol* 54 (Marcovich 108–109; Barnard, 62). Justin believed that power of Christ was prophesied; see Erwin Goodenough, *The Theology of Justin Martyr* (Jena: Frommann, 1923), 245.

similarities between Christ and the gods, and proved the superiority of Christ.[25] The prediction that Justin connects to Asclepius, a reference from Ps. 19:5, was ambiguous, although it likely followed his previous line of argumentation that pagan gods were invented in response to prophecies that specifically referred to Christ. Justin continued in this vein throughout his *First Apology*: "From what has been said you can understand how the demons, in imitation of what was said through Moses, contrived also to raise up the image of the so-called Kore."[26] The contrivances of the non-Christians included the elevation of Asclepius to the divine. Justin repeatedly claimed that Judeo-Christian prophecy compelled the non-Christians to put forward an alternative deity. Imitation was not the sincerest form of flattery; it was a clever tactic in a war for religious supremacy.

Justin argued that Asclepius was an imitator of Christ more explicitly in his *Dialogue with Trypho*. In chapter 69, Justin recalled the same line of evidence, citing the passage from Psalms: "And when it is asserted that Herakles, the son of Zeus and Alcmene, was strong and traversed the whole earth, and that, after death, he, too, ascended into heaven, ought I not conclude that the scriptural prophecy about Christ, 'strong as a giant to run his course,' was similarly imitated?"[27] Justin moved on to Asclepius, arguing, "And when the devil presents Asclepius as raising the dead to life and curing all diseases, has he not, in this regard, also emulated the prophecies about Christ?"[28] In the *First Apology* and the *Dialogue*, Justin made it clear that worship of Asclepius was derivative of worship of the first physician, Christ. Ultimately, no healing cult could claim superiority to Christ the Physician, since Christ was the first and therefore the supreme physician. Justin did not mention Asclepius by name in his *Second Apology*, although he did recall this argument of supersession: "For next to God, we worship and love the Word who is from the unbegotten and ineffable God, since also he became man for our sakes, that, becoming a partaker of our sufferings, he might also bring us healing."[29] Jesus, existing before the beginning of time, became the great Physician in our time to ease the maladies of our existence. The apologists were promoting Christ as a superior healer to their audience.

25. See Robert M. Grant, *Greek Apologists of the Second Century* (Philadelphia: Westminster, 1988), 62.

26. Justin, *1 Apol* 64 (Marcovich, 124).

27. Justin, *Dial.* 69.3 (Marcovich, 189–90), trans. Thomas B. Falls (Washington, DC: Catholic University Press, 2003), 108.

28. Ibid.

29. Justin, *2 Apol*, 13 (Marcovich, 157; Barnard, 84).

Later Greek writers followed Justin in asserting Christ as a physician without explicitly referring to Asclepius.[30] Clement of Alexandria, writing later in the second century, paralleled Justin's argument for the preexistence of the Logos along with his assertion of Christ as a physician. In *The Instructor*, he called Jesus "Our Instructor, the Word, [who] therefore cures the unnatural passions of the soul by means of exhortations. For with the highest propriety the help of bodily diseases is called the healing art, an art acquired by human skill. The Logos of the Father is the only Paeonian physician for human infirmities."[31] And further, "the Logos of the Father, the creator of man, cares for all our nature, healing it in body and soul alike."[32] Although the pagan god is not explicitly named in these examples, Clement may be referring to a rivalry between Asclepius, or other healers, and Christ. Clement was possibly insisting that Christ is the superior physician since he heals not only the body but also the soul, and justly is called "savior":

> Thus, therefore, the Word has been called also the Savior, seeing He has found out for men those rational medicines which produce vigor of the senses and salvation; and devotes Himself to watching for the favorable moment, reproving evil, exposing the causes of evil affections, and striking at the roots of irrational lusts, pointing out what we ought to abstain from, and supplying all the antidotes of salvation to those who are diseased. For the greatest and most regal work of God is the salvation of humanity.[33]

The actions of Christ that Clement described resemble the actions that took place at the Asclepieion or under the care of a Late Antique physician. Priests at the temple would prescribe changes in diet, as would a physician. The difference was that Christ purged the body and the soul, earning the title "savior," a title also bestowed upon Asclepius before Clement. Clement most likely knew that Asclepius was characterized as "savior," just as Aristides knew

---

30. Athenagoras of Athens mentioned the resurrection myth of Asclepius without providing much detail of the competition with Christ in his *Embassy*, 29 (PG 6, 957B). But in his treatise on *The Resurrection of the Dead* 1 (PG 6, 976C), he characterized Christ as "the physician" who introduced salvific medicine for his people. Also see Theophilius of Antioch, *Letters to Autolycus* 1.7 (PG 6, 1036A; *ANF* 2.91): "Entrust yourself to the Physician, and He will couch the eyes of your soul and of your heart. Who is the Physician? God, who heals and makes alive through His word and wisdom."

31. Clement of Alexandria, *The Instructor* 1.2.6 (PG 8, 256B; *ANF* 2.210); see Dumeige, "Le Christ Médecin," 125–29.

32. Ibid.

33. Clement of Alexandria, *The Instructor* 1.12.100 (PG 8, 369C; *ANF* 2.235).

of it decades before this text was written. Clement would not have mentioned the traits of the physician in order to juxtapose Christ with local physicians, since local physicians scarcely posed a threat to the Christians.

The juxtaposition between Asclepius and Christ is clearer in Clement's *Exhortation to the Greeks*, where Clement does mention Asclepius by name, calling him an "invented savior . . . Asclepius the doctor."[34] Clement argued that Asclepius was no savior. He was merely a man, not a god.[35] Given the direct citation in Justin's *Apology*, Asclepius posed a serious problem to Christians, leading Clement to further emphasize Christ's attributes as a physician and as a salvific figure. More importantly, Justin, Clement, and Origen asserted Jesus as the preexistent Logos, exhibiting in accordance with a reading of John's gospel.

ORIGEN

In his response to Celsus, Origen inserted the image of Christ the Physician at critical junctures, further exhibiting a rivalry between Christ and Asclepius. To counter Celsus's praise of Asclepius for "healing men, and doing good and predicting the future," Origen emphasized Christ as Asclepius's counterpart, using similar phrasing as Celsus.[36] In the third book of his *Against Celsus*, Origen embarked on a long tirade against Asclepius among other gods. Origen first debunked the validity of Asclepius's divinity.[37] Origen questioned whether the gods of the pantheon that had lived as mortals, such as Hercules and Asclepius, could simply be referred to as "heroes." Origen also alluded to Asclepius's death by Zeus's thunderbolt as evidence of a divinely mandated death.[38] Jesus' death, in contrast, was caused not by a god but by mortals, and it did not resemble Asclepius's demise in any way.[39] Origen defended the veracity of Jesus' work and ministry on the basis of the many testimonies of his disciples. There were witnesses to Jesus' miraculous work, while Asclepius's miracles had no reliable witnesses; "the great multitude of Greeks and barbarians" that

34. Clement, *Ex.* 2.23 (PG 8, 97A; *ANF* 2.178).

35. Clement, *Ex.* 2.24.

36. Origen, *Against Celsus*, 3.24 (PG 11, 947A-C; Chadwick). See ch. 2, n. 22. Also see Michael Frede, "Origen's Treatise *Against Celsus*," in *Apologetics in the Roman Empire: Pagans, Jews and Christians*, ed. Mark Edwards, Martin Goodman, and Simon Price (Oxford: Oxford University Press, 1999), 131–55.

37. Origen, *Cels.* 3.22 (PG 11, 944C). Origen also mentioned the Titans throwing down the gods from their heavenly throne.

38. Ibid. Origen did not explicitly reference Pindar as the source of his material as Tertullian and Clement do (although he knew Pindar, as he quotes in 3.26). Rather, he cites Homer as a classical tale in his argument against the divinity of the gods.

39. Origen, *Cels.* 3.23 (PG 11, 945C).

Celsus refers to are nonexistent.[40] Still, Origen allowed that Asclepius may have worked as a healer (albeit possessed by a "demon"). Such a concession did not prove that Asclepius was either a god or even a good being, since Asclepius's healings did not institute any moral reformation. The divinity of Asclepius or any other god was not self-evident.[41] Origen believed that if a god's divinity was in question, then it was ludicrous to venerate the god. Only Christ could make the claim to pure goodness; all other healers or miracle workers could not be proven to be good.[42] In this way, Origen cast doubt upon the ability of Asclepius as well as his divinity, while deepening the divide between Christ and his non-Christian adversaries.

Origen's comments regarding the competition between Asclepius and Christ were relegated to his response to Celsus. He was much more expansive in his characterization of Christ the Physician. Although his citations of Christ as the Physician did not specifically identify the rival god of healing, they were not independent of the competition with Asclepius. According to Harnack, Origen depicted Christ as a physician "more frequently and fully than anyone else."[43] Evident in this bounty of depictions was Origen's acknowledgment of Asclepius as a threat to Christ. Against Celsus's charge that Jesus was a *magos*, Origen responded that Jesus was rather a physician (ἰατρός): "And our Lord and Savior came as a good physician among men laden with sins."[44] Origen was quick to emphasize Jesus as a physician and savior in contrast to Asclepius: "The Divine Logos was sent as a physician to sinners."[45]

Origen expounded on the efficacy and superiority of Christ's healing power in his homily on Leviticus:

> Now look at Jesus the heavenly physician. Come inside his room of healing, the church. Look at the multitude of impotent folk lying there. Here comes a woman unclean from childbirth, a leper expelled from the camp owing to his unclean disease; they ask the physician for aid, for a cure, for cleansing; and because this Jesus the Physician is also the Word of God, he applies, not the juices of herbs, but the sacraments of the Word to their diseases. . . . But he who ultimately discovers that Christ has a medicine for souls, will find from these

40. Origen, *Cels.* 3.24 (Chadwick).
41. Origen, *Cels.* 3.25 (PG 11, 947D).
42. Origen, *Cels.* 3.24.
43. Harnack, *Mission and Expansion*, 110, n. 4.
44. Origen, *Cels.* 2.67 (PG 11, 901C; Chadwick).
45. Origen, *Cels.* 3.62 (PG 11, 1002B; Chadwick).

books which are read in the churches, as he finds from mountains and fields, that each yields healing herbs, at least strength won from words, so that any weakness of soul is healed not so much by leaf and bark as by an inward virtue and juice.[46]

Like Justin and Clement, Origen clearly depicted Christ as the Divine Logos. Origen stressed that the remedies of Christ the Physician were superior to the prescriptions of the healing cult, to any local physician or homeopathic remedy: "Jesus is the only Physician of the body and the soul."[47] No herbalist could heal as Christ the Physician did, for it was the word of Christ that brought instant relief. Origen emphasized the healing power of Christ the Physician as embodied in Scripture, a healing power that was not necessarily tangible. For Origen, the reading of the word healed and was infallible evidence of the salvific nature of Christ.

TERTULLIAN

The early Latin church authors continued to depict Christ as the supreme physician, and in doing so often evoked the competition with Asclepius. Arguably, no early Christian writer expressed more hatred of idolatry than Tertullian, who called it "the principal crime of the human race" and placed it at the top of his list of primary sins.[48] Included in Tertullian's understanding of idolatry was any worship of a deity other than the one true God. Tertullian made his antipathy toward Asclepius abundantly clear and derided him as a bastard. In Tertullian's words, Asclepius "was said to have restored the dead to life by his cures. He was the son of Apollo, half human, although the grandson of Jupiter, and great-grandson of Saturn (or rather of spurious origin, because his parentage was uncertain."[49] Tertullian showed a great familiarity with the cult of Asclepius and the corpus of writings concerning its foundation. In *To the Nations* and his *Apology*, he referred to the poet Pindar and his role in popularizing certain sentiments about Asclepius:

46. Origen, *Homily on Leviticus* 8.1.9 (PG 12, 402D; Barkley).

47. Origen, *Homily on Leviticus* 7.1 (PG 12, 476B; Barkley); also see *Cels.* 1.9; 2.67; *Commentary on John* 1.20, where Origen also notes the Physician of body and soul.

48. Tertullian, *Idolatry* 1.1 (CSEL 20.30; see *ANF* 3.61): "The principal crime of the human race, the highest guilt charged upon the world, the whole procuring cause of judgment, is idolatry." And *Against Marcion* 4.9 (CSEL 47.441–442): "idolatry, blasphemy, murder, adultery, fornication, false-witness, and fraud."

49. Tertullian, *To the Nations* 2.14.42 (CSEL 20.127; *ANF* 3.144).

Pindar, indeed, has not concealed his true desert; according to him, he was punished for his avarice and love of gain, influenced by which he would bring the living to their death, rather than the dead to life, by the perverted use of his medical art which he put up for sale. It is said that his mother was killed by the same stroke, and it was only right that she, who had bestowed so dangerous a beast on the world should escape to heaven by the same ladder. And yet the Athenians will not be at a loss how to sacrifice to gods of such a fashion, for they pay divine honors to Asclepius and his mother amongst their dead.[50]

In his *Apology*, Tertullian cited Pindar again; the poet had chronicled how Asclepius's avarice had caused him to make improper use of his healing power, a crime for which he was justifiably killed by Jupiter.[51] The charge of greed was often levied against Asclepius in order to explain his death by Zeus.[52] Tertullian did not mince words regarding Asclepius; he was a beast, a bastard, and his cult was a problem for Christians. A follower of Asclepius was in league with the demons, and Tertullian further discredited the efficacy of their healings, saying "First, they injure; then, they teach remedies new or contradictory to the point of miracle; after that they cease to injure and are believed to have healed."[53] Anyone who followed such a cult, "if they do not confess they are demons," would face divine judgment.[54] Tertullian was battling against the followers of Asclepius who filled his temples in search of cures. Tertullian devoted attention to slandering the cult of Asclepius among others, and along with other Latin authors, he tried to construct the metaphorical and allegorical symbol of Christ the Physician as an alternative.

FOURTH-AND FIFTH-CENTURY WRITINGS

The dialogue concerning Asclepius continued in writings of the early church after Tertullian. Authors such as Arnobius of Sicca and Augustine of Hippo in North Africa, Athanasius of Alexandria, and Ambrose of Milan were still finely

50. Tertullian, *To the Nations* 2.14.45 (CSEL 20.127).

51. Tertullian, *Apol.* 14.4-6 (CSEL 69.38): "the man of lyrics Pindar sings of Asclepius being thunderstruck . . ."

52. The same story from Pindar that Tertullian related twice was also cited by Clement in his *Exhortation to the Greeks*: "You have also a doctor, and not only a brass-worker among the gods. And the doctor was greedy of gold; Asclepius was his name. I shall produce as a witness your own poet, the Boeotian Pindar." Clement of Alexandria, *Ex.* 2.25-26 (PG 8, 101B).

53. Tertullian, *Apol.* 22.11 (Rendall, LCL).

54. Tertullian, *Apol.* 23.6.

aware of the danger of the Asclepius cult as well as the power and usefulness of promoting Jesus as a great healer and physician. The textual examples of the fourth and fifth century reveal a progressive interest in promoting Jesus as a more powerful healer at a moment when images portraying Christ the Miracle Worker were being produced in North Africa and the Italian peninsula. Text and art were useful tools to utilize in a war to win influence.

ARNOBIUS OF SICCA

Arnobius of Sicca, a fellow North African writing a hundred years after Tertullian in the early fourth century, denounced Asclepius while advancing the image of Christ the Physician. Arnobius was a convert to Christianity, and his major treatise, *Against the Pagans,* was possibly an affirmation of his Christian beliefs rather than an actual apology.[55] Arnobius was a consistent voice against the cult of Asclepius and defended Christ as the supreme physician.[56] Because Arnobius was a fairly new convert at the time of his writings, he relied heavily on his North African forebears for help in developing his apologies. This influence was particularly evident in his attacks against Asclepius.[57] Arnobius employed the story from Pindar, a text that Tertullian and Clement had also used, in order to depict Asclepius as greedy: "That because of his greed and avarice, even as Pindar of Boeotia sings, Asclepius was transfixed by the thunderbolt."[58] Asclepius's death was still useful in Christian polemic because it exhibited a case of a deified human being. Arnobius pointed out this hypocrisy:

55. Arnobius was a difficult figure to interpret. His writings have been noted by scholars for their inconsistent theology, and the picture he painted of persecution-era North Africa was far from lucid. For further reading, see Michael B. Simmons, *Arnobius of Sicca: Religious Conflict and Competition in the Age of Diocletian* (New York: Oxford University Press, 1995), 6–7, 236–40; H.A. Drake's review in *CH* 66, no. 2 (June 1997): 305–307.

56. See Jerome, *Chronicon,* trans. Malcolm Drew-Donalson (Lewiston, NY: Mellen University Press, 1996). Jerome writes of Arnobius in *On Illustrious Men* 79, "Arnobius was a most successful teacher of rhetoric at Sicca in Africa during the reign of Diocletian, and wrote volumes *Against the Pagans* which may be found everywhere." See George E. McCracken's translation, *Ancient Christian Writers* series, (Westminster, MD: Newman, 1949). McCracken believes Jerome's story of Arnobius's motives should not be discounted (1.16). Also see Louis J. Swift, "Arnobius and Lactantius: Two Views of the Pagan Poets," *Transactions and Proceedings of the American Philological Association* 96 (1965): 439–48; and Mark Edwards, "The Flowering of Latin Apologetic," in Edwards, Goodman, and Price, eds., *Apologetics in the Roman Empire,* 197–221.

57. See Simmons, *Arnobius of Sicca,* 186. Arnobius did not relegate his vitriol to the god Asclepius; he also ridiculed other pagan gods. Arnobius reserved much space for the Saturn cult that was resurgent in North Africa at the time of the Diocletian persecution. See Fichtner, "Christus als Arzt," 9. Arnobius may have influenced Lactantius in juxtaposing Asclepius and Christ.

"And yet, you who laugh at us for worshipping a man who died ignominiously . . . have you not proclaimed the discoverer of medicines, Asclepius, the guardian and protector of health, well-being, and safety, after he suffered the penalty and punishment of being struck by lightning."[59] Arnobius manipulated the various myths of Asclepius to his advantage, never letting his audience forget that the pantheon included mortals as well.

Arnobius painted Asclepius as a flawed healer. He diametrically compared the imperfect healings of Asclepius to the positive healings of Christ.[60] He emphasized the theological differences between Christ and Asclepius: Christ healed both sinners and the righteous, while Asclepius healed only the good, not the bad.[61] Christ restored to health "a hundred or more afflicted with various weaknesses and diseases."[62] Arnobius acknowledged that the method of Christ's healings was different from that of cults and physicians.[63]

> This only I desire to know: whether it was without adding any substance, that is, any medication, by mere touch, he bade the diseases to fly away from men; commanded or brought it about that the cause of the ailment ceased to exist and the bodies of the sick returned to their natural state. For we know that Christ, by applying His hand to the ailing part or by a single command, opened the ears of the deaf, removed blindness from eyes, gave speech to the dumb, loosened the stiffness of joints, gave power to walk to the paralytic, regularly healed with a word and cured by a command skin diseases, agues, dropsical diseases, and all other kinds of ailments. . . .

58. Arnobius, *Against the Pagans* 4.24 (CSEL 4.161; McCracken). It is unclear whether Arnobius borrowed this story from Tertullian or from Clement. Arnobius undoubtedly was influenced by Tertullian. However, George McCracken in his introduction believes Arnobius utilized Clement in this instance; see his 47–48. After Arnobius's conversion, the works of Clement, Tertullian, and Minucius Felix's *Octavius* would have been accessible in North Africa.

59. Arnobius, *Against the Pagans* 1.41 (CSEL 4.27; McCracken). Here the Latin may be helpful: "nonne Aesculapium medicaminum repertorem post poenas et supplicia fulminis custodem nuncupauistis et praesidem sanitatis valetudinis et salutis?" In this instance, Arnobius may be responding to Porphyry's accusation that Christians worship a man who died an ignominious death; see Simmons, *Arnobius of Sicca*, 257.

60. Arnobius, *Against the Pagans* 1.49 (CSEL 4.33).

61. Arnobius, *Against the Pagans* 1.37–46; 3.24 (CSEL 4.24–31; 4.128). Asclepius healed the *boni*, not the *mali*.

62. Arnobius, *Against the Pagans* 1.46 (McCracken).

63. Arnobius, *Against the Pagans* 1.48 (CSEL 4.32; McCracken).

What similar act have all these gods done by whom you say aid was borne to the sick and the critically ill? For if they ever, as the story goes, ordered by some to be given medicine, or certain food to be taken, or a potion of any particular kind to be drunk, or a poultice of plants and grasses to be laid on the places causing distress; or that persons should walk, rest up, or refrain from anything harmful: then it is clear this is no remarkable thing and deserves no respect at all. If you care to give it attentive examination, you will discover that physicians heal in this same way.[64]

Arnobius particularly distinguished the healing action of Christ from the divine prescriptions of the healing cult. He was careful to point out that Christ healed only with the power of his touch and command, with no added method, prescription, or instrument: "But it is agreed that Christ did all He did without any paraphernalia."[65] The healing prescriptions of the healing cult, including medicine, alterations in diet, or exercise, were analogous to those that Aristides catalogued in his *Sacred Tales*.[66] However, a divine prescription was still a prescription. Christ did not provide prescriptions, but rather instant relief from suffering. Arnobius was emphasizing that Christ eradicated the need for the prescription that was a critical element in the healings at the Asclepieion. Christ healed with the power of touch, while Asclepius healed through the use of prescriptions procured from sleeping in the temple.

Arnobius followed the list of possible prescriptions with the observation that these cures were neither divine nor transcendent, since they resembled those obtained from a mortal physician. For Arnobius, prescriptions from the Asclepieion or from the local physician were all secondary to the healing power of Christ. Moreover, the health of the body was only one part of the equation, and visiting the healing cult jeopardized the health of one's soul. According to Arnobius, true health could be restored only by turning to Christ the Physician. Good health could not be attained by idolaters or unbelievers. The health that Christ offered, and that Arnobius and earlier church writers advocated, was the health of the soul in the final resurrection; in other words, salvation. Thus, Christ's healings supplanted any other remedy. As one can discover in examining the visual art of the fourth century, these works clearly focus on the healing touch of Christ.

64. Arnobius, *Against the Pagans* 1.48 (McCracken).

65. Arnobius, *Against the Pagans* 44 (CSEL 4.29).

66. Aristides, *Sacred Tales* 48.47–48.

ATHANASIUS

Fourth-century Christian writers continued to throw barbs at Asclepius.[67] Arnobius's pupil Lactantius followed his teacher in calling Asclepius disgraceful and a chief among demons.[68] While he credited Asclepius as the founder of medicine, he remarked that any worship of him was as ludicrous as worshiping the inventor of shoemaking.[69] Lactantius followed his apologetic forebears in arguing that Asclepius deservedly died by the thunderbolt, for "he was a man, not a god."[70] Eusebius also saved some poisonous words for the healing god, saying that Asclepius "sometimes restored the diseased to health, though on the contrary he was a destroyer of souls, who drew his easily deluded worshipers from the true Savior to involve them in impious error."[71] Asclepius was "surely no god, but a deceiver of souls who had practiced fraud for many long years."[72]

Athanasius, who was Origen's fourth-century Alexandrian successor, also juxtaposed Asclepius with the true savior, Christ. Although writing a number of years later, Athanasius reflected the earlier work of Justin, Clement, and Origen in asserting the special nature of Christ in opposition to Asclepius. In *On the Incarnation*, Athanasius argued that Christ was a superior healer to Asclepius, since he healed body and soul: "Asclepius was deified by the Greeks because he practiced the art of healing and discovered herbs as remedies for bodily diseases, not, of course, forming them himself out of the earth, but finding them out by the study of nature. But what is that in comparison with what the Savior did when, instead of just healing a wound, He both fashioned essential being and restored to health the thing that He had formed?"[73] Athanasius stated

67. See Arthur Stanley Pease, "Medical Allusions in the Works of St. Jerome," *Harvard Studies in Classical Philology* 25 (1914): 74. According to Pease, Jerome was directly affected by the multiple references of Christ the Physician that appear in Origen. Scholars point to Origen's influence as the reason there are even some scattered references to Asclepius in Jerome. Pease believes even these random citations of Asclepius are the reflection of Origen's writings painting the god as an important opponent. See his 74–75.

68. Lactantius, *Divine Institutes* 1.10.1; 4.27 (CSEL 19.33; 19.387), written between 303 and 310 CE. On the matter of Lactantiius's being one of Arnobius's pupils (and the doubts raised), see one of W. H. C. Frend's last essays, "Some North African Turning Points in Christian Apologetics," in *JEH* 51, no. 1 (January 2006): 1–15.

69. Lactantius, *Inst.* 1.18.21 (CSEL 19.70).

70. Lactantius, *Inst.* 1.19.3 (CSEL 19.71).

71. Eusebius, *Life of Constantine* 3.55-56 (PG 20, 1120-1121; *NPNF* 2.1.535). He went on to record in his hagiography of Constantine how the emperor ordered the Asclepieion in Cilicia to be destroyed so "that not even a vestige of the former madness was left remaining there."

72. Ibid. Eusebius also mentioned the Pindar myth that Tertullian, Clement, and Arnobius refer to: "when in the myth he was struck by lightning."

that Asclepius did not heal by his own power, while the healings of Christ the Physician were entirely restorative and indicative of his superior power. Athanasius further distinguishes Christ from Asclepius by saying that Christ the Physician was in effect creating a "new person" through his healings and discarding the old. Athanasius employed the physician image effectively: "But once man was in existence, and things that were, not things that were not, demanded to be healed, it followed as a matter of course that the Healer and Savior should align himself with those things that existed already, in order to heal the existing evil."[74] Athanasius realized the value of utilizing the image of Christ as the great physician who offered new life in addition to health, as it contributed to his explanation of why Christ came to live among men at all: "Let them know that the Lord came not to make a display, but to heal and teach those who were suffering."[75]

Quite typically patristic endorsements of visual imagery are slightly ambiguous, and any description is usually focused upon the personhood of Christ. Athanasius offered a distinct portrait of the importance of miracles in his *On the Incarnation*.[76] Athanasius specifically mentioned the use of imagery at one point in his treatise, emphasizing the necessity of "seeing" Jesus' miracles. Witnessing the actions that Jesus performed while in his fleshly body allowed one to realize his divine nature: "Taking to himself a body like the others, and from things of earth, that is by the works of his body (he teaches them), so that they who would not know him from his providence and rule over all things, may even from the works done by his actual body know the Word of God which is in the body, and through him the Father."[77] Athanasius believed that the healings Christ performed were crucial to inculcating belief in doubters: "Or who that saw him healing the diseases to which the human race is subject, can still think him man and not God? For he cleansed lepers, made lame men to

73. Athanasius, *On the Incarnation* 49 (PG 25, 184C; A Religious).

74. Athanasius, *On the Incarnation* 44 (PG 25, 173C; A Religious).

75. Athanasius, *On the Incarnation* 43 (PG 25, 172C; A Religious).

76. Athanasius, *On the Incarnation* 19; but more extensively in 38 (PG 25, 129B-C; 161B-C). John Chrysostom reiterated the importance of "seeing" the miracles as inculcating faith in the restorative power of Christ, just as the centurion in Matthew 8:5 was driven to faith by the healing of his servant. *Homilies on Matthew* 26.6. Also see H. J. Frings, *Medizin und Arzt bei den griechischen Kirchenvätern bis Chrysostomos* (Bonn: Dissertation privately printed, 1959).

77. Athanasius, *Incarn.* 14.8 (*NPNF* 2.4.44; PG 25, 120C-D). Athanasius was not speaking entirely about metaphorical "seeing." It is questionable whether he was referencing tangible images of Christ. The early-fifth-century author Theodore of Mopsuestia mentioned imagery as it pertains to the personhood of Christ. Theodore, like Athanasius, understood the power and effectiveness of the visual form, as he describes Christ as an icon. *On the Incarnation*, 13.7 (PG 66, 989A-C).

walk, opened the hearing of deaf men, made blind men to see again, and in a word drove away from men all diseases and infirmities: from which acts it was possible even for the most ordinary observer to see his Godhead."[78] Athanasius appeared to believe that it was not just the recognition of Christ as the son of God that won converts but bearing visual witness of his healings that dispelled unbelief.

For whatever reason, the attacks on Asclepius in the mid to late fourth and fifth centuries were not as severe as in earlier texts.[79] However, that the criticisms became less vehement should not be taken to indicate the cult's demise. The Asclepius cult continued to have its adherents in the late fourth and fifth centuries.[80] Jerome remarked upon the faithful crowds that continued to sleep at the site of the old Asclepieion.[81] Even though the temple had been destroyed, the area was still attended by believers in the healing god.

AMBROSE AND AUGUSTINE ON CHRIST THE PHYSICIAN

The image of performing miracles and healings in a Christian context steadily increased in the later fourth century. The physician was a powerful image and in greater demand in post-Constantinian Christianity than ever before. Christianity was more established during this period than during the time of Tertullian or Arnobius. Asclepieia were destroyed or overtaken and rededicated by the Christians.[82] The persistence and increase of the Physician and Miracle

78. Athanasius, *Incarn.* 18.4 (*NPNF* 2.4.46).

79. Rudolf Arbesmann, "The Concept of 'Christus Medicus' in St. Augustine," *Traditio* 10 (1954): 4. Rudolph Arbesmann writes, "The chief target of the Christian writers is no longer the worship of Asclepius, but the Oriental cults of Isis, Mithras, and Sarapis, which now fascinate the masses by the magic spell of their gorgeous and mysterious ritual." Attention to Isis and Sarapis occurred far earlier than the fourth century, and Arbesmann does not take the writings and actions of Julian the Apostate into account. Material evidence of Asclepius lessened, as the last coins depicting Asclepius come from the time of the emperor Valerian (253–260 ce). Otfried Deubner reports this in *Das Asklepeion von Pergamon* (Berlin: Verlag für Kunstwissenschaft, 1938), 20.

80. It is apparent in the writings of Julian that Asclepius worship was still prominent. Julian's friend and teacher Libanius credited Asclepius with healing his foot. See Libanius, *Ep.* 1383; *Ep.* 1303.

81. Jerome, *On Isaiah* 18.65. René Rüttimann, *Asclepius and Jesus: The Form, Character and Status of the Asclepius Cult in the Second Century CE and its Influence on Early Christianity,* Harvard University (Ann Arbor, MI: UMI Dissertation Services, 1987), on 207 cites the philosopher Plutarch sleeping in the temple in 423 ce.

82. The destruction of the Sarapieion in Alexandria at 391 is an oft-cited example of Christian destruction of a pagan temple, but destruction affected the cult of Asclepius as well. For example, the Asclepieion at Corinth was destroyed in the 520s around Alaric's invasion and rededicated as a Christian church and cemetery. The cult enjoyed some longevity at Corinth. Excavations have unearthed Christian epitaphs at the site. See Carl Roebuck, "The Asklepieion and Lerna," in *Corinth,* vol. 14 (Princeton, NJ:

Worker images in text and art indicated an anxiety that the replacement was not possible. While the Asclepius cult was less of a problem, Christ still had a significant void to fill. The Christian populace needed to be continually reminded that Christ was the healer par excellence who could embrace them body and soul. The effort of church leaders to deter people from returning to the non-Christian fold was ongoing. Late-fourth-century Christian leaders were in a more precarious position than before. They could not afford a misstep that might lead the public to fall back into their old beliefs. Christ as the supreme physician had to be insisted upon repeatedly. The most obvious platform from which to transmit this message to the people was the church pulpit. Ambrose made the image of Christ the Physician part of his preached theology. In one sermon, he tells his listeners, "We have taken refuge with the physician. He has cured our former wounds, and if any pain remains, a remedy will not be wanting. Although we have done some injury, He will not be mindful of it who has once forgiven. Although we have committed grievous faults, we have found a great physician; we have received the great medicine of His grace; for great medicine removes great sin."[83]

Some have argued that the lack of references to Asclepius diminished the impact of the image of Christ the Physician.[84] However, this does not appear to be the case, and it is a mistake to make such a determination. The importance of the physician metaphor is apparent in the multiple references made by Ambrose and Augustine. The lack of Asclepius references does not mean that Asclepius cannot be witnessed in patristic literature. The healings of Christ in the gospels were not stories that Christian bishops would deemphasize in preaching to their congregations, and it did not mean that every sermon had Asclepius in mind. However, the manner in which Ambrose and Augustine characterized Christ the Physician does warrant some investigation.

In Ambrose's treatise concerning widows, the bishop expanded on the healing account in Luke 4:38 of Peter's mother-in-law:

American School of Classical Studies at Athens, 1951), and see the notes in Helen Saradi-Mendelovici's "Christian Attitudes toward Pagan Monuments in Late Antiquity and Their Legacy in Later Byzantine Centuries," in *DOP* (1990): 44:47–61.

83. Ambrose, *On Elijah and Fasting* 20.75 (CSEL 32.458; Buck): Ambrose refers to Jesus as the great "physician" who takes away sin. Also see his *Commentary on Luke* 4.67 where he advocates his listeners to seek out the great physician Christ. See the French edition *Traité sur l'évangile de S. Luc, Texte Latin*. SC (Paris: Éditions du Cerf, 1956).

84. Arbesmann, "The Concept of 'Christus Medicus,'" 5; See Fichtner's characterization of these citations in his "Christus als Arzt," 8–11. Fichtner notes that the roots of the designation of Christ the Physician lie in the competition with Asclepius, but he offers other alternatives as well, including the Cynic tradition.

The Physician is then here asked for. Do not fear, because the Lord is great, that perhaps He will not condescend to come to one who is sick, for He often comes to us from heaven; and is wont to visit not only the rich but also the poor and the servants of the poor. And so now He comes, when called upon, to Peter's mother-in-law. . . . He disdains not to visit widows, and to enter the narrow rooms of a poor cottage. As God He commands, as man He visits.[85]

Ambrose states that Christ attended not only to the rich but also to the poor. More importantly, Christ visited the sick, even the lowly widows in their modest houses. "Patients" did not have to go to him; he made house calls to them, unlike other healers whose adherents were obliged to undertake a journey to the temple.

Ambrose's text also reveals an important difference between the healing action of Asclepius and that of Christ:

Do you see what kinds of healing are with him? He commands the fever, he commands the unclean spirits, at another place he lays hands on them. He was wont then to heal the sick, not only by word but also by touch. And do you then, who burn with many desires, taken either by the beauty or by the fortune of some one, implore Christ, call in the Physician, stretch forth your right hand to Him, let the hand of God touch your inmost being, and the grace of the heavenly Word enter the veins of your inward desires, let God's right hand strike the secrets of your heart.[86]

In this passage, Ambrose, like Arnobius, highlighted the physical nature of Christ's healings in contrast to those of Asclepius. Christ healed by touch; he placed his hands upon his recipients. Furthermore, Ambrose made it clear that Christ the Physician is healer of body and soul, as the preexistent Word enters the body and cleanses the soul of any impurities.

At other points Ambrose expounded on the remedies Christ provided, differentiating Christ not only from worldly healers but from the divine healing of the non-Christians: "This medicine Peter beheld, and left His nets, that is to say, the instruments and security of gain, renouncing the lust of the flesh as a leaky ship that receives the bilge, as it were, of multitudinous passions. Truly a mighty remedy, that not only removed the scar of an old wound, but

---

85. Ambrose, *Concerning Widows* 10.60 (*NPNF* 2.10.401; PL 16, 266).

86. Ambrose, *Concerning Widows*, 10.62.

even cut the root and source of passion. O Faith, richer than all treasure-houses; O excellent remedy, healing our wounds and sins."[87] Christ the Physician's remedies scoured away scars, provided new flesh, and most importantly, removed sin. The fact that Ambrose chose the image of the physician for his sermons exhibits how steadfastly the image endured well into the fourth century.

Unlike Ambrose, Augustine did mention Asclepius by name in his writings, which suggests that the god was still on Augustine's radar.[88] That being said, the references to the god cannot compare to the sheer volume of citations of Christ the Physician in his work. Out of all the early church authors, Augustine employed the terms *medicina* and *medicus* more than any other in contexts regarding not physical health but moral health.[89] A large amount of the evidence for this is found in Augustine's sermons.[90] The physician was a very serviceable image for Augustine to emphasize a key point in his theology: that is, warning his audience against the critical sin of pride. The physician

87. Ambrose, *Exposition on the Christian Faith* 2.11.92 (CSEL 78.90; NPNF 2.10.236). At other points, Ambrose recounted healings of Jesus as indicative of the present action in healing the sinful. See *On the Mysteries* 4.24 (CSEL 73.98-99).

88. Augustine did mention Asclepius by name in his *City of God*. In these references, he generally listed Asclepius along with other pagan gods deemed as demonic, although he did mention the advent tale to Rome, further indicating the longevity of this legend: "Asclepius left Epidaurus for Rome, that in this foremost city he might have a finer field for the exercise of his great medical skill." Augustine also mentioned the legend at another point, criticizing the story as proof that the god deserves no special attention, since the Asclepius stories cannot compare to the stories of miracle concerning God's people. See *City of God* 12 (CSEL 40.122-123). Also see 4.21; 4.22; 4.27; 8.5; 10.16 (CSEL 40.189, 190, 198, 362, 474).

89. Arbesmann, "The Concept of 'Christus Medicus,'" 2 and 7. Paul Monceaux uncovered an inscription in Timgad that invoked the image of Christ the Physician. "Une invocation au *Christus medicus* sur une Pierre de Timgad," in *Comptes rendus de l'Acad. des Inscr.* (Paris: De Boccard,1920), 78ff. As this discovery occurred in Timgad, late antique Thamugadi, it is probable that it was a Donatist inscription, proving that the image was not solely popular with Catholic or Donatist audiences, but cut across fractious lines in North African Christianity. For further reading, see W. H. C. Frend, "The *Memoriae Apostolorum* in Roman North Africa" *JRS* 30, no. 1 (1940); and Jane Merdinger, "Optatus Reconsidered," *Studia Patristica* 22 (Louvain: Peeters, 1989), 294–99.

90. Arbesmann, "The Concept of 'Christus Medicus,'" 7. "For the figure, if used expertly by a preacher, is especially well-adapted for explaining to a congregation the nature of the Redemption." Also see Sister Mary Keenan, "Augustine and the Medical Profession," *Transactions of the American Philological Association* 67 (1936): 169. While Pease's work focuses solely on Jerome, Keenan still offers one of the more extensive treatments of medical terminology in Augustine. Keenan has noted that Augustine's references to medicine usually include mention of the physician, the disease, the patient, and his knowledge of anatomy and physiology. While she argues that most of Augustine's uses are figurative, in order for them to be effective, they "must have had some connection with actual practice and custom."

is described as a humble figure who "cures" humanity of the deadly disease of pride.[91] Augustine was not ignorant of physical health procedures such as surgical techniques or of the actual methods of healing that his congregation might pursue. In his *Confessions*, he called the doctor named Vindicianus a "skilled and renowned physician."[92] In his sermons, Augustine utilized medical terminology as a vehicle to drive home the danger of pride to his audience, often characterizing pride as a tumor that could only be cured through the process of Christian humility.[93] Clearly, Augustine's use of medical imagery was grounded in his social context and his recognition of the needs of his congregation. Using healing language as a metaphor supports Augustine's interest in the moral well-being of his congregants. Emphasizing the "inward" moral healing that Christ can accomplish characterizes Jesus as a healer of the soul as well as the body.

Quite often in his sermons, Augustine treated Christ as a physician who prescribed humility to his "patients." He placed the cause of human ills squarely on the shoulders of Adam, who had committed the sin of pride: "Through the pride of the first parents then have we so fallen as to become subject to this mortality. And because pride has wounded us, humility makes us whole. . . . For a Physician (Christ) does not care what a deranged patient says to him. . . . So too the Lord came to a sick man . . . by this very attitude he was preaching humility, and it was only by being taught humility that they would be healed of their pride."[94] In other preaching, Augustine was even more explicit, preaching that because of the great sin of pride, God came amongst men to treat the disease of humanity's souls, "the Omnipotent Physician" was drawn "down from heaven."[95]

In Augustine's sermons on John's gospel, the bishop repeatedly referenced the image of the physician, inextricably linking it to the action of Christ: "Now the sick confess that they are sick; let the physician come to heal the sick.

---

91. Arbesmann, "The Concept of 'Christus Medicus,'" 9. Augustine, *City of God* 10.29 (CSEL 40.499). The Latin may be helpful to note Augustine's usage of *medicus*: "Ut parum sit miseris quod aegrotant, nisi se etiam in ipsa aegritudine extollant et de medicina, qua sanari poeterant, erubescant. Non etiam hoc faciunt ut erigantur, sed ut cadendo grauius adfligantur." Pride and humility were key issues Augustine addresses in *City of God*, occasionally employing a medical metaphor to stress his point. Due to their hubris, the Platonists deprived themselves of the "medicine which could cure them." (Augustine, *City of God* 10.29).

92. Augustine, *Confessions* 4.3.5 (CSEL 33.67; Chadwick).

93. Augustine, *Expositions on the Psalms* 118.9.2 (CCSL 40.1690).

94. Augustine, *Exp. Ps.* 35.17 (CCSL 38.335).

95. Augustine, *Exp. Ps.* 18.2.15 (CCSL 38.112; trans. author).

Who is the Physician? Our Lord Jesus Christ. Who is our Lord Jesus Christ? . . . He is the complete Physician of our wounds."[96] While Augustine firmly established the image of the Physician, he emphatically stated that Christ, "and no other" is the ultimate Physician, reminding his audience that any adversary of Christ was no equal. Augustine was possibly alluding to Asclepius, magicians, or local physicians. As can be seen in the writings of Aristides and Julian Apellas, Asclepius was known by supplicants as a healer of the body and soul. Still, Augustine's choice of metaphorical language in the context of healing emphasizes Jesus as a healer of body and soul in a way that sets the divine physician apart from any other.

Augustine was fully aware of the healing treatments that were available in North Africa. He understood the tradecraft of the physician and the suffering that a patient often underwent in order to be cured. At moments in his sermons and his treatises, he vividly described the removal of sin as to a painful purging, cauterization, or surgical operation that must take place: "A sick person likewise begs many things from the physician which the physicians does not grant; he will not accede to the patient's whims, because he means to satisfy the real will to health. . . . What remedies he (God) will apply to cure you, he knows; what surgery, what cauterizations, he knows. You brought your sickness on yourself by sinning; he has come not merely to coddle you, but to cut and burn."[97] Salvation did not come without pain. Augustine argued that just as a human physician may hurt the patient in order to heal, so did Christ the Physician: "Truly, as a faithful Physician, with the healing knife of preaching in his hand, he has cut away our wounded parts."[98] Augustine employed surgical imagery quite often, for the image could impress upon the audience that the severity of the contagion of sin was akin to the contagion of physical disease:

> He is the doctor, and he knows about cutting off a decaying part,
> to stop the decay spreading from it to other places. "One finger," he
> says, "is cut off here; because it is better for one finger to be shorn

96. Augustine, *Tractates on the Gospel of John*, 3.2 (CCSL 36.21; NPNF 1.7.19).

97. Augustine, *Exp. Ps.* 85.9 (CCSL 39.1184; Boulding).

98. Augustine, *Exp. Ps.* 93.7 (CCSL 39.1309). "The human race is sick, not with physical disease, but with sins. . . . To heal this gigantic invalid there came down the all-powerful doctor . . . . Don't let anyone start saying, 'the world used to be better before than it is now; from the moment this doctor began practicing his skills, we've seen many horrible things here.' Do not be surprised. Before anyone was treated and cured, the doctor's surgery and operating theater were clean of blood; well you, then, as you see the blood now, shake yourself free of the empty pursuit of pleasure, come to the doctor." *Sermons* 87.13 (PL 38, 537; Hill). The complaint Augustine listed recalls Pliny the Elder's suspicion of and ire concerning physicians.

off smooth, than for the whole body to rot." If a human doctor does this by his medical skill, if the art of medicine can remove one part of the body to save them all from decay, why should God not cut out whatever he knows to be rotten in people, so that they may attain salvation?[99]

Augustine appeared to be utilizing his medical knowledge and his audience's proclivity to believe in the ineffable to his advantage.[100] The image of Christ the Physician was obviously one that had an impact on Augustine's congregation. Augustine's understanding of its value is apparent in his frequent use of the term in his sermons. "Sickness" and "disease" were characterized as maladies of pride and greed affecting the soul that only Christ the Physician could heal.[101]

Augustine indirectly portrayed Christ the Physician as superior to any possible opponents. In his homily on Psalm 44, he depicted Christ as attending to Peter: "The Physician had felt his pulse, and knew what was going on within his patient's soul: the patient knew it not."[102] Only Christ could diagnose problems of the soul as well as the body, even without the patient's knowledge. Ambrose and Augustine needed to make their message clear in order to prevent any lapse into idolatry: the healer of body and of soul was Christ. The homiletic image of Christ the Physician detailed the healing power of Christ, the only healer who could bring about salvation of the soul. Ambrose and Augustine emphasized the miracle working of Christ for a similar end—to remind their congregations of Christ's authority in a landscape that still offered religious alternatives.

AMBROSE AND AUGUSTINE ON MIRACLES

The stress on healings and miracles in the early Christian texts is quite evident. A natural question arise: Why was the image of Christ the healer and miracle worker so omnipresent in Christian scripture and patristic texts? The answer

---

99. Augustine, *Serm.* 113A.13 (PL 46, 930; Hill). Also see *Serm.* 88.7-8, recalling Matt. 9:12 ("We have already begun to get ill, we are feverish, we are lying on a bed of sickness"); and *Serm.* 30.5 of the physician calling his patients while the sick quarrel.

100. See Augustine, *Ep.* 38.1 (CSEL 33.64-65). For further reading of Augustine's medical knowledge, see Augustine's *Confessions* where he recalled his critical fever while at Rome (5.9); a digestive attack he endured as a child (1.11); and a toothache he suffered from (9.4). See Anne Elizabeth Merideth, *Illness and Healing in the Early Christian East* (Ann Arbor, MI: UMI Dissertation Services, 1999), 26.

101. See Augustine, *Serm.* 46.13, where Augustine relates the paralytic story to the idea that studying the Scriptures allows the physician to be lowered through the roof.

102. Augustine, *Exp. Ps.* 44.16. (Latin 43; *NPNF* 1.8.144).

is partly that the image of Christ the Physician addressed the common interest in physical health. The precarious nature of life in Late Antiquity made people particularly susceptible to belief in miracles. Such belief among the Christian populace was out of the control of the bishops, as Augustine's wavering stance suggests. Despite some clerical resistance, miracles became a present reality as church leaders ultimately acquiesced to the people's desires. Eventually, bishops realized how miracles could be manipulated to their advantage, whether for political gain or congregational discipline.

Belief in the existence and efficacy of miracles was not related to class, a matter of highbrow versus lowbrow culture, or of elitist versus common beliefs. Augustine stated as much in *City of God*, claiming that the "wise" are not saved by their education and rationality: "God knows their thoughts, how futile they are."[103] The understanding of the importance of healings and miracles cut across social and educational divides. The reality and efficacy of healing miracles was shared among the elite and the commoner.[104] The church historian William Babcock comments that religious conversions in antiquity, lowbrow or otherwise, demonstrate the tension between the "elite" and the "masses," and conversions represent a common frame to exhibit the full religious import of the Christian religion.[105]

Healings and miracles also embodied a common frame to display the same religious import Babcock states; however, healings and miracles were not consigned to just one genre. Visual art in which Christ is depicted performing healings and miracles was another method to speak to Christians. While such images were popular in the early stages of Christian art, they became increasingly dominant in the fourth century, especially in a funerary context, where they brought comfort and also served as a reminder of the ultimate "healing" Christ the Physician provided in life after death.[106] After Constantine, at a time when Christ appeared to have won the battle against Asclepius and his other rivals, images of Christ performing healings and miracles were abundant.

Given their predominance in material art, it is useful to explore how healings and miracles actually took place in the life of the Christian congregation. In the late fourth century, healings and miracles were performed by Christian relics, which raised another issue for church leaders such as Ambrose and Augustine. Ambrose and Augustine's writings indicated a shift in

---

103. Augustine, *City of God* 22.4 (CSEL 40.587; Bettenson), from Ps. 94:11.

104. See Paulinus of Nola, *Ep.* 31.1; 32.17. The fragment Paulinus sent came from Melania the Elder, a gift from John of Jerusalem. He describes the splinter in detail at 32.11.

105. Babcock, "MacMullen on Conversion: A Response," 89.

106. The visual evidence will be introduced later in this book.

the procurement and efficacy of healings and miracles. The person of Christ was continually proclaimed as the supreme healer and physician. His healing power could be transferred to the saints, and consequently any primary or secondary material attached to the saints could have a healing effect. The text of Acts 19:11 instituting *brandea* (ordinary objects that come into contact with holy people or places) suggests this transition: "And God did extraordinary miracles by the hands of Paul, so that handkerchiefs or aprons were carried away from his body to the sick, and diseases left them and the evil spirits came out of them." Relics of Christ and the saints began to grow in number in the middle of the fourth century, beginning with the discovery of the true cross that established the pilgrimage routes.[107] Divine healings continued in the Christian guise, and the physical proof of Christ the Physician could be offered. Christ the Physician could tangibly act through the material relics, healing those who encountered the relics, drawing visitors to churches that housed the miracle-working objects.[108]

This new understanding of the transference of healing power was in its early stages in late-fourth-century Milan with Ambrose and his catechumen, Augustine. Ambrose's letter to his sister describing the discovery of the relics of Gervase and Protase provides valuable insight into the bishop's notion of miracles. According to this letter, the discovery took place after his congregation had pleaded with him to consecrate his new church in Milan: "At once a kind of prophetic ardor seemed to enter my heart."[109] Upon the consecration, he immediately found the burial place of the saints: "We found two men of marvelous stature, such as those of ancient days. All the bones were perfect, and there was much blood."[110] Following the unearthing of the holy remains, as if to legitimate the discovery, a blind man's sight was restored.

---

107. If the dawn of the reliquary era can be traced, it may point to the discovery of the true cross in Jerusalem. See Eusebius, *Life of Constantine* 3.41-43. Cyril mentioned the sites of Bethlehem and the Ascension in reference to the site of the Resurrection, without mention of Helena. *Catechetical Lectures* 4.10. Interestingly, Ambrose may have been the first to widely propagate the attribution of Helena in reference to the true cross as he spoke of this association in his funeral oration to emperor Theodosius, *Oration on the Death of Theodosius* (CSEL 73.3923-401), stating that Helena witnessed the true cross. See Annabel Jane Wharton, "The Baptistery of the Holy Sepulcher in Jerusalem and the Politics of Sacred Landscape," in *DOP* (Washington, DC: Dumbarton Oaks Center for Byzantine Studies, 1992), 46:323.

108. Just as the afflicted traveled to the temple of Asclepius, so did ailing pilgrims travel to churches housing relics. See Katherine Park, "Medicine and Society in Medieval Europe, 500–1500," in *Medicine in Society* (Cambridge: Cambridge University Press, 1992), 72.

109. Ambrose, *Ep.* 77 to Marcellina (CSEL 82/3.126ff; letter 22 in the Benedictine manuscript; *NPNF* 2.10.437).

110. Ambrose, *Ep.* 77.2.

The discovery and subsequent miracle provided Ambrose with political capital as well. The finding of the relics was a well-orchestrated spectacle intended to boost Ambrose's standing with the masses.[111] The doubters Ambrose cited in his sermon reflect the negative Arians in his episcopate who questioned the efficacy of this miracle and the subsequent healings. Ambrose equated the healing miracles wrought by the relics to the miracles of Christ:

> But many not improperly call this the resurrection of the martyrs; whether they have risen for themselves is another question, for us beyond a doubt they are risen. You have heard, nay, yourselves have seen, many cleansed from evil spirits; many also, after touching with their hands the garments of the saints, delivered from the infirmities under which they suffered: you have seen the miracles of old time renewed, when through the coming of the Lord Jesus, a fuller Grace descended upon the earth; you see many healed by the shadow, as it were, of the holy bodies. How many napkins are passed to and fro? How many garments placed on these holy relics, and endowed by the mere contact with the power of healing are reclaimed by their owners. All think themselves happy in touching even the outer-most thread, and whoever touches them will be made whole.[112]

Ambrose claimed that the miracles of old were being repeated; the miracles wrought by the saints' relics were no different than the miracles of Christ and the disciples. The bishop was establishing that the transference of miraculous power was indeed real and efficacious.

Ambrose was also defending the veracity of the relics of Gervase and Protase by insisting that the blind man had in fact been cured. He told his sister that the man himself had testified to his own healing: "He declares that when he touched the border of the garment with which the martyrs' bodies were clothed, his sight was restored to him." Ambrose then asks, "Is not this like what we read in the Gospel? For the power which we admire proceeds from one and the same Author."[113]

---

111. See John Moorhead, *Ambrose: Church and Society in the Late Roman World* (London: Longman, 1999), 152–53; and Neil B. McLynn, *Ambrose of Milan: Church and Court in a Christian Capital* (Berkeley: University of California Press, 1994), 212–14.

112. Ambrose, *Ep.* 77.9 (*NPNF* 2.10.438).

113. Ambrose, *Ep.* 77.17–18. Augustine provides a similar eyewitness endorsement of the miracle's occurrence in *City of God* 22.8 (CSEL 40.596–597).

Augustine's explanation of miracles was much more cautious than Ambrose's and offers a rare opportunity to witness Augustine reversing his earlier position. Early in his priesthood, Augustine was didactically negative about the contemporary occurrence of miracles. In 390, Augustine wrote a treatise titled *Of True Religion* that reveals he had stopped being a disciple of Mani and describes his early theories on the dispensation of grace. Augustine sent the treatise to Paulinus of Nola, who called it "his Pentateuch against the Manichees."[114] In the treatise, Augustine argued that Christ was a true complement to the philosophy of Plato and stated that philosophers were beginning to turn to Christianity. In order to accommodate the rationally minded philosophers, Augustine had to explain miracles that occurred in the New Testament. He asserted that miracles had been relevant for early Christians but were not needed today:

> We have heard that our predecessors, at a stage in faith on the way from temporal things up to eternal things, followed visible miracles. They could do nothing else. And they did so in such a way that it should not be necessary for those who came after them. . . . On the one hand miracles were not allowed to continue till our time, lest the mind should always seek visible things, and the human race should grow cold by becoming accustomed to things which when they were novelties kindled its faith. On the other hand, we must not doubt that those are to be believed who proclaimed miracles. . . . At that time the problem was to get people to believe before anyone was fit to reason about divine and invisible things.[115]

Augustine conceded the veracity and necessity of New Testament miracles. However, he argued that these miracles had occurred at a time before Christians could "reason" about the ineffability of the divine. Thus, miracles had no purpose in Augustine's world since humanity now used rational inquiry to understand divine things.

In *On the Usefulness of Belief*, written shortly after Augustine's ordination, the presbyter argued further that the miracles of the gospels during the time of Jesus were real. Miracles performed during Christ's ministry helped to instill Christian faith in those who witnessed them. For Augustine, anyone who continued to believe in miracles after that period was foolish, since he or she relied on the eyes and not on the rational mind: "Miracles must be presented

---

114. Augustine, *Ep.* 25 (CSEL 34.78ff), a letter from Paulinus.

115. Augustine, *True Religion* 25.47 (CSEL 77.33; Burleigh).

to the eyes, of which fools are much readier to make use than of the mind. . . . [Christ] did miracles in order to incite us to follow God."[116] Miracles were tools to enlighten dull minds. Augustine went on to differentiate between miracles in which Christ played no part and the miracles of Christ:

> But again, there are two kinds of miracle. Some there are which merely cause wonder; others produce gratitude and good will. If one sees a man flying one merely marvels. . . . But if one is affected by some grave and desperate disease and at a word of command immediately gets better, love of one's healer will surpass wonder at one's healing. Such things were done when God appeared to men as true Man, as far as was necessary. The sick were healed. Lepers were cleansed. To the lame the power to walk was restored, to the blind, sight, to the deaf, hearing. The men of that time saw water turned to wine; five thousand satisfied with five loaves of bread, waters walked on, the dead raised. Of these miracles, some looked to the body . . . but all of them had regard for men, bearing testimony to them of the majesty of Christ.[117]

In these few lines, Augustine conclusively explained why the figure of Christ the Physician was consistently employed and why the iconographic image of Christ performing healings and miracles was so significant and pervasive during his time: the image instilled faith. Christ's miracles were useful promotional tools, akin to church billboards on a highway; they demanded attention and inculcated belief. In these early works, Augustine was arguing against the contemporary existence of miracles. Miracles were for the dull, not for the wise: "Christ's miracles, therefore, were done at the most opportune moment so that a multitude of believers might be drawn together."[118]

As Augustine progressed through his priesthood and episcopate, he lucidly outlined his position to his congregation during his sermons. Just as the image of Christ the Physician appeared frequently in his sermons, Augustine quite often addressed the subject of miracles. In his early sermons, he played the image of the physician off the ridiculousness of miracles. Augustine understood that the proclivity to believe in miracles was due to the occurrence of Jesus' miracles in the gospels. Nonetheless, he exhorted his congregation to abandon any belief in contemporary miracles, citing that "better are those that do not see and

---

116. Augustine, *The Usefulness of Belief* 15.33 (CSEL 25.41; Burleigh).
117. Augustine, *The Usefulness of Belief* 16.34 (CSEL 25.42; Burleigh).
118. Ibid.

believe."[119] Augustine wanted his audience to focus not on what could be seen with the "outer eye," but on what could be absorbed by the "spiritual eye." To this end, he stressed how the senses could deceive: "Therefore the Bridegroom has cautioned us that we ought not to be deceived by miracles."[120] Augustine emphasized that superficial demonstrations of miracles, fantastic events that can be physically seen, were unreliable.[121] Furthermore, it was not miracles that cleansed the body of sin, but only the prescriptions of Christ the Physician. Augustine used the image of Christ the Physician as a metaphor of rationality to motivate his audience to focus on Christ and not on external signs or miracles.

As Augustine moved deeper into his episcopate in the early fifth century, his perception of miracles underwent a noticeable shift. This occurred when the relics of the martyr Stephen arrived in North Africa.[122] Just as the relics of Gervase and Protase healed in Ambrose's Milan, so did the relics of Stephen in Augustine's Hippo. The subject of miracles and healing subsequently became a focal point in the life of Augustine's episcopate. Augustine referred to the existence of Stephen's relics in a sermon given around 416: "And this is now certainly made known to almost all nations in the revelation of the body of the blessed Stephen."[123] In his sermons from 425, he preached on the efficacy of the miracles wrought by these relics. God "grants us such favors from the dust of the dead." according to Augustine.[124] This put him in an awkward position however, given his earlier stance on contemporary miracles, and in one particular instance, he was compelled by his congregation to acknowledge their current reality.[125]

Toward the end of his career, then, Augustine conceded that miracles did in fact occur in the contemporary world: "And in fact, even now miracles are being performed in Christ's name."[126] After the arrival of the relics of Stephen, the bishop expressed his desire to record the many accounts of true miracles in

119. Augustine, *Serm.* 88.2 (PL 38, 540). Also see 88.7-8.

120. Augustine, *Trac. Jo.* 13.17 (CCSL 36.140; *NPNF* 1.7.93).

121. Augustine also employed metaphors from his understanding of the natural world, such as the springing of an olive tree in *On Marriage and Desire* 1.21 (CSEL 42.234); *Ep.* 137.10 (CSEL 44.110).

122. In 415, a priest named Lucian discovered the remains of Stephen through revelation in a dream. It usually is cited that Orosius is responsible for returning with the relics of Stephen in 416. This is clouded slightly by *City of God* 22.8 (CSEL 40.604), where Augustine refers to Bishop Praejectus bringing the relics of Stephen. It is more likely that Augustine was referring to a specific establishment at Aquae Tibilitanae, rather than the general advent of the relics of Stephen into North Africa.

123. Augustine, *Trac. Jo.* 120.4 (CCSL 36.662; *NPNF* 1.7.435).

124. Augustine, *Serm.* 317.1 (PL 38, 1435; Hill).

125. Augustine, *Serm.* 323.4 (PL 38, 1440).

126. Ibid. (Hill).

his episcopate. Augustine noted that if he recorded all of the miracles, then he would never finish writing, even if he restricted himself to miracles of healing at Hippo and Calama. Augustine stressed his concern "that such accounts should be published because I saw that signs of divine power like those of older days were frequently occurring in modern times too, and I felt they should not pass into oblivion, unnoticed by the people in general."[127] The people of Augustine's episcopate had no problem accepting the miracles. Augustine finally relented and viewed the incidents in Hippo not through the eyes of a skeptic but through the eyes of his people. Only then did he admit the reality and veracity of miracles.

Augustine attempted to explain his reversal in the composition *Retractations*, which he wrote in his twilight years. In his recollection of his work *Of True Religion*, Augustine claimed that current miracles did not occur in the same way as they had in the New Testament. For instance, no one was healed by a minister's shadow, the way Peter's shadow healed in Acts. He vociferously claimed, "But I should not be understood to mean that today no miracles are to be believed to happen in the name of Christ," citing as evidence the fact that he had witnessed Ambrose's discovery of Gervase and Protase as evidence.[128] In his review of *On the Usefulness of Belief*, Augustine argued that his point about Christ's miracles having their time and place did not mean "that such great miracles do not happen now, not that no miracles happen even today."[129]

The popularity of Stephen's shrine may partly explain why Augustine reversed his earlier position on miracles. The attention given to the shrine may have been a burgeoning trend over which the bishop realized he had no control. Miracles, particularly miracles involving healing, elicited sincere devotion and faith. Miracles also addressed the maladies of human existence that afflicted the general population. An argument for rationality could not quell the desire to believe in miraculous cures, such as those brought about by the relics of Stephen. At the time of the relics' arrival in Hippo, there may have been a need for a viable healing option. Augustine recognized the value of miraculous healings wrought by the relics of Stephen.[130] The healing miracles not only

127. Ibid.

128. Augustine, *Retractations* 1.13.7 (CSEL 36.62; Bogan). This is also not the only time Augustine altered his stance on an issue. During the Donatist controversy, he was forced to adapt his position on baptism and reappropriated the writings of Cyprian, especially the letters.

129. Augustine, *Retract.* 1.14.5 (CSEL 36.70).

130. See Peter Brown, *Augustine of Hippo: A Biography*, repr. ed. (Berkeley: University of California Press, 2000), 418–22.

educed faith, they also provided comfort; and comfort in fifth-century Hippo was likely difficult to come by. Augustine provided enough gory detail of the horrors of surgery and disease to make this need for comfort obvious: "As to bodily diseases, they are so numerous that they cannot all be contained even in medical books."[131]

Augustine softened his stance on miracles, since he realized that the relics fulfilled a need in his congregation and were not severely detrimental to the church. He stated in his *City of God* that regardless how a miracle was wrought, "they all testify to the faith in which the resurrection to eternal life is proclaimed."[132] As Peter Brown points out, the later Augustine realized that it was the nature of human frailty to focus attention on the future resurrection of the body.[133] To counteract the physical illness that plagues the body in life, Augustine preached the cure of *Christus medicus* that takes place in the physical cleansing of the resurrection of the body. Augustine's shift on miracles demonstrates the evolving nature of his role as shepherd to his flock and the newly focused attention on the role of the saints.

CONCLUSION

The early Christian texts emphasize Christ as a physician and worker of miracles, as a figure dominant to any religious opponent. The position of Christian supremacy had to be continually upheld, and the populace needed to be reminded of the superior authority of Christ. The best vehicle to drive home this message was the image of Christ healing and working miracles—what I have labeled Christ the Miracle Worker. The image of Christ the Miracle Worker in text and art allowed the listener and viewer to realize the uniqueness of Christian "healing," the salvation of the soul procured by Christ and his power over death. The frequency with which this message appears in early church polemic is matched by its appearance in visual art. This connection is not unintentional and reveals an effort to maintain the image of Christ the Miracle Worker in the minds of the populace. Ambrose and Augustine preached the supremacy of Christ in their sermons. The visual representations of Christ the Miracle Worker would reinforce that message.

---

131. Augustine, *City of God* 22.22 (CSEL 40.638; Bettenson).
132. Augustine, *City of God* 22.9 (CSEL 40.613; Bettenson).
133. Brown, *Augustine of Hippo*, 421.

4

Images of Christ Healing

As Christians began to develop their visual language and realize the narrative and nonnarrative functions of art, the figure of Christ became a useful tool in promoting Christianity over other religions. Shortly after the beginning of Christian art, Christ as a healer became a primary theme. Early Christian images predominantly appeared in sepulchral settings such as the catacombs. Christ healing the sick and raising the dead were apt funerary themes because they were reminders of the ultimate resurrection vouchsafed by Christ. Thus, these images had a viewing audience that was very much alive, as different members would visit the dead and realize the message visually depicted by the art. The catacombs provided further space to perform the crucial ritual of burying as well as physically interacting with the dead through their presence at the catacomb crypts. The martyrs' underground tombs commemorated Christian heroes and provided a space where Christian memory was preserved and could proliferate.

The rituals in the catacombs could be somewhat frightening, especially given the physical characteristics of a sepulchral crypt. Jerome attests to such trepidation as he recalls childhood visits to the catacombs in his *Commentary on Ezekiel*: "And often did I enter the crypts, deep dug in the earth, with their walls on either side lined with the bodies of the dead, where everything is so dark that it almost seems as if the psalmist's words were fulfilled: 'Let them go down alive into hell.'" For a child, descending into a dark, damp area that housed the dead would understandably cause anxiety. One of the functions of the further development of Christian iconography was to alleviate the darkness with light and make the catacomb space visually appealing to its visitors. The Christian poet Prudentius noted such developments in his description of the tomb of Hippolytus. He described the gleams of light in the confined area dancing off the precious metals used to adorn the worship space where the congregation partook of the Eucharist. Obviously, viewers of the early Christian images of Christ responded to narrative art as in the salient visual theme of the miracle-working Christ. In a realm celebrating the dead, the art was for the living.

By contemplating an image of Jesus, viewers such as the young Jerome could reflect upon the final resurrection secured by the ultimate healer.

The early images of Christ the Miracle Worker wove together several components of existing visual traditions. Early Christians adopted the artistic influences of their immediate neighbors. Such appropriations do not imply that the Christians lacked originality; instead, the tendency reveals a deeper methodological goal. Non-Christian imagery was appropriated to portray rival deities as inferior to Christ. Christian imagery was a useful platform, and the images of healings were constructive in promoting the powerful abilities of Christ as superior to any non-Christian figure. This chapter will examine images of Christ's curative ability by focusing on the three scriptural motifs that illustrate his ability: the healing of the paralytic, the woman with the issue of blood, and the healing of the blind. Healing and restoration were prominent themes that were well suited to a funerary setting, and they additionally illustrated the powers of Christ. Finally, this chapter will discuss the visual appearance of Jesus and the god Asclepius, where their connection and rivalry illustrated in the writings treated in the previous chapter can be witnessed visually.

Clearly early Christians were influenced by the non-Christian use of art either in icon devotion or in other material forms. Eusebius recorded a possible appropriation in his history describing a statue at Paneas (Caesarea Philippi). Eusebius described the statue as an artwork erected in gratitude for Jesus healing the woman with the issue of blood:

> For they say that there stood on a lofty stone at the gates of her house a brazen figure in relief of a woman, bending on her knee and stretching forth her hands like a suppliant, while opposite to this there was another of the same material, an upright figure of a man, clothed in comely fashion in a double cloak and stretching out his hand to the woman; at his feet on the monument itself a strange species of herb was growing, which climbed up the border of the double cloak of brass, and acted as an antidote to all kinds of disease. This statue, they said, bore the likeness of Jesus.[1]

---

1. Eusebius, *Ecclesiastical History* 7.18 (PG 20, 679C; Oulton, LCL). The statue was also mentioned in Sozomen (*Hist. eccl.,* 5.21) and Philostorgius (*Hist. eccl.* 7.3). The late-fourth-century poet Prudentius was similarly accommodating to pagan statues that had come under the aegis of a Christian empire. In his reply to Symmachus, he exhorted Romans to abandon idolatry, but not to destroy pagan statues: "Let your statues, the works of great artists, be allowed to rest clean; be these our country's fairest ornaments,

Eusebius's description of the statue, particularly the detail of the growing curative plant, makes it unlikely that this statue was originally intended to depict the healing of the woman with the issue of blood. His characterization of non-Christian image devotion, of the tendency to regard the statue as "Savior," implies that the Christians appropriated and altered a pagan statue. Eusebius's statements regarding imagery should not be construed as negative. He noted existing images of Paul, Peter, and Jesus without any reservation. His criticism of image devotion gently reminds his readers of their non-Christian neighbors' proclivities. For the Christians, the natural subject to transpose from the pagan oeuvre was related to Christ performing healings and miracles.

Eusebius's description of the statue also invites an intriguing comparison. The statue at Paneas may in fact originally have been a statue of Asclepius. The growing herbal plant could have been a Christian rendition of the serpent-entwined staff. The local population at Paneas obviously interpreted the statue as a healer, which influenced the Christian population to model it after a Christian healing story. Although impossible to prove, the suggestion is an interesting one to debate. To imbue a non-Christian image with a Christian meaning certainly would not be unprecedented.[2] Even Adolf von Harnack was obliged to make the comparison between the two: "If the statue originally represented Asclepius as the curative plant would suggest, we should have here at least one step between 'Asclepius the Savior' and 'Christ the Savior.' But this interpretation of a pagan savior or healer is insecure."[3]

Harnack perceived Eusebius's statue as possible visual evidence of a rivalry between Asclepius and Christ. What can be drawn from Eusebius's account, regardless of the origin of the statue at Paneas, is that Christians were developing a visual language to propagate a message of Christ as a healer and worker of miracles. Eusebius's text apparently shows that the early Christians were discovering the utility of art and imagery, were capitalizing on the influences of their non-Christian neighbors, and were placing that imagery in the context of healing.

---

and let no debased usage pollute the monuments of art and turn it into sin." *Against Symmachus* 1.502 (Thomson, LCL).

2. See Steven Bigham, *Early Christian Attitudes towards Images* (Rollinsford, NH: Orthodox Research Institute, 2004), 188–89. Bigham follows Murray's position, particularly on Eusebius's stance on images. He does allow the possibility that the statue at Paneas could be Asclepius.

3. Adolf von Harnack, *The Mission and Expansion of Christianity in the First Three Centuries*, trans. and ed. James Moffatt (New York: Harper, 1962), 119.

THE HEALING OF THE PARALYTIC

At its inception, Christian art was narrative art. Images served as "pages," with the wall painting serving as the manuscript. For example, images of Daniel relate to images of Jonah and Noah; they cannot be interpreted in isolation from one another. The images are integrated and intentionally placed within the surrounding examples, creating a symphonic tableau instead of singular "staccato" notes. The narrative aspect of Christian art dwindled after Constantine as the image of Jesus, among others, assumed a more dogmatic meaning as a divine symbol.[4] But at the catacomb of Callistus and the third- and early-fourth-century catacombs, the images were narrative in nature.[5]

The portrayal of the baptism of Christ in the catacomb of Callistus is one of the earliest depictions of baptism. As with most images in this catacomb, the facial expressions and figural depictions are faded and difficult to interpret. Immediately adjacent to the scene of Christ's baptism is an image of the healed paralytic. This scene does not include an image of Christ. Rather, the solitary figure of the healed paralytic is shown holding his pallet above his head in a manner that becomes emblematic of the healing act of Christ (Figure 2). The position of this scene next to the scene of Jesus' baptism is appropriate. The healing of the paralytic is among the first miracles of Christ's ministry in the synoptic gospels.[6] Mark begins with Jesus' baptism, and immediately follows with several of Christ's healings and miracles. Matthew, Mark, and Luke include the healing of Peter's mother-in-law as well as the cleansing of a leper directly after Jesus' baptism and before the healing of the paralytic. The Gospel of John uses the episode in the healing scene at the pool of Bethesda in John 5:2-9. Christ encounters an invalid near the healing pool and orders him to take up his mat and walk.

Why the Christians at the catacomb of Callistus chose to depict the paralytic rather than the earlier scenes of Jesus' healing is curious. If one is to read the images chronologically, following Jesus' baptism, a scene where he heals the leper or casts out demons would logically follow. However, there are few depictions of such exorcisms in the corpus of early Christian art. Similarly,

4. Robin M. Jensen, *Understanding Early Christian Art* (New York: Routledge, 2000), 90–91.

5. Mathews disputes the long-held view that early Christian images held no connection from one image to another to create a programmatic whole. He uses the musical term *staccato*, which refers to a musical note that is brief and separate from other notes on a sheet of music, to criticize Grabar's interpretation of early Christian images. Thomas Mathews, *The Clash of Gods* (Princeton, NJ: Princeton University Press, 1993), 13.

6. Mark 2:1-12; Matt. 9:2; Luke 5:17. For Peter's mother-in-law, see Mark 1:29-31; Matt. 4:1-11; and Luke 4:1-13.

the cleansing of the leper was not a depiction included in the catacombs.[7] The healing of the paralytic was a popular story due to its dramatic assertion that Jesus is the Son of Man and that Christ was unique. Another obvious reason for its inclusion in a catacomb environment is its symbolism. Jesus orders the paralytic to "Get up" (?γείρω), which the King James Version translates as "Arise." Such language serves as a metaphor for resurrection. Just as the paralytic rises up, so do the Christian dead. Mark and Luke ended the miracle narrative with the crowd exclaiming, "We have never seen anything like this" (Mark 2:12; Luke 5:26). Jesus' healing ability was witnessed by a large crowd of people who are duly awed by his powers. Early church authors such as Augustine found the paralytic story useful in preaching of the curative power of Christ. Augustine demanded that his listeners lower Christ the Physician through the roof of their homes by expounding on Scripture, thereby binding up any fractures or maladies caused by greed or pride.[8]

Few catacomb examples of the healing of the paralytic have been recovered.[9] Along with the representation at the catacomb of Callistus, there is another at the catacomb under the Vigna Massimo and another in the catacomb of Peter and Marcellinus. In the Vigna Massimo catacomb, Christ is depicted on a lower-register relief amid several other scenes, including those of Daniel, Tobias with the fish, and the figure of Job (Figure 3). Jesus is depicted next to the boy carrying his mat above his head. While the image is damaged, it appears that Jesus is not only gesturing toward the boy but also touching him. The late-third-century catacomb of Peter and Marcellinus includes the image of the paralytic in a ceiling relief next to an image of Daniel. Daniel, naked and flanked by two lions, was also understood as a baptismal figure. His nudity may suggest baptism as well as resurrection, and his experience in the lion's den marked him as the prototypical martyr.[10] This image of Daniel may not be much different from the image at the catacomb of Callistus with its context

7. It is extremely difficult to depict an exorcism, and there was no direct precedent in pagan or Jewish art for such a scene. Consider Bosio's drawing, where the interpretation remains unclear; cf. Finney's figures 41.3 and 40.2 in "Do You Think God Is a Magician?" in *Akten Des Symposiums Früchristliche Sarkophage* (Marburg: Deutches Archäologisches Institut, 1999).

8. Augustine, *Serm.* 46.13.

9. Josef Wilpert, *Die Malereien der Katakomben Roms* (Freiburg im Breisgau: Herdersche Verlagshandlung, 1903), 218–24. Some themes are more prominent than others, as Wilpert noted fifteen instances of the healing of the paralytic and seven instances of the healing of the blind man compared with sporadic instances of the healing of the leper and of the woman with the issue of blood that appear in the catacomb of Praetextus and the catacomb of Peter and Marcellinus.

10. See Tertullian, *Antidote for the Scorpion's Sting* 8; and Cyprian, *Eps.* 57.2; 67.8; *On the Lapsed* 19. Cyprian states that Daniel was the model of the martyr confessor. In *On the Lapsed*, Cyprian cites Daniel

of baptism. The inclusion of a naked Jonah underneath the gourd also suggests baptism and resurrection. Daniel and Jonah's nudity cannot be explained in the narrative context, but their nudity in art refers to the ritual nudity of baptism. Nudity has ritual connotations in early Christian sacramental practice. Cyril, bishop of Jerusalem in the mid-fourth century writes of baptismal nudity in his catechetical instructions: "Truly you bore the image of the first-formed Adam, who was naked in the garden and 'was not ashamed.'"[11] Theodore of Mopsuestia also echoes the theme of Adam in his baptismal homilies comparing the baptisand's ritual nudity to the nudity of Adam.[12] Both Cyril and Theodore evoke an understanding of baptism so clearly represented by Paul in his letter to the Romans: that the ritual represents baptism into the death of Christ.[13] A nude Daniel and a nude Jonah reflect this fourth-century understanding and similarly imply baptism and resurrection in a funerary environment.

A feature shared by the Callistus and the Peter and Marcellinus images is that Jesus is absent from the scene. Instead, only the paralytic is shown holding his mat and following Jesus' command to walk. Only the paralytic bears witness to the healing performed by Jesus. The scenes at the catacomb of Callistus and the catacomb of Peter and Marcellinus are temporally separated by just under a century. This separation in time indicates that the image consistently operated on a symbolic level, echoing the healing power of Christ without Christ ever being represented. On relief sculpture, Jesus is represented along with the paralytic; however, the depiction of the paralytic remains consistent. The catacomb examples, particularly the paintings at the catacomb of Callistus and the catacomb under the Vigna Massimo, are integrated into the other scenes. Christ's ability to heal is symbolized by the paralytic now walking, and with the image of Christ's baptism or with Daniel, the rejuvenating effects of baptism are emphasized as well.

In the catacombs, the paralytic scene conveys the nature of narrative imagery in early Christian art and correlates to the cognate images in its immediate environment. While the paralytic scene is not the most duplicated of all the scenes depicting Christ as healer, it does portray a successful healing; the paralytic is walking proof of Christ's powers. While restoring sight to the blind,

as the most glorious martyr, asking, "Who more strong for suffering martyrdom in firmness of faith" than Daniel? Also see Jensen, *Understanding Early Christian Art*, 174–76.

11. Cyril of Jerusalem, *Mystagogical Catechesis* 2.2 (*NPNF* 2.7.147).

12. Theodore of Mopsuestia, *Commentary on the Lord's Prayer, Baptism and the Eucharist*, trans. A. Mingagna (Cambridge, UK: W. Heffer and Sons, 1933), 4

13. Both Cyril and Theodore cite and reflect upon Rom. 6:3-4, stating clearly that one is baptized into the death of Christ.

healing the woman with the issue of blood, or even raising Lazarus emphasizes the dramatic moment of the miracle itself, the healing of the paralytic more deeply captures the end result of the healing—the restored life of the man who was healed. Later examples of the paralytic in Christian art will follow the precedent set by the catacomb examples. The boy walking with the mat above his head becomes the symbol of a successful healing. Other examples of Christ's healing emphasize the power of his touch.

RELIEF SCULPTURE

The iconography of the paralytic scene in Christian relief sculpture is very similar to the scene's representation in the catacombs.[14] The standard of portraying the young man as little more than a boy, carrying his mat after the act of healing, continues in the sarcophagus frontals (Figures 4–7). In the relief sculpture scenes, there are more surrounding figures. The disproportionate size of the figures in the art is significant. Christ is depicted on a larger scale than the recipients of his healing power; the paralytic, as well as the woman with the issue of blood, the blind man, Lazarus, and Jairus's daughter are all portrayed as much smaller than their healer and miracle worker.

While Christ is large compared with the supplicants, he is of equal height and stature to the disciples who flank him in the sarcophagus images. This size difference is common in Greco-Roman depictions of the gods. The inferiority of those being healed is signified by their diminutive size, and the figures requiring Christ's aid are easily identified at the feet of their savior. The discrepancy in height can partially be explained as due to spatial considerations on such a limited surface. While such size differentiation does occur in images of Christ in the catacombs, there is less space for the artist to use in the medium of relief sculpture. Yet the larger stature of Christ and his disciples reveals who the powerful characters in the drama are. Christ and the disciples have power relative to those who receive their power. The focus in the healing and miracle scenes is obviously on Christ and his disciples.

The healing of the paralytic is classically depicted with Christ in the act of speech towering over the paralytic who carries his mat above his head. The paralytic carrying his mat in this manner denotes the healing power and authority of Christ. Several examples of relief sculpture in the Museo Pio Cristiano portray the boy seated or lying on his mat while Christ is depicted directly next to him, issuing his edict (Figures 8–9). The figure of Christ is akin to the images of Christ in the catacombs. He is depicted either beardless

---

14. See Jensen, *Understanding Early Christian Art*, 95.

or bearded with short, curly hair, draped in a robe and wearing sandals. This is not an image of Jesus meant for veneration; rather, it emphasizes the narrative drama that is taking place.[15] Usually, scenes of Christ performing his healing are flanked by multiple other scenes of his miracles (Figures 4–5). Occasionally, sculpted columns or barriers frame each scene. With few significant narrative details, the identification of each scene usually relies upon repeated symbols such as the paralytic's mat.

While the boy carrying his mat clearly signifies the paralytic account in the Synoptic Gospels, there is one particular example that recalls the Johannine account of the pool at Bethesda (Figure 6). In this sarcophagus, now in the Museo Pio Cristiano, there is an indication of a pool in the scene that recalls the Bethesda miracle in John 5. In the central scene separating the upper and lower zones, a carved barrier with wavy striated lines suggests water. Since this central scene involves a ritual at a pool, the typical interpretation is that it recalls baptism.[16] The association between water and a healing signals the restorative washing that takes place during this event. What makes this sarcophagus unique is the illustration in the central panel. In the lower register, the paralytic is lying on his bed in the posture of Jonah/Endmyion (the mythic figure lured into eternal sleep by the moon goddess Selene) although the paralytic is not nude. The figure represents one of the disabled people whom John describes lying near the pool.[17] Above the carving of the paralytic lying in repose, Christ orders him to walk, gesturing toward the paralytic with his hand, almost appearing to touch the top of his mat.

The boy carrying his mat is depicted low on the Bethesda relief, and is quite small, while Christ is shown gesturing toward the top of the mat with his hand.[18] Whether Christ is actually touching the mat, making this a healing by the power of touch, is unclear. Images of the paralytic in relief sculpture such as the Bethesda example follow the gospel accounts specifying that the healing occurred through the speech of Christ, not through the power of his touch.[19] Christ's hand is in the gesture of speech, three fingers closed, with one or two

15. See Jensen, *Face to Face: Portraits of the Divine in Early Christianity* (Minneapolis: Fortress Press, 2005), 151–52.

16. David Knipp, *"Christus Medicus" in der frühchristlichen Sarkophagskulptur: Ikonographische Studien der Sepulkralkunst des späten vierten Jahrhunderts* (Leiden: Brill, 1998), 154–56. However, he points out that it also reflects a competition with the Asclepius cult, arguing that this scene is a representation of a successful healing similar to the incubation treatment in a temple of Asclepius.

17. This before-and-after portrayal of the scene is unique to this particular sarcophagus, dating from 375 CE.

18. It should also be noted that in Figure 4, the figures on the right half of the frontal have been restored. Unfinished faces of figures, or damaged figures, have been noticeably repaired and carved.

fingers extended. Due to the lack of space, it does appear that Christ touches the mat in the Roman examples, but the depictions of the scene also appear to stay true to the gospel: the boy walks with his mat after Christ issues his verbal edict. This is clearer on a double register sarcophagus dating from 300 to 325 CE, also at the Vatican, where the figures are carved even smaller (Figure 7).[20] Christ still stands over the boy and his mat; however, his hand hovers directly over the mat and is clearly not touching it.

In two examples in the Museo Pio Cristiano and at Arles, a seated paralytic is portrayed as the viewer glimpses the moment of healing rather than the proof of its efficacy (Figures 8–9). Christ is directly next to the paralytic, who is sitting on the edge of his mat, and Christ's hand is directly above his head, appearing to touch him. In the example at Arles, Christ's hand seems to touch the head of the paralytic as well as indicate speech, signaling that his edict heals as well as the power of his touch. Christ holds a scroll in his left hand while his right hovers over the boy's mat, yet the power of touch is still emphasized in these enigmatic instances. The focus is the moment of Christ's edict before the paralytic takes up his mat and walks, proving the authority and power of Christ. Christ holds a scroll in his other hand as in cognate representations, emphasizing his authority, just as the biblical scene affirms his authority to forgive sins on earth. With few exceptions, in Christian relief sculpture, the healing of the paralytic is a scene emphasizing the authority of Christ noted by the scroll and the healing act marked ambiguously by Jesus' gesture of speech or more blatantly through the touch of his hand.

The Woman with the Issue of Blood

Another scene highlighting Jesus' healing ability is that of the woman with the issue of blood.[21] While the narrative asserts that the woman's faith made her

19. As in any aspect of early Christian art, there are always exceptions. In Figure 4, Christ is clearly touching the mat with his hand. However, this section of the fragment was restored—quite noticeably, given the color of the stone compared with the previous section, as well as the facial features of the characters. It may well be that during restoration, the hand was altered so that it touched the mat. The previous section is unaltered, and the hand is clearly in the gesture of speech, not touching the mat of the paralytic.

20. The sarcophagus is originally from the cemetery of Praetextus. Notice that the boy holds what appears to be a staff, an inclusion that appears in some representations of the blind man as well.

21. The scene occurs in Roman examples thirty-eight times. See G. Bovini and Hugo Brandenburg, *Repertorium der christlich-antiken Sarkophage*, Band 1, *Rom und Ostia*, ed. F. W. Deichmann (Wiesbaden: F. Steiner, 1967), 123. It occurs fifteen times in examples from Gaul and North Africa. See Brigitte Christern-Briesenick, *Repertorium der christlich-antiken Sarkophage*, Band 3, *Frankreich, Algerien, Tunesien*, ed. T. Ulbert (Wiesbaden: F. Steiner, 2003), 301.

well, touch is still emphasized in the story, although the normal direction is reversed. The woman touches Jesus out of her desire to be healed. The story appears in all three Synoptic Gospels, while it is absent from the Gospel of John.[22] The scene of the woman with the issue of blood is depicted in catacomb art that emphasizes the healing power of Christ's touch. At the catacomb of Peter and Marcellinus, the woman kneels below the figure of Christ, clutching the hem of his tunic (Figure 10). Christ is not touching the woman; the woman is touching him, recalling the moment when Christ realizes the healing power "goes out from him." Christ gestures toward the woman with his hand, possibly in recognition of the event or in blessing.

The woman with the issue of blood appears rarely in the catacomb evidence that has been uncovered. Only one other instance has been discovered in addition to the image at Peter and Marcellinus, and that is at the catacomb of Praetextus.[23] With little direct evidence, there is no real way of knowing whether many other catacomb representations of the woman with the issue of blood existed. However, if the dating of the catacomb of Peter and Marcellinus is correct, the scene of the woman with the issue of blood was completed at the end of the third century, just under a century removed from the earliest iconography of the catacomb of Callistus. That the image of the woman with the issue of blood was included in this later catacomb and persistently appears on sarcophagi of the same time period indicates that the image was entering into the repertoire of depictions of Christ in the act of healing. Viewed in the wider context of Roman Christian art, the woman with the issue of blood was a fairly prominent image in the late third century. Its inclusion in the corpus of healing images is not unexpected, as it captures a successful healing through physical interaction with the figure of Christ.

RELIEF SCULPTURE

Christian relief sculpture depicts the scene of the woman with the issue of blood in a way similar to the catacomb painting of Peter and Marcellinus (Figure 10). Jesus stands over a kneeling woman, who clutches the hem of his robe. Jesus either touches the woman's head or motions his hand toward her in the gesture of speech, as he does in the scene of the healing of the paralytic.

A column sarcophagus at the Vatican is indicative of the typical portrayal of this scene (Figure 11). Christ touches the woman while she touches him;

22. For the woman with the issue of blood, Mark 5:21-34; Matt. 9:18-26; Luke 8:40-48.

23. See Josef Wilpert, *Die Malereien der Katakomben Roms* (Freiburg im Breisgau: Herdersche Verlagshandlung, 1903), 218–24. In Roman catacomb art, there are fifteen examples of the paralytic but only two examples of the woman with the issue of blood.

it is a scene centered upon physical contact. Some examples include only the woman touching Jesus' robe, while others show Christ not touching the woman's head but motioning toward her in the gesture of address (Figures 10, 12). Knipp discusses a unique example of the image on the sarcophagus of San Celso, dating from the late fourth or early fifth century.[24] In the scene, the woman clutches at the hem of Christ's robe. However, the woman is not kneeling at Christ's feet as in other portrayals, but leaning down. Christ is positioned away from the woman and is looking back at her. The scene captures the moment when Christ becomes aware of his power going out of him. Neither of Christ's hands clutches a scroll or is in the gesture of address. This image, as others in the catacombs, envisage the entire narrative through symbolic art; however, the positioning of Christ as portrayed in this image is unique.

In certain examples of Christian relief sculpture, it may appear that the woman is included in the scene of the raising of Lazarus (Figure 13). In such representations, Jesus is portrayed in the act of resurrection while a woman kneels at his feet touching his robe.[25] She is in a similar position to the woman with the issue of blood; however, the figure is meant to depict Lazarus's sister, either Mary or Martha, as the image follows the text from John quite closely. Martha's presence in the text is important, as she recognizes Jesus as the Messiah (11:27). Her presence announces Jesus as the "resurrection and the life" just as Jesus restores Lazarus to new life. An identification of the figure as Martha is obviously appealing. Examples of relief sculpture that contain both images of the woman with the issue of blood and the raising of Lazarus support this conclusion.[26] The woman with the issue of blood was healed by Jesus due to her faith, but the physical nature of Christ's healing is emphasized throughout the representations of this iconographical "note" in the larger symphony of early Christian relief sculpture.

Another "note" in the ensemble of miracle and healing images that depict Jesus' transformative touch in a similar manner is the healing of the blind man. As with the woman with the issue of blood, few instances of the healing of

24. Knipp, *Christus Medicus*, 110ff, and pl. 15.

25. See F. Benoit, *Sarcophages paléochréttiens d'Arles et de Marseille* (Paris, 1954), 50, pl. 19, where he argues that a single relief at Arles shows both Jesus raising Jairus's daughter and the woman with the issue of blood..

26. See W. Kuhn, *Frühchristliche Kunst aus Rom* (Essen: Villa Hügel, 1962), pl. 457 from the grotto of the Vatican, dating from the fourth century. Also see my "Perspectives on the Nude Youth in Fourth-Century Sarcophagi Representations of the Raising of Lazarus," in *Studia Patristica* (Leuven: Peeters, 2013), 59:77–88.

the blind man have been discovered in the catacombs.[27] In paintings at the catacomb of Domitilla and the catacomb of Peter and Marcellinus, Christ is depicted touching the eyes of his patient. In the painting at Domitilla dating from the early fourth century, Christ touches the blind man with his index finger, a motif that is replicated on Christian relief sculpture.[28] Other scenes in the catacombs render Christ touching the patient with his entire hand. The healing of the blind exhibits Christ physically encountering and healing his supplicants. While there are few examples to work with in the catacombs, this healing image is visibly evident in fourth- and fifth-century examples of Christian relief sculpture.

The subject of Christ healing the blind man is the most frequently represented healing image in extant Christian relief sculpture. In the surviving Roman examples, it appears more often than any other healing scene.[29] The scene portrays Christ touching the patient, emphasizing his power and his status as the supreme healer. Unlike the healing of the paralytic represented in relief sculpture, which includes several divergent representations, those that portray Christ healing the blind man are fairly consistent. The representation consists of the comparatively large figure of Christ, touching the eyes or face of the patient, who is depicted on Jesus' left or right (Figures 14–15). All of the gospels include the story of Christ healing blind persons. Some accounts describe the events as predicated by the patients' faith, as Christ affirms that their faith has healed them. Other accounts detail Christ's healing touch as the catalyst of the event.[30] In Christian relief sculpture, the representations of Christ healing the blind man follow the accounts that describe the power of Christ's touch. That is, instead of emphasizing the gesture of Christ's speech, as in the paralytic scene, the healing power of Christ's touch is on display in the healing of the blind man.

Two representative examples of the scene in relief sculpture from Rome and Gaul offer insight into its significance.[31] Examples of relief sculpture now in

27. Wilpert, *Die Malereien der Katakomben Roms*, 218–24. Some themes are more prominent than others. Wilpert noted in the catacomb of Praetextus and the catacomb of Peter and Marcellinus fifteen instances of the healing of the paralytic and seven instances of the healing of the blind man compared with sporadic instances of the healing of the leper and the woman with the issue of blood.

28. Sadly, the Domitilla fresco is now lost. The original image has been preserved as a line drawing.

29. There were seventy-one occurrences as recorded by U. Lange, *Ikonographisches Register für das Repertorium der christlich-antiken Sarkophage*, ed. F.W. Deichmann (Dettelbach: Röll, 1996), Band 1:123, and forty-four in examples from Gaul and North Africa; see ibid., Band 3:299.

30. The gospel accounts of these events include the healing of blind Bartimaeus by faith in Mark 10:51; Jesus healing two blind men with the power of touch in Matt. 9:27-30 and 20:29-34; healing by faith in Luke 18:35-43; and healing with touch in John 9:1-41. Jesus healing the blind man at Bethsaida in Mark 8:22-26 is unique to Mark.

the Museo Pio Cristiano and at Arles include the healing of the blind man along with other representations of miracles and healings. The blind man is usually depicted as much smaller than the figure of Christ, and he is shown holding a staff similar to the one the paralytic boy occasionally wields (Figure 14). Christ places his hand or fingers on the blind man's face or touches the top of his head (see Figure 4, 5). The scene stresses Christ's touch; his fingers upon the face of the afflicted are shown in detail, and occasionally the blind man's sightless eyes are given definition.[32] Christ holds the face of the afflicted as he covers the blind man's eyes with his fingers (Figures 14–15).

As in the scene of the paralytic, here Christ is usually portrayed clutching a scroll in his other hand. The sarcophagus in Saint-Victor, Marseille, dating from the first half of the fifth century, contains a scene of the *traditio legis* (giving of the law) in the central panel with a scene of Christ healing the blind next to it.[33] In the scene, Christ's fingers are placed on the patient's eyes. On the sarcophagus example at Arles, Christ holds his scroll and places his thumb directly on one of the eyes of the afflicted, who holds a staff or cane in this portrayal (Figure 15). Whether the depictions of Christ healing the blind man follow the Matthean, Lukan, or Johannine account is unclear. The synoptic accounts only mention Jesus touching the man's eyes. The account in John is more detailed, as it describes Jesus spitting, mixing mud, and rubbing it on the man's eyes. Regardless of which account the images follow, or whether the images are closely reflective of the biblical text, they refer to episodes from Scripture to emphasize the power of Christ's touch.

Images that feature the healing touch of Christ have an underlying message. His touch demonstrates his curative power, since his healings were a result of real physical interaction between physician and patient. Asclepius's remedies were provided through the power of dreams. Temple priests would supply a prescription after the patient had slept in the Asclepieion. An image of Christ healing through touch spread the message of his superiority, since his healing power was depicted as a tangible action taking place between healer and patient. The power of the healer is promoted in these images. In other words, Jesus healed his patients immediately in the physical world, not through the power of dreams. While the power of Jesus is promoted, the images also reveal the importance of the faith of the patient. For example, the faith of the woman

31. See Benoit, *Sarcophages paleochrétiens*, 39, 51.

32. See the ivory Andrews diptych (450–460 CE), now at the Victoria and Albert Museum, London, and in Jensen, *Understanding Early Christian Art*, fig. 48.

33. Knipp, *Christus Medicus*, devotes a large section of a chapter to this sarcophagus beginning on p. 24.

is indicated by Jesus as part of the healing process ("your faith has made you well"), and the viewing audience would be reminded of the text by witnessing the image in a funerary context.[34] And in a funerary context, the connection between faith "making one well" in this world and faith in the resurrection also can be realized visually.

THE VISUAL APPEARANCE OF JESUS AND ASCLEPIUS

Asclepius enjoyed a fair amount of prominence in the iconography of the Late Antique Mediterranean world. Images of Asclepius proliferated around the centers of healing in each town, which were known as Asclepieia. The images corresponded with and reflected the healing action that took place in the immediate location. Asclepius, most often depicted in statuary form or carved upon *stelai*, had a definitive and thus easily recognizable appearance. Clad in a *himation* (cloak) that exposed his chest, Asclepius is depicted holding a scepter or scroll in one hand and his staff entwined with a serpent in the other (Figure 16). Ovid referred to this familiar portrayal in his *Metamorphoses*, as the god speaks to a Roman crowd exhorting them, "Only be sure to note this snake that twines about my staff, and mark it well to fix it in your mind!"[35] The snake and the staff are representative of Asclepius and are much more reliable indicators of his identity than hair or beard.

Asclepius in statuary form is consistently portrayed standing or leaning on his serpent-entwined staff, bearded or beardless with curly hair and occasionally accompanied by the smaller figure of Telesphoros.[36] While many images of Asclepius were destroyed after the ascension of Christianity following Constantine in the fourth century, numerous images of Asclepius still survive. In several instances, Asclepius was captured in statuary form as an Apollonian youth, beardless and leaning on his staff, shifting his weight to his front foot.[37] In later examples from Epidauros and Athens, Asclepius appears as Jupiter or Sarapis, fully bearded and with flowing hair.[38] Pausanias described a statue of Asclepius in his book on Corinth, remarking that the Corinthian statue was half as tall as the Olympian Zeus. It was made of ivory and gold and depicted

34. Luke 8:48.

35. Ovid, *Metamorphoses* 15.650ff (Melville).

36. Telesphoros was the hooded nocturnal god who accompanied Asclepius, reminding of the healing action that had taken place while the patient was asleep at night. His name literally means "The Finisher," just as death is the finisher.

37. See *Lexicon Iconographicum Mythologiae Classicae*, comité de redaction, John Boardman, et al. (Zurich: Artemis, 1981–97), "Asklepios," figs. 22–29.

38. See ibid., fig. 321.

Asclepius with his staff and serpent.[39] This trend in the depiction of Asclepius is unvarying in representations throughout the Late Antique Mediterranean world. In statuary examples from North Africa (now Tunisia and Algeria), Asclepius appears the same as he does in representations in Athens; fully bearded, draped in his *himation*, and bearing his snake-entwined staff.[40]

In statuary, Asclepius is never portrayed in the act of healing, and on two-dimensional *stelai*, such depictions are exceedingly rare. On those few occasions when Asclepius is depicted healing, the image portrays him arriving while the patient is asleep, and while the god appears to physically touch the patient and administer some form of cure, it is apparent that the encounter occurs in a dream.[41] Such is also the case in a relief at the Asclepieion at Piraeus: Asclepius is depicted approaching the slumbering patient, suggesting that the god's healing action is taking place through the power of dreams.[42] This does not diminish the encounter, although the images of Christ healing recall rather more direct encounters with his supplicants.

Asclepius is also not alone. In two-dimensional art, he is repeatedly accompanied by the figure of Hygieia.[43] The cult of Asclepius desired to attract not only the sick and the needy, but the healthy as well. Hygieia, the personification of Health, was incorporated into the iconography of Asclepius to express this message.[44] With the dual personifications of healing the sick and preserving the healthy, the cult could presumably draw larger crowds to the temples. While Asclepius required another figure to represent Health in order to gain "patients," Jesus was not portrayed with any such figure in the visual representations of his healing. The message conveyed by the Christians was that

39. Pausanias, *Description of Greece* 2.27.2. Pausanias calls the staff a *bakteria* (small staff), not a *virga*; see chapter 7.

40. See *LIMC*, figs. 276–77.

41. See the damaged relief at Athens, *LIMC*, fig. 56.

42. This work dates from 400 BCE. For the image, see the plate in C. Kerényi, *Asklepios: Archetypal Images of the Physician's Existence* (New York: Pantheon, 1959), pl. 18.

43. *LIMC*, 631. Out of almost four hundred cataloged images, at least a fourth contained Hygieia, fifty-five of them appearing on *stelai*. Occasionally with Hygieia are the goddesses Akeso, Iaso, and Panakeia, as well as his sons Machaon and Podaleirios. The presence of Hygieia may appear to cast doubt on the derivation of the statue Eusebius described. However, it could be that the woman with the issue of blood was originally Hygieia (or Telesphoros) and was recast as the woman. It is impossible to know what Eusebius's statue originally looked like.

44. Michael T. Compton, "The Association of Hygieia with Asklepios in Graeco-Roman Asklepieion Medicine," in *Journal of the History of Medicine and Allied Sciences* 57, no. 3 (2002): 325. Especially see "Asklepios," fig. 252 in *LIMC*, 654, where Asclepius and Hygieia are depicted side by side, as co-deities in prominence, flanked by snakes.

healing the sick and preserving the healthy could be completely accomplished by one persona, not two, and that Christianity was thus superior to any healing cult.

Since the advent of the cult in Greece, the manner in which Asclepius was depicted was rarely altered. A pagan or a Christian could identify his figure by his snake-entwined staff or the presence of Hygieia. The early Christian references and Emperor Julian's appraisal of Asclepius suggest that the cult of Asclepius posed a challenge to early Christianity.

The manner in which the figure of Christ was depicted is consonant with other Greco-Roman prototypes. Christ is portrayed in the typical dress of a tunic and mantle, sometimes called a *pallium*. The way in which the figures are clothed is important in any discussion of visual appearance. The *pallium* refers to a long outer robe, very much like a toga but less voluminous.[45] Just as manner of depiction changes over time in the contemporary world, so it did in Late Antiquity. The Greek and Roman style of dress shifted to include the use of a *pallium*, sometimes worn with a tunic or undergarment, called a *chiton*. Portrayals of a philosopher usually omit the undergarment, leaving the chest bare.[46] There is no particular term to describe the dual use of a *pallium* and *chiton*.[47] The Christ that is depicted in the catacombs wears such a dual garment, which certain scholars have dubbed the "robe."

From a contemporary point of view, it may appear problematic for Christians to dress themselves in the manner of their rivals and to depict Christ in such a way. That early Christians embodied a pristine form of Christianity, unique and unspoiled and completely distinct from outsiders, is a false notion. Christians would logically wish to look like any other ordinary citizens, to blend in and not draw attention to themselves. As depiction in the art, Christ's dress was typical for a citizen of the empire, and it also demonstrates that Christians did not erase their Roman identity. A Christian was a member of the faith but, like Paul, could also possibly be a Roman citizen. Pliny the Younger,

45. See Erwin Goodenough, "Catacomb Art," *JBL* 81, no. 2 (June 1962): 117. Goodenough is not exactly reliable; however, he provides some of the few academic criticisms concerning the "Anatomy Lesson" catacomb painting discussed below and thus must be begrudgingly considered.

46. Such portrayals suggest the peripatetic nature of the wandering teacher and the ascetic lifestyle embodied by a disregard for worldly goods. Also see Jensen, *Face to Face*, 146. To be clear, a *pallium* is not a toga, and occasionally one arm rests in a sling-like fold.

47. Goodenough, "Catacomb Art," 118. A dalmatic was a flowing robe with wide sleeves; Noah appears in art wearing one occasionally. Jensen usually refers to the dress as a tunic and *pallium*; see *Face to Face*, 149. Goodenough is useful for his comments on dress but must be used cautiously overall, given that more recent work has occasionally refuted his views on iconography.

governor of Bithynia-Pontus, indicates that possibility in his correspondence to emperor Trajan in 111–113 CE. Pliny describes to Trajan his actions against professed Christians. Some Christians (noncitizens) were executed, and some who were Roman citizens were transferred to Rome to stand trial.[48] Christians were members of Late Antique society and, as such members, dressed in the manner typical of the times.

Tertullian characterized the dress of Christians in third-century Carthage according to changing times and shifting fortunes. The manner of dress in which a garment was thrown over the shoulder, baring the chest, was reserved for the priestly class within non-Christian cults: "The garment of the mantle extrinsically—itself too quadrangular—thrown back on either shoulder, and meeting closely round the neck in the gripe of the buckle, used to repose on the shoulders. Its counterpart is now the priestly dress, sacred to Asclepius, whom you now call your own."[49] Tertullian identified the *pallium* as equivalent to what he calls the "mantle." The "mantle" indicated leisure and was also an identifier of professional intellectuals such as the Cynic philosophers. The popular dress of Tertullian's Carthage included wearing an undergarment with the mantle, similar to Christ's "robe." Christians wore similar dress to their non-Christian counterparts, which prompted an explanation from Tertullian. A shift in clothing was practical, as Tertullian advocated its virtues, "What is your first sensation in wearing your gown? Do you feel yourself clad, or laded? Wearing a garment, or carrying it?"[50] The new dress was easier to manage and covered the shoulders equally. He called the clothing the suitable garment for a Christian: "But I confer on it likewise a fellowship with a divine sect and discipline. Joy, Mantle, and exult! A better philosophy has now deigned to honor thee, ever since thou hast begun to be a Christian's vesture."[51]

The dress Tertullian described, the dress of a Christian living in the empire, was the typical manner of dress used to portray Christ in visual imagery. Christ as depicted in the catacombs did not appear in the same dress as that of the Asclepius statuary that was in existence. Asclepius was usually depicted in a Greek *himation*, with or without one fold draped over the shoulder, and with his chest bare. In the catacomb paintings, Christ wears the dress that Tertullian described, with the inclusion of the *chiton* underneath the *pallium*. Such a guise would have been familiar to his audience and would not have seemed unusual or foreign. Christ looks like everyone else in the paintings, and likely

---

48. See Pliny, *Letters* 10.96.

49. Tertullian, *The Pallium* 1.1 (*ANF* 4.5).

50. Tertullian, *The Pallium* 5.1 (*ANF* 4.11).

51. Tertullian, *The Pallium* 6.2 (*ANF* 4.12).

resembled the fourth-century audience viewing the paintings. He appeared like an everyman, albeit a fairly prosperous everyman. What set him apart from all the other figures was his miracle-working acts.

Indeed, it can be argued that the catacomb Christ wearing the robe, short haired and often beardless, does not resemble Asclepius at all.[52] The attributes of Asclepius in iconography were his staff, his bare chest, and quite often his beard. The appearance of the beard in visual representations of Asclepius and Christ requires some explanation. In the third- and fourth-century Roman catacombs, Christ is not uniformly depicted with a beard. In large part, the catacomb paintings of Christ portray him without a beard; however, there are exceptions, and the bearded Christ becomes standard after the sixth century.[53] Instances of a bearded or beardless Christ do not reflect a direct connection with Asclepius, since there were many representations of gods fully bearded. Asclepius is normally portrayed with a full beard as in the statue that resides now in the Capitoline Museum in Rome.[54] Asclepius was also not the only god depicted with a beard: Jupiter, Neptune, Mars, and Sarapis were all portrayed with full heads of hair and lustrous beards.[55]

The issue of the beard urges a pair of questions: Does a beard recall Asclepius? And if the beard was so critical, why does the catacomb Jesus appear beardless in many instances?[56] The beardless examples in the catacombs reveal that the Christians were utilizing several elements of familiar Greco-Roman

52. See James Breckenridge's findings in his *Likeness: A Conceptual History of Ancient Portraiture* (Evanston, IL: Northwestern University Press, 1968), 249.

53. Even then, there are beardless representations; instances of Byzantine art portraying a beardless Christ include San Vitale in Ravenna (546 CE). The earliest example appears on the coffered ceiling of cubiculum N5 at the catacomb of Commodilla, where Christ is bearded with a nimbus and a flanking alpha and omega. This image would become a typical mode of depicting the "cosmic Christ" in fourth- and fifth-century Christian art.

54. However, it was not uncommon to depict Asclepius beardless. See Pausanias, *Description of Greece*, 2.10.3; also see 2.13.5, "an image of the god not having a beard" (Jones, LCL); Cicero, *On the Nature of the Gods* 3.34.83 (Rackham, LCL); Emma J. Edelstein and Ludwig Edelstein, *Asclepius: A Collection and Interpretation of the Testimonies* (Baltimore: Johns Hopkins Press, 1945), 1:359-368. Edelstein suggests that the beardless Asclepius is a relic of the past before the bearded Asclepius became the normative manner of depiction. A beardless Asclepius would be an apt choice of depiction, as the cult was beginning to replace the cult of Apollo (traditionally depicted beardless) and capitalize on its status as the preeminent healing cult in the Roman world. Edelstein, *Asclepius*, 2:220. These texts are balanced by recollections of the bearded Asclepius. See Minucius Felix, *Octavius* 23.5; and Lucian's entreaty to Apollo to "not play the boy with us, Apollo. Say what you think boldly and don't be sensitive about speaking without a beard when you have such a long-bearded, hairy-faced son in Asclepius." Lucian, *Jupiter the Tragedian* 26 (Edelstein, T. 684). Note Augustine's comments in *Sermon* 24.6 that Hercules's strength was in his beard.

55. For further reading, see Jensen, *Face to Face*, 62.

iconographic precedents to depict their subject.[57] Christians were influenced by the existing non-Christian iconography, which included bearded gods and youthful beardless gods such as Apollo (and in some cases Asclepius).

The figures in the catacombs serve a narrative purpose to convey a message. Exhibiting Christ as a teacher of wisdom, miracle worker, or healer shows the special nature of Christ. Examining how Christ was visually portrayed—his dress and so forth—permits an understanding of the Christian conception of Christ. In addition to the physical depiction of Christ, the context and the action of the figures in the scenes also reveal an appropriation. In the catacombs, Christ is largely portrayed beardless or with a slight trace of a beard, more akin to representations of youthful gods than the older gods. Christ is also portrayed in these instances healing or performing feats of wonder and acting as a savior. Thus, Christ's appearance or dress may not reflect Asclepius at all. But his action in these scenes arguably does. Christ performs acts of healing and works miracles in a different manner than Asclepius, occasionally using touch and often with the staff. Whether with a hand or staff, bearded or beardless, the images of Jesus attempt to convince the viewer that Jesus is a greater healer than any other representative from pagan traditions.

While for the most part, Jesus and Asclepius bear little physical resemblance to each other in the art of Late Antiquity, some unique examples show a strong physical similarity. One particular example of relief sculpture deserves mention. A fragment at the Terme museum in Rome includes some pertinent images of Christ healing and raising the dead that closely resemble Asclepius (Figure 34). In the fragment, Christ is portrayed healing the paralytic, dividing the loaves, raising the widow's son at Nain, and addressing the crowd. Touch is emphasized, as his hand rests upon the head of the afflicted; however, it is Jesus' dress that has caused scholars to comment. Jesus is not dressed in his typical robe with *chiton* and *pallium*, as in the catacombs and in other sarcophagus scenes. Instead, his chest is bare, with one fold of material draped over the shoulder, representing him as a philosopher and also akin to representations of Asclepius.[58] The facial appearance approximates that of Asclepius, as Christ has

56. However, Erich Dinkler has argued that a bearded Christ begs a direct relation to Asclepius and was modeled upon Asclepius. See Erich Dinkler, *Christus und Asklepios* (Heidelberg: Carl Winter, 1980), 15. Dinkler believes this is so and is rejected by Bovini, et al, *Repertorium der christlich-antiken Sarkophage*, Band 1, *Rom und Ostia*, ed. F. W. Deichmann (Wiesbaden: F. Steiner, 1967), 161; and Paul Zanker, *The Mask of Socrates* (Berkeley: University of California Press, 1995), 100.

57. Also see Jensen, *Face to Face*, 159, and the preceding pages on her treatment of the beard.

58. John Dominic Crossan has insisted that the fact Jesus holds the scroll in his hand and is dressed in such a way intentionally recalls Cynic philosophers. A Cynic association is a leap;. The bare chest and

curly hair and is fully bearded.[59] More than in any other piece of evidence in early Christian art, Christ appears in the guise of Asclepius.[60] However, there is no other cognate piece of relief sculpture quite like the Terme fragment, making any overarching conclusion nearly impossible.

Given the absence of consistent stylistic traits between the two figures, there is little to compare. Still, the catacomb images of Jesus exhibit the polyvalent quality of early Christian art by including influences from non-Christian sources. And the healing and miracle images show an awareness of the Asclepius cult in the subject matter and context of the images. Jesus may not look like Asclepius, but Jesus does not need to appear like the healing god to be portrayed as superior. While Christ is certainly a chameleon in catacomb art, Jesus shown successfully restoring a patient to life exhibits an awareness of Asclepius, especially when the narrative features Jesus triumphing where Asclepius failed.

CONCLUSION

Numerous scenes in the catacombs and on funerary relief sculpture exhibit Jesus raising the dead to life. According to the early Christian authors, Asclepius did not have the divine authority to perform resurrections.[61] Asclepius was killed by Zeus for raising the dead; he did not have authority over life and death. The early church authors knew this quite well, as this lack of divine authority was the tactic of choice when deriding Asclepius. Christ exhibited in the act of raising the dead is evocative of Asclepius's failure. Instead of narrowly

clutched scroll does not necessarily support such a conclusion. John Dominic Crossan, *Jesus: A Revolutionary Biography* (San Francisco, CA: Harper San Francisco, 1994), v.

59. See Erich Dinkler, *Christus und Asklepios* (Heidelberg: Carl Winter, 1980), 66. Dinkler asserts a comparison between the Terme Jesus and Asclepius due to their resemblance. He also believes the scroll to be the Law of the Old Testament; see Paul Zanker, *The Mask of Socrates*, (Berkeley: University of California Press, 1995), 300. Zanker disagrees with Dinkler on the Asclepius comparison, however he argues that any association with Cynic philosophy is erroneous; rather he claims the image bears a relation to "pagan holy men."

60. See Mathews, *The Clash of Gods*, 69–70. Mathews makes an apt connection regarding the fragment, but he should note that the Terme fragment is a unique instance in early Christian art. Mathews is also not the first to rest his argument on this particular object. L. de Bruyne realizes its import in his "L'imposition des mains dans l'art chrétien ancien," *RAC* 20, nos. 1-4 (1943): 113–278, albeit without making the connection between Jesus and Asclepius.

61. Justin, *1 Apol.* 21 (critical edition: *Iustini Martyris Apologiae Pro Christianis* and *Dialogus cum Tryphone*, ed. M. Marcovich [Berlin: De Gruyter, 2005], 63.2-6); Clement, *Ex.* 2.24 ; Origen, *Cels.* 3.22 (PG 11, 944C); Tertullian, *To the Heathen* 2.14.45 (CSEL 20.127). Also in Arnobius, *Against the Pagans* 4.24 (CSEL 4.161); and Lactantius, *Inst.* 1.19.3 (CSEL 19.71).

examining the physical stylistic traits of images of Jesus and images of Asclepius, thematic imagery could reflect such a comparison. The miracle of raising the dead demonstrates that Christ requires no authority to resurrect a person, a miracle of charity and benevolence.

The healings of Jesus were emphasized in early Christian art just as they were in the gospel texts. The healing of the paralytic, the healing of the woman with the blood issue, and the healing of the blind man all promote Jesus as the great physician, a healer with no earthly or heavenly rival. The images of these episodes in the catacombs and on relief sculpture portray Jesus as the supreme healer, just as Scripture does. And these portrayals in art do not occur in a vacuum. The context of healing in Late Antiquity reveals a potent rivalry between Jesus and the healing god Asclepius. Images of Jesus successfully healing sufferers of chronic illness exhibit him as a healer like Asclepius but greater, since Jesus the physician heals directly through physical touch. The historical context also helps any understanding of the multiple instances of Jesus raising the dead to life, an act symbolizing the divine mandate of Jesus as well as highlighting the shortcomings of the god Asclepius. It is to these pervasive instances in the canon of early Christian art that we now turn.

5

Images of Christ Raising the Dead

Though the third and fourth centuries saw a significant amount of growth in Christian theology, the visual language of Christianity was still developing. The imagery of the catacomb of Callistus marked the dawn of Christian art around the year 200 CE, and as late as the fourth-century catacomb at Via Latina, Christians were still appropriating and transforming images and themes from a Greco-Roman social context (Figure 17).[1] Many of the images on the walls and the ceilings of the catacombs have non-Christian prototypes; however, they reflect pertinent themes and issues that the early Christian community desired to portray in a funerary environment. Resurrection was a central theme that reflected the comfort of immortal life after death. The theme of resurrection well demonstrated the superiority of Christ. Pagan heroes as well as scriptural heroes from the Old Testament such as Moses were incorporated into Christian art in order to highlight the attributes of Jesus.

This chapter will begin by exploring the use of figures such as Hercules, Orpheus, and Asclepius to stress the theme of resurrection and the powers of Christ. This theme displays the syncretism in early Christian art as early

---

1. For an extensive, and the earliest, discussion of Via Latina, see Antonia Ferrua, S.I., *Le Pitture della Nuova Catacombs di Via Latina*, Monumenti di antichita cristiana, ser. 2, vol. 8 (Vatican City: Pontificio Istituto di Archeologia Cristiana, 1960); and, with reservations, Erwin Goodenough, "Catacomb Art," *JBL* 81, no. 2 (June 1962): 113–42. See William Tronzo, *The Via Latina Catacomb: Imitation and Discontinuity in Fourth-Century Roman Painting* (University Park: Penn State University Press, 1986), 10–11. Tronzo points out that the early dating of Ferrua (315/20–350) and the late-fourth- to early-fifth-century dating of Deichmann and Dorigo are both correct. See Wladimiro Dorigo, *Pittura tardoromana* (Milan: Feltrinelli, 1966), 221; F. W. Deichmann, "Zur Frage der Gesamtschau der frühchristlichen und frühbyzantinischen Kunst," *Byzantinische Zeitschrift* 63 (1970): 50. Also see F. W. Deichmann and Theodor Klauser. *Frühchristliche Sarkophage in Bild und Wort* (Olten: Urs Graf, 1966). The construction likely began in the 320s and extended into the late fourth century. Also see André Grabar, *The Beginnings of Christian Art, 200–395* (London: Thames and Hudson, 1966), 231, who supports a later dating of the catacomb. Norbert Zimmermann, *Werkstattgruppen Römischer Katakombenmalerei*, JAC 35 (Münster: Aschendorff, 2002), 67, reviews the arguments for dating.

Christians appeared to adopt themes and motifs from these pagan figures. Next, I will examine the predominant images of raising the dead in early Christian art, such as Jesus raising Jairus's daughter, the widow's son at Nain, Christ as Ezekiel in the Valley of the Dry Bones, and the raising of Lazarus, this last example being a frequently used theme in Christian funerary art.

THE CONTEXT OF RESURRECTION IMAGES IN ART

The second-century apologist Justin Martyr mentioned the similarities between the hero Hercules and Christ: "And when it is asserted that Herakles, the son of Zeus and Alcmene, was strong and traversed the whole earth, and that, after death, he, too, ascended into heaven, ought I not conclude that the scriptural prophecy about Christ, 'strong as a giant to run his course,' was similarly imitated?"[2] In his *Exhortation to the Greeks*, Clement cited Euripides's words to depict Orpheus as a predictor of Christ.[3] Just as Orpheus lured the wild beasts to peacefulness with the music of his lyre, Christ lured men as the Divine Logos.[4] The comparison between the deities was made by pagans as well. In his polemic, Celsus attacked Jesus' divinity by slandering him as a magician and suggested there were several other heroes who were much more dignified than Jesus. Celsus offered some alternatives by claiming, "If Herakles, Asklepios, and others held in honor long ago did not please you, you had Orpheus, a man, as all agree, with a divine spirit who also died a violent death himself; but perhaps he had already been chosen by others. . . . You regard someone as a god who lived a most infamous life and died a most miserable death."[5] Moreover, Celsus suggested alternatives within the Christian tradition who would be more suitable than Jesus: "How much more suitable than him [Jesus] would Jonah

2. Justin, *Dialogue with Trypho* 69.3 (PG 6, 636C–637B; Falls).

3. Clement, *Exhortation to the Greeks* 7.28. See *Ex.* 1.1: "that Thracian Orpheus."

4. See Mary Charles Murray, *Rebirth and Afterlife, Rebirth and Afterlife: A Study of the Transmutation of Some Pagan Imagery in Early Christian Funerary Art* (Oxford: BAR International Series, 1981), 47ff. She argues that Clement conveyed a meaning of Orpheus beyond the metaphorical and really saw Plato in the figure of Orpheus. This is not uncommon, given Orpheus's attraction to the realm of philosophy, although it is harder to make the case that the catacomb artists were seeing Orpheus with Clement's eyes when they constructed their paintings. It could be they only saw Christ as the New Orpheus. Murray believes that Clement revealed a Christianizing of the Orpheus tradition. "The Christian Orpheus," *Cahiers Archéologiques* 26 (1977): 19–27.

5. Celsus in Origen, *Against Celsus* 7.53 (Chadwick). Celsus also accuses Christians of reading and blaspheming the Sibylline Oracles. Also see William S. Babcock, "Image and Culture: An Approach to the Christianization of the Roman Empire," in *Perkins Journal* 81, no. 3 (July 1988): 4–6, as he ruminates on the importance of Jonah/Endmyion and its emphasis on the fleshly resurrection.

have been for you with his gourd, or Daniel escaped from the beasts, or others whose stories are even more miraculous than these."[6]

Origen did not accept Celsus's attack on Jesus' divinity. In a rational response to the latter's suggestions, Origen pointed out that Jonah and Daniel were admirable, but they were not as heroic as Christ.[7] Instead of elevating Jonah and Daniel as types of Christ, he stated that these were figures to be emulated in prayer, since they were examples of those whose prayers had been answered.[8] Jonah and Daniel, along with the three youths in the fiery furnace, became parallels to Hercules and Orpheus, figures mentioned by Celsus.[9] All three subjects can be read christologically—that is, as implying resurrection. Origen's response to Celsus is not the only text that made the christological use of these figures explicit. The fourth-century *Apostolic Constitutions*, a collection of liturgical documents found in Syria, mentioned Jonah, Daniel, and the three youths as symbolizing resurrection:

> Besides these arguments, we believe there is to be a resurrection also from the resurrection of our Lord. For it is He that raised Lazarus when he had been in the grave four days, and Jairus' daughter, and the widow's son. It is He that raised Himself by the command of the Father in the space of three days, who is the pledge of our resurrection. For says He, "I am the resurrection and the life." Now He that brought forth Jonah in the space of three days, alive and unhurt, from the belly of the sea monster, and the three children out of the furnace of Babylon, and Daniel out of the mouth of the lions does not want power to raise us up also. But if the Gentiles laugh at us, and disbelieve our Scriptures, let at least their own prophetess Sibylla oblige them to believe who says thus to them.[10]

---

6. Origen, *Cels.* 7.53 (Chadwick).

7. Origen, *Cels.* 7.57.

8. Origen, *Exhortation to Martyrdom* 5.33: "But we . . . shall imitate those holy youths." Origen mentions them again in a similar context, as well as Daniel and Jonah, as examples of those whose prayers were answered. *Prayer* 13.2; 16.3.

9. The nudity of Jonah and Daniel is vexing, since along with Adam, they are the few figures that are uniformly depicted nude. Their nudity may be explained due to their Greco-Roman stylistic prototypes, or it could be a reference to the ritual of baptism. See Robin M. Jensen, *Understanding Early Christian Art* (New York: Routledge, 2000), 174–76. Jensen offers a similar interpretation of a nude Daniel as an image connoting resurrection, akin to Jonah. Jensen states that Daniel's nudity can suggest baptism as well, absent any water imagery that appears in the image of Jonah. Daniel's nudity represents the ritual nudity that took place during the rite.

The author of the *Apostolic Constitutions* described Jonah, Daniel, and the three youths as types of Christ—the very figures with which early Christians adorned their catacomb walls. More importantly, the author cited the resurrections of Lazarus, Jairus's daughter, and the widow's son at Nain. The text reveals the great attention given to Christ's miracles. Since the *Apostolic Constitutions* were found in Syria and deal mainly with Christian ritual, it is highly unlikely that there is a direct correlation between the *Apostolic Constitutions* and the art of the Roman catacombs. The text does highlight themes and motifs that early Christians obviously found universally compelling. The author of the *Apostolic Constitutions* included these incidents from Scripture to emphasize Jesus' superiority over preexisting figures. The art of early Christianity similarly exhibits Jesus as a greater hero than any other figure, including the heroes that Celsus mentioned in his polemic.

Hercules and Orpheus are represented frequently in the art of Late Antiquity, a body of work that includes Christian art. There is evidence of pagan objects that bear their depictions.[11] Images of Hercules and Orpheus declined considerably after the time of Constantine, but instances were still in existence.[12] Paintings of Hercules' deeds were included in the catacomb on the Via Latina as late as 350 CE. Hercules was a suitable subject for devotees, since he connoted divine aid and strength. The story of Hercules's resurrection of King Admetus's wife Alcestis was apparently of interest to early Christians, as indicated by its inclusion in a cubiculum at Via Latina (Figure 18). The depiction demonstrates Hercules's ability to travel to the underworld and overcome death on behalf of another. Moreover, the death of Alcestis, sacrificing herself for someone she loved, would have appealed to Christians, who might have recognized Christ's sacrifice in the story. In Late Antiquity, Hercules was revered less as a god and more as a divine helper and occasionally

10. *Apostolic Constitutions* 5.1.7 (*ANF* 7.440). The author of the *Apostolic Constitutions* not only cited the figures from Scripture, but also pointed the unbelievers to look at the Sibylline Oracles as well. The oracles were the very works that Celsus believed the Christians misused (Origen, *Cels* 7.53) and Lactantius appropriated (see *Inst.* 4.18-19; 4.15), although Augustine discouraged their influence (*Against Faustus* 13.1-2).

11. The Boston Sarcophagus features Orpheus. See A. Van den Hoek and J. J. Herrmann, "Celsus' Competing Heroes: Jonah, Daniel, and their Rivals," in *Poussières de christianisme et de judaïsme antiques* (Lausanne: Éditions du Zèbre, 2007), 326–27.

12. See Van den Hoek and Herrmann, "Celsus' Competing Heroes," 333. As evidence, the authors cite the small amount of post-fourth-century imagery of Hercules in the *LIMC*. The same can be said for Asclepius. No coins were pressed with either image of the god. See Otfried Deubner, *Das Asklepeion von Pergamon* (Berlin: Verlag für Kunstwissenschaft, 1938), 20. However, there were scattered images of Asclepius and Hygieia in the fifth century.

as a defender against disease. The shrines at Attica and Huettos drew visitors seeking healing remedies.[13] Hercules was notably associated with Chiron, the centaur healer who legendarily taught Asclepius. The hero god was revered as a protector against evil. Clement of Alexandria noted a house that had inscribed over the door, "Hercules, for victory famed, dwells here; let nothing bad enter."[14] Philostratus connected Hercules to the healing of a plague in Ephesus, as his cult statue was regarded as the averter of evil.[15] In Philostratus's text, Apollonius claimed that the god had helped him to stop a pestilence since the "temple of Hercules . . . averts disease." He went on to recall how Hercules had purged the city of Elis of plague by stemming the disease-ridden river tide.[16]

Hercules's legend associated him with healing. Ovid's *Fasti* described Hercules's visit to Chiron, who had also taught the hero Achilles peaceful arts such as medicine, astronomy, and music.[17] Pausanias noted that in Olmones, he found "a temple of Hercules, from whom the sick may get cures."[18] The warlike nature of Hercules was drawn upon less in Late Antiquity, when the military conflicts of the Greek states were over. Hercules's softer attributes as a helper, comrade, and healer became more prominent in his cult. Hercules's status as a medicinal god lasted until the end of paganism. Farnell noted that some gods were converted into Christian saints; an anonymous epigram in the Greek Anthology recorded Hercules reminding his devotees that he was not actually "Lucius," although they shared the designation of physician.[19] Sickness was occasionally understood as the absence of the soul from the body.[20]

13. See Lewis Richard Farnell, *Greek Hero Cults and Ideas of Immortality* (Oxford: Clarendon, 1921). Farnell describes the exclusion of women at shrines to Hercules, although occasionally slave women were allowed to enter (161–63).

14. Clement, *Miscellanies* 7.4 (*ANF* 2.529). Clement is citing Diogenes Laertius here.

15. Philostratus, *Life* 4.10.

16. Philostratus, *Life* 8.7.

17. Ovid, *Fasti* 5.379-414. Hercules's visit sadly results in Chiron's death, as one of his poisoned arrows strikes the foot of the centaur. The presence of Hercules and Achilles suggests the foreshadowing of their own deaths: Hercules's death by the blood of the centaur Nessus, and Achilles's with an arrow in a part of his foot, his heel. Also see Ian Brookes, "The Death of Chiron: Ovid, *Fasti* 5.379-414," *Classical Quarterly* 44, no. 2 (1994): 444–50.

18. Pausanius, *Description of Greece* 9.24.3 (Jones, LCL). He also notes that a statue of Hercules was erected in thanks for healing the plague at Athens.

19. *Greek Anthology* 11.269: "I, victorious Hercules, the son of Zeus, am not really Lucius, but they compel me to be so." It is possible the association with Luke is implied here; however, W. R. Paton believes it is a jibe at the statue of Commodus/Hercules, "Lucius Commodus." See Paton, LCL, vol. 4; Farnell, *Greek Hero Cults*, 151.

Hercules' journey with Alcestis exhibited his status as a type of healer, one who could travel to the underworld and restore the soul to the body. It is a pagan resurrection story that even the bishop Epiphanius of Salamis recognized in the fourth century.[21] The existence of Hercules's iconography in Cubiculum N of the Via Latina catacomb, including scenes with Alcestis, fit in a funerary environment (Figures 17–18). The scene portrays a healing in a sense—the victory of life over death.

Orpheus, like Hercules, journeyed to the underworld on behalf of another, although his resurrection of Eurydice ended tragically. There are six recovered wall paintings of Orpheus in the catacombs, the oldest of which was found in the catacomb of Callistus.[22] Orpheus is often depicted seated with a lyre and with one or more animals. At the catacomb of Callistus and the catacomb of Peter and Marcellinius, the figure of Orpheus is surrounded by sheep; at the catacomb of Domitilla, the animals also include birds, a lion, a horse, a mouse, a snake, and several other undetermined breeds (Figure 19). The pastoral nature of the images of Orpheus led early commentators to claim that the image of the Good Shepherd was modeled after Orpheus, prompting art historians to label catacomb images of Orpheus as "Christ-Orpheus with the gentle animals."[23] Floor mosaics found north of Lepcis Magna in North Africa certainly influenced such a connection, as they also portray Orpheus with his harp and surrounded by animals, akin to the pastoral image of the Good Shepherd.[24] Mary Charles Murray has argued instead that these representations are distinct to catacomb art, given the fact that the Orpheus of Christian art is not consistently depicted in garb associated with the Good Shepherd. The

20. Edwin Eliott Willoughby, "The Role of Hercules in the Resurrection of Alcestis," *Classical Journal* 22, no. 5 (February 1927): 380.

21. Epiphanius, *Ancoratus* 85 (PG 43.176). Epiphanius also mentions Asclepius and Castor and Pollux in terms of resurrection.

22. These are found at Callistus, two each in Peter and Marcellinus and Domitilla (one destroyed), and a destroyed one at Priscilla catalogued by G. B. De Rossi in 1877. See Paul Corby Finney, "Orpheus-David: A Connection in Iconography between Greco-Roman Judaism and Early Christianity," *JJA* 5 (1978): 6–15. The argument that the David figure at the Dura synagogue is Orpheus and that the Christians were influenced in their usage of Orpheus by a Jewish "David-Orpheus" was introduced by H. Stern in "Orphée dans l'Art Paleochrétien," *Cahiers Archéologiques* 23 (1974): 1–16. His position of a Jewish influence was rebutted by Murray in "The Christian Orpheus," 19–27. At Dura, it may not be Orpheus at all.

23. G. B. De Rossi, namely, but also Grabar, pl. 84. See Théophile Roller, *Les catacombes de Rome: Histoire de l'art et des croyances religieuses pendant les premiers siècles du Christianisme* (Paris: Vve. A. Morel & cie, 1881), 244–49.

24. Murray, "The Christian Orpheus," 25.

only really consistent attribute shared by the images is the appearance of sheep.[25] The image of Orpheus singing to the animals was important enough to early Christians for them to depict it visually. The Christians saw something in the image that a biblical scene did not provide. Orpheus was popular in pagan imagery and respected in antiquity as a peaceful figure, a patron of music and the arts, and as supporting a moral life. As Murray states, the result in Late Antiquity was that Orpheus attracted several different groups of devotees and served as a unifying religious figure.[26]

Orpheus in the context of a Christian catacomb need not necessarily be identified as a hybrid, "Christ-Orpheus," but as the pagan god. Thus, the images of Hercules or Orpheus in the catacombs are not actually representations of Christ; they are depictions of Hercules and Orpheus.[27] Their appearance in the catacombs may reveal a Christian appropriation of these heroes and show the influence the Roman world naturally had on the creation of Christian art. The early Christians took figures from the Roman realm and transformed them into figures of cultural unity and types of Christ.

The painting of Hercules and Alcestis in Cubiculum N of the Via Latina catacomb may have been chosen by the patron to represent marital devotion.[28] Scenes of spouses reuniting after death are nonexistent in the Christian canon, likely since there was no narrative as familiar as the Alcestis story. At Via Latina, a spouse possibly chose the Alcestis narrative for this reason. Such figures and themes that are pagan in genesis fit nicely in a mixed catacomb at a time when the world was becoming increasingly Christianized. The Alcestis story of deathly sacrifice does have christological overtones. Hercules and other figures from the pagan pantheon represented well-known tales that Christians could recognize as compatible with a funerary environment and not as idolatrous threats.[29]

Cubiculum N can be dated to the period of 350–370 ce.[30] This was a period of confrontation between pagans and Christians with the apostasy of Emperor Julian and the altar of victory dispute in Rome. Thus, in the Via Latina catacomb, the conflation of pagan and Christian themes does not

25. Murray, *Rebirth and Afterlife*, 42.

26. See ibid., 46, and her entire chapter on the Christian Orpheus.

27. Ibid. Murray claims these figures "are Christ himself."

28. See Beverly Berg, "Alcestis and Hercules in the Catacomb of Via Latina," *VChr* 48, no. 3 (September 1994): 220.

29. During the Reformation, the Cranach workshop's visual art incorporated mythological themes such as the Three Graces, Venus and Cupid, and Hercules and Omphale. Christian art could utilize these figures, since they represented certain themes that were compatible with Christianity.

30. Tronzo, *The Via Latina Catacomb*, 17.

appear antagonistic. Adjacent to Cubiculum N, in Cubiculum O, is the scene of the raising of Lazarus (Figure 31). Antonio Ferrua noted that the hallway leading into the Lazarus cubiculum exhibits painted representations of Ceres and Proserpina, and they appear again on the ceiling of the chamber.[31] The pagan goddesses possibly guide the viewer from one chamber emphasizing marital devotion with the scene of Hercules and Alcestis to a chamber containing a primary scene of resurrection in the raising of Lazarus. Arguably, the patrons chose the Lazarus painting as the ultimate scene of resurrection for the person lying at rest in the cubiculum.

Whether the Via Latina patrons were Christians or pagans, they found utility in images of Hercules and images of Christ. The iconography, even in a unique catacomb like Via Latina, leads one to believe that Christian viewers found both pagan and Christian images and themes suitable in some capacity. Early Christians could exhibit images of Hercules or Orpheus and project Christian themes. Both figures embodied charity and were able to exert a level of control over the dead, and they both enjoyed a heroic apotheosis.[32] Orpheus and Hercules were raised to divinity after a period of suffering—Hercules with his labors, and Orpheus with the tragic loss of his love and subsequent death. With the Christian visual lexicon still developing, it is apparent that non-Christian themes and prototypes were ripe targets for appropriation by early Christians.

Images of Asclepius, unlike those of Hercules or Orpheus, do not exist in Christian environments. Arguably, the cult of Asclepius was more prominent than the cults of the other two figures. Asclepieia covered a vast range and were scattered throughout the empire, playing a pivotal role in Late Antique health care. The healing cult of Asclepius certainly engendered popular devotion and fervor in Late Antiquity.[33] The Corinthian Asclepieion enjoyed some longevity prior to its destruction in the 520s.[34] Jerome remarked on the continued practices of the Asclepieion in his commentary on Isaiah, and the philosopher Proclus was extremely devoted to the god up until his death in 485.[35] In

31. Ferrua, *The Unknown Catacomb*, 119.

32. See David Aune, "Heracles and Christ: Heracles Imagery in the Christology of Early Christianity," in *Greeks, Romans, and Christians*, ed. David L. Balch, Everett Ferguson, and Wayne Meeks (Minneapolis: Fortress Press, 1990), 3–19. The comparisons that Aune cites are not unique to Hercules, but are also embodied by Asclepius. His usage of Aristides fails to mention the effect Asclepius had on his writings.

33. See Aristides, *Sacred Tales* 48.13; *Oratio* 39.5; and Julian, *Against the Galileans* 1.200B. Also see *Oration* 4.144B, where Julian juxtaposes Asclepius to Christ; and 153B for his claim of Asclepius as "the savior."

34. See chapter 2, note 111.

Marinus's biography of the Neoplatonist, he recorded Proclus praying at the temple of Asclepius on behalf of a friend, calling the Asclepieion the "temple of the savior" and describing the subsequent healing: "for the savior, being a god, healed her [Proclus's friend] easily."[36] In the fifth century, the Asclepius cult was still celebrated, and the god was remembered as a "savior." Even as late as the eighth century, Alcuin of York referred to Asclepius as the false Christ.[37] Alcuin's comment shows the enduring perception of Asclepius as an opponent of Christ. The observance of the cult, albeit scattered, and the persistent references in Christian texts suggest that the Christians in Late Antiquity were aware of the Asclepius cult as a continuing and competing faith.

Although Asclepius is nonexistent in Christian iconography, the image of Christ healing and working miracles may still recall the pagan cult. In the absence of images of Asclepius or images of Christ rendered as Asclepius, it is the subject matter of the images that bears the most resemblance.[38] Depictions of the feats of Christ may be an obvious choice for a Christian catacomb; however, a scene such as Christ healing the paralytic places Christ in the realm of Asclepius. Asclepius is possibly appropriated by portraying Christ performing healings and miracles. Christ is not evoking a generic physician; the scenes recall the gospel episodes involving chronically ill supplicants. The images of Christ healing illustrate a divine healing, an arena occupied by the cult of Asclepius, not Late Antique physicians. In these scenes, Christ is often directly encountering his "patients" and physically touching them, something Asclepius accomplishes through dreams. In the Christian iconography, Christ's touch is prominently featured. Christ raising the dead exhibits Christ performing a feat that Asclepius was killed by Zeus for performing. Thus, the depiction of Christ raising the dead raises the question whether a resurrection can even be considered a healing.

35. Jerome, *On Isaiah*, 65; Farnell commented that if only the cult of Asclepius had a genius or true prophet touting its fame, instead of Aristides and Julian, then the cult could develop a high theology and create an even greater problem for the Christians. *Greek Hero Cults*, 279. The continued references, however, reveal that Asclepius was not a light threat.

36. Marinus, *Life of Proclus* 29 (Edwards). Also see 31–32 for other healings attributed to Asclepius. The temple Proclus prayed in was at Lydia. See Mark Edwards, *Neoplatonic Saints: The Lives of Plotinus and Proclus by their Students* (Liverpool: Liverpool University Press, 2000).

37. Alcuin, *Ep.* 245 in Ernst Dümller's *Monumenta Germaniae Historica* (Berlin: Brepols, 1891–97). Alcuin calls the false Christ, "Scolapius falsator." See Edelstein, 2:134, n. 6, which cites the substitution of Asclepius's name for Christ's during the Renaissance, when words foreign to classical Latin were forbidden. It is an example of the continuing juxtaposition of Christ and Asclepius.

38. In Mathews, *The Clash of Gods*, figs. 48–49.

While it is debatable whether a resurrection is healing or not, Christ performing a resurrection recalls Asclepius, as it has more to do with divine authority than with healing. Libanius praised Julian the apostate emperor: "You were, for the body of our world, what in legend Asclepius was for Hippolytus."[39] As Hippolytus was raised from the dead by Asclepius, so Julian raised the people from darkness by restoring pagan religion. However, Asclepius was killed by Zeus for his act of resurrection. The church fathers knew this quite well, as this lack of authority was the argument of choice when denouncing Asclepius. Justin, Clement, Origen and Tertullian all point out that Asclepius's downfall was due to his lack of authority, since he was not really a divine agent.[40] Christ's act of raising the dead evokes Asclepius's shortcoming, as it shows that Christ required no authority to raise the dead. Further, it was a miracle of charity and benevolence, not greed, as Jesus required no payment. Outside of the debate over whether a resurrection is a healing, an early Christian viewer may see Christ performing an action that sets him apart from any opponent from pagan tradition, including Asclepius.

Early Christian art adapted and utilized Greco-Roman images and themes. The heroes Orpheus and Hercules occur as types of Christ in catacomb art. While the figure of Asclepius is absent, the healing god is evoked as the Christians demonstrate a degree of innovation by transposing themes of healing and resurrection onto the person of Christ. In early Christian art, this recollection of Asclepius can be witnessed in images of Christ healing the paralytic and the woman with the issue of blood and of Christ raising the dead. This last miracle likely held the most resonance with the Asclepius cult. Jesus restoring the dead to life exhibits the divine authority of the Christian figure, while the non-Christian god was punished for performing the same deed.

SCENES OF CHRIST RAISING THE DEAD

The act of raising the dead to life exhibits the power and authority of the miracle worker on a grand scale. Unlike any typical healing by a physician or other healer, raising the dead restores life rather than just health. The authors of the canonical gospels obviously realized the power of raising the dead, and portrayed Jesus performing the miracle in several different scenes. And these scenes are visualized when early Christians crafted their visual language. While

---

39. Libanius, *Orations* 13.42 (Norman, LCL).

40. Justin, *1 Apol.* 21 (PG 6, 360A); Clement, *Ex.* 2.24; Origen, *Cels.* 3.22 (PG 11, 944C); Tertullian, *To the Heathen* 2.14.45 (CSEL 20.127). Also in Arnobius, *Against the Pagans* 4.24 (CSEL 4.161); and Lactantius, *Inst.* 1.19.3 (CSEL 19.71).

the story of raising Lazarus from the Gospel of John is typically the most popularly depicted scene in art, other scenes from the Gospels are also visualized in the artistic canon.

THE WIDOW'S SON AT NAIN

The gospels include accounts of the resurrection of individuals as cited by the *Apostolic Constitutions*: "We believe there is to be a resurrection also from the resurrection of our Lord. For it is he that raised Lazarus when he had been in the grave four days, and Jairus' daughter, and the widow's son." [41] The three figures identified by the author of the *Apostolic Constitutions* are readily apparent in Christian art. In early Christian art, Christ is usually the only figure depicted with the power to raise the dead; no figures from the Old Testament are portrayed as possessing this power. In some rare instances in the fourth century, Peter is possibly depicted raising Tabitha from the dead; however, the figures in the scene closely resemble Jesus and Jairus's daughter, which makes the identification of Peter questionable. [42]

Four major scenes of raising the dead are in the record of early Christian art: Jesus raising the widow's son at Nain, Jesus raising Jairus's daughter, Jesus appearing as Ezekiel in the Valley of the Dry Bones, and Jesus raising Lazarus. [43] Typically, the scene features Jesus gesturing toward a body with his miracle-working implement, beckoning the figure to awake and rise. The raising of Lazarus is the most easily identifiable, since it normally features a mummified body within an *aediculum* (burial house). The other three scenes are slightly more challenging to identify, since they do not bear the iconographic hallmarks of the Lazarus scene. In the other three scenes, Christ is depicted touching either the bed of Jairus's daughter, a burial box containing a rising figure, or a figure lying inert at the feet of Jesus with his staff (Figure 20). The viewer must make

41. *Apostolic Constitutions* 5.1.7 (*ANF* 7.440).

42. In later instances of Christian art on ivories in the British Museum, Christ grasping Jairus's arm becomes Peter raising Tabitha, visually emphasizing Peter as Christ's heir. See Herbert Kessler, "Scenes from the Acts of the Apostles on Some Early Christian Ivories," in *Gesta* 18, no. 1 (November 1977–February 1978): 112. Kessler cites a possible example of Peter raising Tabitha at Arles (however, it is unclear what image he is referencing), but it is not conclusive whether it is Peter, and more likely it is Christ raising Jairus's daughter along with the healing of the woman with the issue of blood. Benoit suggests that it is Christ raising Jairus' daughter, *Sarcophages paleochréttiens* 50, pl. 19. Benoit does indeed label a fragment at the collection of Arles the Raising of Tabitha (*Sarcophages paleochréttiens* 39, pl. 7), although this also is debatable.

43. The Lazarus account is in John 11; the widow's son in Luke 7:11-17; and Jairus's daughter in Mark 5:35-43; Matt. 9:18-26; and Luke 8:40-56. Ezekiel and the Valley of the Dry Bones appears in Ezek. 37:1-14.

some interpretive decisions in order to discern which resurrection narrative is being depicted.

Outside of the raising of Lazarus, all early Christian scenes of Jesus raising the dead include a body being restored. The Valley of the Dry Bones scene has several distinctive aspects, such as skulls or body parts lying adjacent to the prostrate figure. The scene of Jairus's daughter usually includes some type of bed, which recalls the gospel story. The scene of the widow's son at Nain is the only one that does not contain such telling iconographic clues. While the supine figure may be confused with the figure in the scene of Christ in the Valley of the Dry Bones, the absence of signs to indicate the Ezekiel text or the bed of Jairus's daughter makes it more likely that the scene is that of the widow's son at Nain.

The story of the widow's son at Nain appears only in Luke 7. In the gospel, Jesus encounters a widow whose only son has died, leaving her financially destitute. Jesus feels compassion for the widow; he touches the son's coffin and tells him to rise. The miracle involves touch and a vocal command, resulting in a successful resurrection. In Christian art, a coffin is not uniformly shown in this scene; rather, Jesus is portrayed touching an inert figure with his miracle-working staff, as in the example from the Museo Pio Cristiano (Figures 8 and 20). A naked figure is depicted next to the inert body. Such a figure also appears in early Christian relief sculptures representing the raising of Lazarus. Instead of evoking a secondary character, the nude figure likely represents the restored widow's son or the restored Lazarus. Just as nudity symbolically represents baptism or new birth, nudity in this context refers to the newly restored life granted to the individual. The nudity resembles nudity in the final sense, symbolizing paradise.

JAIRUS'S DAUGHTER

Identifying the raising of Jairus's daughter leads one to believe that the artisans were paying strict attention to the scriptural narrative. Jairus's daughter is not on a bier or in an *aediculum,* or burial box, but on a bed. In a fragment housed in the Museo Pio Cristiano, Jesus is shown pulling an awaking figure into a sitting position on a bed (Figure 21). In this scene of Jairus's daughter, Jesus does not resurrect with a staff but uses the power of touch directly. This identification is appropriate, as Jesus is captured in the drama of awaking a "sleeping" child who was once dead, as told in Luke's gospel: "And Jesus said 'She is not dead but asleep'" (Luke 8:52).

A unique and well-preserved depiction of this scene from the late fourth century appears on the reliquary box of Brescia, known as the Brescia Casket

(Figure 22). Two resurrection scenes can be seen on the box: the raising of Lazarus and the raising of Jairus's daughter.[44] The depiction of the scene of Jairus's daughter is much the same as that on the fragment at the Museo Pio Cristiano. Christ grasps the wrist of the girl who lies on a bed and pulls her into a sitting position. Although these are similar to the scenes of Christ healing a seated paralytic, these are not scenes of the healing of the paralytic (Figures 8–9). In the rare instances that the paralytic is on a mat during the healing event, the patient appears to be in a sitting position, not waking from sleep in the manner of Jairus's daughter. From the recovered evidence, scenes of the resurrection of Jairus's daughter were rarely duplicated, in contrast to those of the widow's son and the raising of Lazarus.

VALLEY OF THE DRY BONES

The image of Christ as Ezekiel in the Valley of the Dry Bones appears with some frequency in Christian funerary art (Ezek. 37:1-14). While the figure in the image could be Ezekiel, it is likely a depiction of Christ touching an inert body in the same manner as in other scenes.[45] The inclusion of the Ezekiel text from the Old Testament demonstrates Christ fulfilling an earlier prophecy. In the scene of Christ in the Valley of the Dry Bones, Jesus points his staff downward toward a figure lying prone on the ground (Figure 23). The figure is not in a coffin, nor in any type of structure as Lazarus' body was, but out in the open.

A representation of Ezekiel in the Valley of the Dry Bones occurs in a Jewish context in a recovered wall painting from the Dura synagogue of the third century (Figure 24). In this image, strewn body parts (heads, feet, hands, and arms) are reconstructed into persons by the hand of God.[46] In Christian

44. See Catherine Brown Tkacz, *The Key to the Brescia Casket: Typology and the Early Christian Imagination* (Paris: University of Notre Dame Press; Institut d'Etudes Augustiennes, 2001), 105. Tkacz makes the argument that there is an attention to the balancing of men and women in the inclusion of the resurrection scenes of Lazarus and Jairus's daughter. It is difficult to make this argument, as Brescia is a well-preserved reliquary with all sides and lids intact, compared with sarcophagus fragments and frontals.

45. G. Bovini and Hugo Brandenburg, *Reportorium der Christlich-Antiken Sarkophage*, Band 1, *Rom und Ostia*, ed. F. W. Deichmann (Wiesbaden: F. Steiner, 1967) is not as useful on this particular subject. Bovini and Brandenburg cite around eleven examples of Ezekiel and the Valley of the Dry Bones in the Roman evidence; however, he tends to cite questionable images as Ezekiel that may in fact be the raising of the widow's son. Bovini and Brandenburg also consistently identify the prone figure, even without remnants of heads or skulls, as the Ezekiel scene, not the widow's son. This is problematic. See Band 1, pts. 1, 11.

46. For plates, see Herbert L. Kessler and Kurt Weitzmann, *The Frescoes of the Dura Synagogue and Christian Art* DOP 28 (Washington, DC: Dumbarton Oaks Research Library and Collection, 1990).

relief sculpture, the actor in this scene is not a disembodied hand but the figure of Christ, touching his staff to the inert body, indicating his power of resurrection.[47] In the passage from Ezekiel, the Lord commands the prophet, "Prophesy to these bones, and say to them: 'O dry bones, hear the word of the Lord. Thus says the Lord God to these bones: I will cause breath to enter you, and you shall live. I will lay sinews on you, and will cause flesh to come upon you, and cover you with skin, and put breath in you, and you shall live; and you shall know that I am the Lord'" (Ezek. 37:4-6). As in the visual example at the Museo Pio Cristiano, the supine figure is often accompanied by standing individuals of various heights; the individuals are naked, indicating that they have been wrapped in new flesh. And several skulls appear nearby, hinting at the bones in the grave.

Christians understood the Ezekiel passage as a proof text of Christ's power of resurrection. Justin Martyr and Cyril of Alexandria both interpreted Christ as the acting figure in the story of the Valley of the Dry Bones.[48] The text in Ezekiel calls the prophet "Son of Man" and says, "These bones are the whole house of Israel. They say, 'Our bones are dried up and our hope is gone; we are cut off.' Therefore prophesy and say to them: 'This is what the Sovereign Lord says: O my people, I am going to open your graves and bring you up from them; I will bring you back to the land of Israel. Then you, my people, will know that I am the Lord, when I open your graves and bring you up from them'" (Ezek. 37:11-14). Predictably, early Christians understood Christ to be represented in this prophetic text. The "Son of Man" in Ezekiel referred to Christ, and bodily resurrection, a distinctive Christian theme, also appeared in the Ezekiel passage. The text fits well with the arguments of patristic authors who asserted that Christ predated creation and was witnessed in the Old Testament texts.[49] The passage also reflects the hope that God will raise humanity up from the grave. Christians could easily recognize Christ in the text, acting as a member of the Godhead, resurrecting the body and binding new flesh.

In a funerary context, any scene with resurrection overtones would be a logical choice to place on a sarcophagus. The notion of physical and bodily resurrection, the refleshing of bones that is described in the Ezekiel passage,

---

47. See Anthony Cutler, "Ezekiel and the Politics of Resurrection" in *DOP* 46 (Washington, DC: Dumbarton Oaks Research Library and Collection, 1992), 47–58. Cutler rejects all of the early Christian evidence to focus on a tenth-century Byzantine ivory containing the scene.

48. Justin, *1 Apol.* 43; Cyril of Alexandria, *Explanation of Teachings* 7.562.

49. Justin, *1 Apol.* 63 (PG 6, 424C); *Dial.* 60; Grant, *Greek Apologists*, 60. See also the discussion on Justin in chapter 3.

is of premier importance to Christians. The image of bodily resurrection is captured in the creeds, recited and reiterated by Christians in Late Antiquity up to the present day. Faith in bodily resurrection is part of Christian belief and is reflected in Christian art in portrayals such as Christ in the Valley of the Dry Bones.[50]

Patristic authors emphasized a final bodily resurrection, often using themes from Scripture as a vehicle to spread their message. The same stress is reflected in Christian art. Tertullian, in his *On the Resurrection of the Flesh,* included Jonah as proof of the eventual fleshly resurrection, which possibly explains the popularity of the figure in visual art as well.[51] Over 150 years later, at the end of the fourth century, church fathers such as Jerome were busy defending themselves against charges of Origenism that denied the full fleshly resurrection of the body. In a response against John of Jerusalem, Jerome stated in a letter that, upon death, the flesh was clothed in heavenly glory in a physical resurrection.[52] Augustine also preached the notion of a physical resurrection. The frailty of human life drove Augustine to preach of the role of Jesus as *Christus medicus* and of the final cleansing that would occur in a physical resurrection.[53] Just as the belief in Christ as the supreme miracle worker was taken to heart by the believing public, so was belief in a physical, bodily resurrection. The bones that reacquire flesh in Ezekiel are akin to Augustine's preaching that the body will reacquire flesh in the tomb.[54] The image of Christ in the Valley of the Dry Bones, and its propensity to appear on fourth- and fifth-century relief sculpture, testifies to this theological development.

50. Note "the resurrection of the body" as part of the Apostles' Creed, dating as early as the second century. And see Justin, *1 Apol.* 18-19, where he discusses our bodies at the resurrection. Also see Jensen, *Understanding Early Christian Art*, 158–59.

51. Tertullian, *The Resurrection of the Flesh* 58; also see William S. Babcock, "Image and Culture: An Approach to the Christianization of the Roman Empire," *Perkins Journal* 81, no. 3 (July 1988): 5–6.

52. Jerome, *Ep. to Pammachus* 23-27. For further reading, see Elizabeth Clark, *The Origenist Controversy: The Cultural Construction of an Early Christian Debate* (Princeton, NJ: Princeton University Press, 1992).

53. See Peter Brown, *Augustine of Hippo: A Biography,* repr. ed. (Berkeley: University of California Press, 2000), 418–22.

54. See Augustine, *Sermon* 242; *City of God* 22.11-22. Augustine is refuting critics such as Porphyry and reminding his listeners that everyone had bodies initially until the first sin resulted in bodily sin. Augustine obviously is aware of Porphyry and understands the danger posed by *On the Return of the Soul.* He sidesteps a direct answer by attacking those who would question the ability of God to make such events as a physical resurrection possible. See Eugene TeSelle, "Porphyry and Augustine," *Augustinian Studies* 5 (1974): 142.

THE RAISING OF LAZARUS

The scene of the raising of Lazarus is another prominent miracle of Christ that is depicted first at the catacomb of Callistus and then at several other catacomb locations; it is also represented frequently on Christian funerary relief sculpture such as sarcophagi.[55] The resurrection scenes are slightly more varied in Christian relief sculpture than in catacomb wall paintings. However, the raising of Lazarus is still a primary motif, along with the healings of the widow's son at Nain and of Jairus's daughter. The raising of Lazarus occurs in 65 extant examples of Roman sarcophagi, and the image appears over 23 times in examples from Gaul and North Africa.[56]

The catacomb of Callistus image of Lazarus, like the paralytic scene, includes several typical elements while at the same time containing key differences (Figure 26). Christ stands to the side of a small *aediculum* (burial house) that houses the figure of Lazarus. The features of Lazarus are indiscernible; it is clear that the figure is not mummified, as in later depictions of this scene, and that he originally had some type of facial features (Figure 25). This is indicative of the novelty of this portrayal of the scene. The wrapped figure became the standard for portraying Lazarus instead of the figure at the catacomb of Callistus, which stands with two feet planted firmly underneath the *aediculum*.[57]

On Christian sarcophagi, in the representations of the raising of Lazarus, he resides within a carved *aediculum*, mummified without any discernible facial features. A larger-than-life Christ touches the *aediculum* with a wand or staff-like instrument, sometimes with Mary or Martha at his feet (Figure 13). As in the previous healing scenes, Jesus is of a stature similar to the other central characters, while the recipients of his power are significantly smaller. Most often, Jesus uses a staff when performing his resurrections while the other hand clutches a scroll (Figure 27). Christ is youthful, with short, curly hair. Sometimes Christ faces toward Lazarus, sometimes not. Lazarus's face is consistently indiscernible in the relief sculpture; burial wrappings cover his face and body.

---

55. Found in Level 2, Area I, Cubiculum A6. Finney, *The Invisible God*, 218.

56. G. Bovini and Hugo Brandenburg, *Repertorium der Christlich-Antiken Sarkophage*, Band 1, *Rom und Ostia*, ed. F. W. Deichmann (Wiesbaden: F. Steiner, 1967), pts. 1, 123; Brigitte Christern-Briesenick, *Repertorium der Christlich-Antiken Sarkophage*, Band 3, *Frankreich, Algerien, Tunesien*, ed. T. Ulbert (Wiesbaden: F. Steiner, 2003), 302. The widow's son and Jairus's daughter occur in sixteen examples in the Roman material, and in eight examples from Gaul and North Africa. See 1:123; 3:301–302.

57. See Maurice Besnier, *Les catacombes de Rome* (Paris: Leroux, 1909) pl.14.

In the image, Christ is wearing his robe, a tunic with a *pallium*, with his right arm extended toward the *aediculum*, emphasizing the miraculous action taking place. In his left hand, he is holding what can be construed as a staff, wand, or scepter. As mentioned previously, this is a telling iconographic feature that appeared at an early stage in Christian art, and it will be discussed in chapter 7. However, it should be noted that the Jesus figure at the catacomb of Callistus is not using the staff as part of his resurrection of Lazarus. Instead of pointing an instrument toward the *aediculum*, to touch the structure or the body of Lazarus and signify the transference of miraculous power, Jesus is gesturing toward the body of Lazarus with his hand—a rather unusual depiction. The scene at the catacomb of Callistus is unique in this rendering of the raising of Lazarus. While the image includes both protagonists in the drama, it captures not the action of the miracle but its successful outcome. The resurrected Lazarus is standing in the foreshortened area in front of the *aediculum*. Christ's gesture toward Lazarus does not show action but indicates Christ praising Lazarus, even saluting him in victory.

In one representation in the catacomb of Priscilla, the image of the raising of Lazarus offers another example of Christ gesturing toward Lazarus with his hand rather than the reed-like staff. The image is badly damaged, but it is clear that Lazarus is mummified, housed in the *aediculum* rather than standing in front of it, as at the catacomb of Callistus (Figure 28). The Priscilla image illustrates that catacomb representations of Lazarus had evolved slightly since the catacomb of Callistus to depict the actual raising of Lazarus. Christ is shown gesturing toward the *aediculum* of Lazarus, emphasizing the action taking place. Given the deteriorated state of the painting, it is unclear whether Christ is holding a staff in his left hand, as at the catacomb of Callistus. It is apparent that a staff is not involved in the gesture he makes with his right hand.

The catacomb of Domitilla offers another example of the evolution of depictions of the Lazarus scene. In the "Red Cubiculum," Christ is shown gesturing toward a mummified Lazarus housed in the *aediculum*. Instead of gesturing with just his hand, Christ is holding the instrument of the staff and physically touching Lazarus with it (Figure 29). The staff is not merely an accessory, as in the catacomb of Callistus image, but is part of the miracle-working action of Christ. Like the mummified Lazarus, the staff became a standard iconographic feature in further depictions of this scene in the catacombs. At the Via Latina catacomb, there is at least one depiction of the raising of Lazarus. In one example in Cubiculum O at Via Latina, Christ is surrounded by his followers and touches the forehead of a mummified Lazarus, inside his *aediculum*, with the staff (Figure 30).

The raising of Lazarus appears in two instances at the catacomb of Peter and Marcellinus. On a wall painting in a cubiculum, Jesus is depicted in a robe with a monogram of the Chi-Rho at the bottom.[58] The figure of Jesus is larger than life, and the *aediculum* of Lazarus, which Jesus touches with his staff, holds a much smaller mummified figure. In these examples, Christ's touch, with hand or staff, reveals his miracle-working power.

In the second image at the Via Latina catacomb, on an arcosolium (arched burial cell) wall of Cubiculum C, Christ is depicted with a band of followers and is touching the *aediculum* of Lazarus, but no body lies within it (Figure 31). The lack of a mummified Lazarus may be evidence that the Lazarus scene was not the original representation. Both of the Lazarus scenes at Via Latina are positioned facing a scene of Moses crossing the Red Sea, balancing a scene of the miracle-working Moses with one of the miracle-working Christ. Due to the Lazarus scene's proximity to the scene depicting the crossing of the Red Sea, Grabar believed that the Cubiculum C image had originally been a scene from Exodus showing the Hebrews crowding into the sanctuary built by Moses with Aaron at the door.[59] William Tronzo argued that since Moses is exhibited adjacent to the image, the scene must naturally progress through the Exodus narrative and thus captures Joshua entering Israel with the twelve tribes.[60] This seems unlikely, considering that the instrument Christ wields was also wielded by Moses, not Joshua, in cognate scenes. Be that as it may, the alteration of the Cubiculum C scene into a scene of the raising of Lazarus signifies the popularity of the Lazarus image and its inherent interpretation of resurrection. Whatever the original depiction, it was altered to become Christ resurrecting Lazarus, adjacent to Moses crossing the Red Sea. The motivation behind such an alteration reveals the close connection in catacomb art between the figures of Jesus and Moses, and between baptism (crossing the Red Sea) and resurrection (Lazarus).

In a ceiling lunette at the catacomb of Peter and Marcellinus, an image of the raising of Lazarus exhibits Christ standing next to the *aediculum* of Lazarus, touching it with his staff. Directly next to the scene is an image of Moses striking the rock, recalling the scene from Exodus 17 and Numbers 20, with

58. See Antonio Ferrua, "Una nuova regione in SS. Marcellino e Pietro," *RAC* 44 (1968): 73. Ferrua points out the slight difference in how Christ holds the staff.

59. Ferrua rejects Grabar's argument based on the attitude of Christ touching the mummified Lazarus. See *The Unknown Catacomb*, 170; Tronzo, *The Via Latina Catacomb*, 53. See also Enrico Josi, "Découverte d'une série de peintures dans un hypogée de la voie Latine," *Comptes rendus de l'Académie des Inscriptions et Belles-Lettres* (1956): 275–79.

60. Tronzo, *The Via Latina Catacomb*, 56.

a similar type of instrument (Figure 32).[61] The connection between these two themes is made clear in several other examples in the catacombs. In the "Red Cubiculum" of Domitilla mentioned above, the raising of Lazarus is balanced on the other side of an image of Moses striking the rock (Figure 29). At the Vigna Massimo catacomb, a series of images including Daniel, Job, and the paralytic also includes balancing scenes on the upper and lower registers of Moses striking the rock and Christ raising Lazarus. The juxtaposition of these two images, which appeared with some frequency in catacomb iconography, demonstrates the early Christian emphasis on the miracle-working power of Christ. Moses was indeed a miracle-working figure within the tradition and could be understood as being in competition with Christ.[62] However, it appears that the early Christians used Moses to highlight Christ as the superior miracle worker and to show Christ as the new Moses. The image of Moses striking water from the rock helps demonstrate their intent in balancing Jesus with an older miracle worker.

The Jesus who is portrayed in the gospels performs miracles differently than Moses or any Greco-Roman god in that he requires no intermediary such as the God of Israel. In Scripture and in Christian art, Jesus heals by virtue of his personal power. With his voice or his touch, Christ heals and performs miracles directly. Christ's touch heals his patients immediately. The catacomb art reflects this aspect of his healing ability. In the catacomb images, Christ touches the blind man, the paralytic, the woman with the issue of blood, and the *aediculum* of Lazarus with a staff. In relief sculpture, the power of Christ's touch is also apparent. In examples of the healing of the blind man, Christ's hands and fingers are the instruments of healing. In the woman with the issue of blood, touch is emphasized. In the miracles that include the use of a staff, such as the resurrection images, touch is still involved. This is all in contrast to the mode of healing of the pagan god Asclepius, which according to the accounts of Aristides did not involve touch or physical interaction but rather a process of dream interpretation and prescription. As Aristides noted, the devotees of Asclepius touted the efficacy of Asclepius, but his methods never relied upon physical touch.[63] Neither were his healings instantaneous like those performed by Jesus.

---

61. This is also not the sole juxtaposition of Moses and Christ raising Lazarus at Peter and Marcellinus. It occurs in at least two other instances. For the images, see Wilpert, *Die Malereien der Katakomben Roms* (Freiburg im Breisgau, 1903).

62. Origen, *Cels.* 1.45.

63. Aristides, *Sacred Tales* 48.21; also see the discussion on Aristides in chapter 2.

CONCLUSION

The early Christian emphasis on resurrection images reiterates Christ's superior divine attributes and offers a window to examine the early Christian adaptation of non-Christian themes. The prominence of resurrection images, albeit a natural choice for a Christian funerary context, can be read as a Christian rebuttal of a non-Christian cult. The raising of Lazarus exhibited Christ performing a successful resurrection; when Asclepius performed the same action, it brought about his death. The scene also established the divine authority of Jesus as compared with Asclepius or any other god. There was no Olympic hierarchy Christ needed to follow, because he himself was divine. In the imagery, Jesus accomplished his miracles through the power of physical touch with hand or staff. Jesus encountered and touched his patients, and he had witnesses to his physical presence and the resulting miraculous act. Indeed, Origen argued against Celsus along these lines, claiming that Christ's miracles were real, since he had eyewitnesses. [64]

Images of Jesus raising the dead were intended to remind viewers of the eternal life that was secured for Christians. The resurrection scenes also reiterated Jesus' power in a very clever way, in that they painted Jesus as looking like other gods and then as performing greater feats than those gods. The images conveyed the unique abilities that set Christ above any other rival and his divine authority, proved by his work as a miraculous healer.

Early Christian art served many purposes in Late Antiquity. Images illustrated scenes from Scripture, exhibited theological understandings of Jesus, and served as propaganda. Images of Christ performing miracles like raising the dead fulfilled all of these functions marvelously.

64. Origen, *Cels.* 24.

6

The Nature Miracles of Christ

Nearly a century after the birth of Christian art in the catacomb of Callistus, the pervasive theme in Christian relief sculpture was the image of Christ the Miracle Worker.[1] On Christian sarcophagi now housed in museums in Rome and Arles, the earliest examples bear a date of the late third century, while most date from the fourth to the fifth centuries.[2] In the fourth century, the catacomb images and sarcophagi share some thematic overlap. In the catacombs of Via Latina and Peter and Marcellinus, images dating from the late third and the fourth centuries feature Christ's healings and miracles, while parallel examples, such as the sarcophagus of Marcus Claudianus, provide multiple portrayals of the miracles of Christ.[3]

Relief sculpture such as sarcophagi continued the popular tradition of depicting Christ's miracles well into the late fourth and early fifth centuries.[4] While difficult to date with any certainty, several of the latest examples bear a provenance of the early fifth century. Several in particular at the Museo Pio Cristiano have a later dating from the end of the fourth century to the beginning of the fifth century (following Bovini and Brandenburg, and the Vatican Museum's own dating): the sarcophagus with the Bethesda miracle (Figure 6), the sarcophagus of the *traditio legis*, and the sarcophagus with

---

1. David Knipp calls this art "Theodosian art" to mark the era of the later emperor—an odd choice, since the dating of artifacts is so difficult and there is obvious overlap with other ruling eras of other emperors. Knipp, *"Christus Medicus" in der frühchristlichen Sarkophagskulptur: Ikonographische Studien der Sepulkralkunst des späten vierten Jahrhunderts* (Leiden: Brill, 1998), 22.

2. These museums are the Museo Pio Cristiano in the Vatican, the Musei Capitolini and Museo Nazionale Romano delle Terme in Rome, and the Musée de l'Arles et de la Provence antiques in France. Deichmann is an invaluable resource for examining the chronology of Christian sarcophagi. For example, in his catalog of sarcophagi at the Vatican, one fragment dates from the late third century (pl. 696). Deichmann's chronology supports an early dating for Christian sarcophagi of the late third century.

3. In the Terme museum in Rome, from the second quarter of the fourth century.

4. See Walther Kuhn, *Frühchristliche Kunst aus Rom* (Essen: Villa Hügel, 1962); and Erich Dinkler, *Der Einzug in Jerusalem* (Opladen: Westdeutscher, 1970).

the crossing of the Red Sea. Images of Christ performing healings, such as the paralytic scene, are interspersed in the same frame with images of Christ dividing loaves and raising Lazarus. Each individual scene displays the triumphant power of Christ. Within the sarcophagus frontal, the individual scenes operate as notes in a symphonic tableau, exuding an overall programmatic message of the superiority and unique nature of Christ.

As late as the fourth century, the early Christians still had not completely developed their own visual language of salvation. Instead, images of Hercules, Orpheus, and the healing god Asclepius were used to evoke Christ. The art seems underdeveloped relative to the theological advancements taking place in fourth-century Christianity. Art, of course, operates differently than philosophy or theology, and the development of Christian art, in particular, was slowed by the fact that Christians did not have much land or capital until the third century. Therefore, it should not be entirely surprising that Greco-Roman images and prototypes were still in use in Christian art into the fourth century. Adaptation and annexation were key components in the construction of Christianity's visual language.

Early Christians experimented with different prototypes in the development of a visual language.[5] Christian art did not arrive *ex nihilo*; the process of establishing visual representations included borrowing elements from outside influences. The evidence reveals that early Christians found the image of Christ's healings and miracles particularly resonant. The early Christians made choices in their iconographical patterns, and several of those choices included representative images of Christ's healings and miracles. These choices in early Christian art not only include representations of Jesus raising the dead, but also show Jesus performing miracles that are not directly related to healing—for example, dividing loaves or turning water into wine. Since these miracles suggest Jesus' mastery over the natural world, they often carry the label "nature miracles," a label that is quite appropriate.

The division of loaves and the Cana miracle are not the only miracles from the gospels that can be labeled "nature miracles." Jesus walking on the water and exhibiting control over the natural world fits under this rubric as well. However, in the canon of early Christian art, only the division of loaves

---

5. Paul Corby Finney, *The Invisible God: The Earliest Christians on Art* (New York: Oxford University Press, 1994), 146; and Finney, "Antecedents of Byzantine Iconoclasm: Christian Evidence before Constantine," in *The Image and the Word: Confrontations in Judaism, Christianity and Islam*, ed. Joseph Gutmann (Missoula, MT: Scholars, 1977), 28. Given the epigraphical evidence in the catacomb and the textual evidence, Finney dates the wall paintings of the catacomb of Callistus to the year 200, plus or minus fifteen to twenty years.

and Cana miracle appear with any degree of consistency. This is unsurprising, given the sacramental connotations of these miracles. Especially in a funerary environment, where the Eucharist was celebrated or families followed the Roman custom of dining with the dead, the two nature miracles featured are entirely appropriate.

"Nature miracles" is also a convenient term to encompass the acts of another figure who features prominently in the images of Christ the Miracle Worker: Moses. The Old Testament figure of Moses is often interspersed with the same image of Christ performing miracles as in the catacomb under the Vigna Massimo painting (Figure 3). Or Moses is depicted performing a miracle of his own, such as crossing the Red Sea, as in the Via Latina catacomb's Cubiculum C and Cubiculum O (Figure 33). Moses's miracles suggest his mastery over the natural world and typologically point to the miracle worker Jesus. But his miracle of striking water from the rock has particular relevance in an early Christian atmosphere. Moses striking water from the rock is a nature miracle that is congruent to a Christian environment, as it emphasizes the sacrament of baptism, forming a couplet with the division of the loaves and the Cana miracle, which together suggest the Eucharist.

JESUS AND MOSES

In the cubiculum next to the image of the baptism of Christ and the healing of the paralytic at the catacomb of Callistus is a wall painting that depicts Moses striking the rock. It is a difficult scene to identify, given its condition (Figure 35a). A figure is prominently standing next to what appears to be a large rock or column, and he holds a type of instrument in his right hand, which is extended toward the rock. Paul Corby Finney believes this to be an image of Moses striking the rock.[6] This scene is the most replicated scene in all catacomb paintings portraying Moses.[7] The scene is also depicted at the catacomb of Callistus in a wall painting that was created later and is much clearer (Figure 35b). The reproduction of the scene at the catacomb of Callistus signifies that the image had become more established in the visual lexicon of early Christians. Moses is standing before the rock, holding his staff, striking the object and

6. Finney, *The Invisible God*, 216. Wilpert, *Die Malereien der Katakomben Roms* (Freiburg im Breisgau, 1903), 266. The image of Moses striking the rock recalls baptism, as Wilpert noted the popularity of the symbol was attached to its insinuation of baptism.

7. Wilpert, *Die Malereien*, 266–81. Wilpert noted that its frequency in depiction, at least sixty-eight examples in the catacombs, indicates its importance to early Christians. In conjunction with the Raising of Lazarus, Moses striking the rock is fairly astounding in its frequency compared with other scenes of works and wonders. Also see Jensen, *Understanding Early Christian Art* (New York: Routledge, 2000), 76.

releasing a stream of water. A smaller figure, presumably one of the Israelites, is shown gathering the water. On a rock behind Moses is another figure, kneeling as if he is removing his sandal.

There are antecedents for such a scene, although they are temporally and geographically separated. In the later catacomb of Callistus scene, Moses is wearing sandals while the figure behind him removes his sandal. There are images at the Via Latina catacomb that show only the figure of Moses removing his sandal. It could be that the catacomb of Callistus image is depicting two different scenes of Moses or that the figure is an Israelite emphasizing the sacred event taking place. Later images of this scene in the catacombs do not replicate the kneeling figure, thus removing any cause for confusion. Instead, the major figures are Moses and the smaller figure gathering the water. The later catacomb of Callistus scene shows how early Christians selected and incorporated characters in their visual narrative as they began to establish how they wanted to depict scenes that were important to them, such as the raising of Lazarus and Moses striking the rock.[8]

The typological connection between Moses and Christ appears quite frequently in patristic texts. Several instances in the church fathers illuminate the significance of particular scenes in catacomb art involving Moses. Justin Martyr provided telling evidence that explicitly connects Moses striking the rock to Christ. Just after he claimed Asclepius to be an imitator of Christ in his *Dialogue*, Justin proved the prediction of the healing action of Christ by quoting a passage from Isa. 35:1-7:

> The wilderness and the dry land shall be glad, the desert shall rejoice and blossom; like the crocus. . . . Say to those who are of a fearful heart, 'Be strong, do not fear! Here is your God, He will come with vengeance, with terrible recompense. He will come and save you.' Then the eyes of the blind shall be opened, and the ears of the deaf unstopped; then the lame shall leap like a deer, and the tongue of the speechless sing for joy. For waters shall break forth in the wilderness, and streams in the desert; the burning sand shall become a pool, and the thirsty ground springs of water.

8. See Umberto Fasola, *Le catacombe di S. Gennaro a Capodimonte* (Rome: Editalia, 1975). The striking of the rock also appears in the catacomb of San Gennaro in Naples, dating from the late third to early fourth century. Moses is depicted striking the rock, and nearby Christ is depicted in a similar manner as at Callistus, merely holding the instrument. Also see the early-fourth-century image in the catacomb of Priscilla of the striking of the rock, also in conjunction with the raising of Lazarus. See fig. 5A in Jeffrey Spier, ed., *Picturing the Bible: The Earliest Christian Art* (New Haven, CT: Yale University Press, 2007).

Justin provides some commentary on the passage: "'The fountain of living water,' which gushed forth from God upon a land devoid of the knowledge of God (that is, the land of the Gentiles), was our Christ, who made his appearance on earth in the midst of your people, and healed those who from birth were blind and deaf and lame. He cured them by his word, causing them to walk, to hear, and to see. By restoring the dead to life, he compelled the men of that day to recognize him."[9]

Justin's words offer an insight into the iconography of Christ in the catacombs. Jesus healed the blind and the deaf, as Justin described; however, what is notable is Justin's language of the "thirsty land" and the "spring of living water" that will gush forth. Jesus wields an instrument akin to the staff Moses wields when he strikes water from the rock, providing relief for the "parched," those people in need. Here Justin connects the action of Jesus to the action of Moses. According to Justin, Christ restoring the dead to life allowed people to recognize him. Miracles served a purpose, as they drew attention, inculcated faith, and showed the power of Christ.

Predictably, the iconography of Jesus' miracles such as the raising of Lazarus incorporated a similar wonder-working instrument as the staff of Moses in the striking of the rock and the crossing of the Red Sea. Justin further implied Jesus' connection to Moses, as he foresaw the argument that Jesus would be derided as a magician: "Yet, though they witnessed these miraculous deeds with their own eyes, they attributed them to magical art; indeed, they dared to call him a magician who misled the people. But he performed these deeds to convince his future followers, that if anyone, even though his body were in any way maimed, should be faithful to his teaching, he would raise him up at this second coming entirely sound, and make him free forever from death, corruption, and pain."[10] Moses was a wonder worker whose actions such as the striking of the rock foreshadowed the coming of Christ, the supreme wonder worker. Moses, portrayed in the catacombs striking the rock and crossing the Red Sea with the use of his staff, like Jesus bore the traits of a magician, and some authors were persuaded that Moses was indeed a magician.[11]

Two centuries later, Augustine reaffirmed the connection between Moses and Christ. In a reply to Marcellinus addressing the issues of Volusian, Augustine named Moses as a great wonder worker, fulfilled by Christ, solidifying any connection: "We read that the magicians of the Egyptians, men

9. Justin, *Dial.* 69.5-7. Justin mentions it again at 86.1-4 and at 131.6: "And water gushed forth from a rock for your benefit" (Falls).

10. Ibid.

11. See chapter 7 for more evidence on the magician.

most skilled in these arts, were surpassed by Moses, the servant of God, for, when they produced certain wonders by their wicked arts, he simply called upon God and destroyed all their devices. But Moses himself and the rest of the most truthful prophets foretold Christ the Lord and gave great glory to him."[12] The inclusion of Moses striking the rock as well as Christ raising Lazarus exhibits Moses as a foretelling of Christ and shows Christ as the Christian patriarch, as a New Moses.[13] Just as Moses led his people to a new land, Jesus was the New Moses who led his people to eternal life. The raising of Lazarus was a funerary theme that emphasized resurrection; however, seen in conjunction with the image of Moses striking the rock as in the catacomb of Domitilla, the combined force of the images shows Christ as the New Moses. The emblematic feature of the staff is the key iconographic component linking the two figures, and the next chapter will focus on this unique feature.

THE WEDDING AT CANA AND THE DIVISION OF THE LOAVES

Along with healing miracles, early Christian art includes multiple instances of the wedding at Cana and the division of loaves, although these do not appear in the earliest catacomb art. At the catacomb of Peter and Marcellinus, Christ is portrayed standing above the baskets of bread in the scene of the division of loaves, and the raising of Lazarus is depicted on the opposite side.[14] In a painting on an arched doorway, the image of Noah separates the flanking images of the division of the loaves and the Cana miracle (Figure 36). In these depictions at the catacomb of Peter and Marcellinus, Christ is using his staff to enact the miracles, as he stands pointing it toward the baskets and the jars. At the Via Latina catacomb, the scene is replicated as Christ uses his reed-like staff to touch the baskets of bread. In this particular Via Latina image in Cubiculum O, Christ is shown with short, cropped hair, and the edge of his robe is marked with an ancient symbol. This same ancient symbol is exhibited on the border of Moses's robe in the crossing of the Red Sea on the opposite wall (Figure 33). The figures are similar in appearance and dress, and Christ performing his miracle with the staff is mirrored by Moses wielding his staff in the crossing the Red Sea. The visual appropriation of Moses's staff in the image of Christ is apparent, as Christ miraculously provides bread for his followers in the guise of Moses, just as Moses provided manna for the Israelites.

---

12. Augustine, *Ep.* 137.13 (Teske).

13. Martine Dulaey claims the rod marks Christ as a new Moses in "Le symbole de la baguette dans l'art paleochrétien," *Revue des études augustiniennes* 19, nos. 1–2 (1973): 7.

14. For the image, see fig. 10B of the appendix in Spier, *Picturing the Bible.*

In the Vigna Massimo catacomb, the division of the loaves is included among other images of the miracles of Christ, along with representations of other scriptural figures such as Moses striking the rock (Figure 3). A scene of the raising of Lazarus accompanies an image of Christ pointing his staff toward several baskets at his feet. Not only does this painting provide evidence of a nature miracle, it also exhibits the tendency in catacomb art to use images as narrative devices. All the themes and figures depicted, including Daniel and Noah at opposite ends of the painting, were likely included as integral elements interpreted as messages of comfort, deliverance, and resurrection in a funerary setting. Early Christians possibly viewed the division of the loaves as an image that emphasized life-giving sustenance, as Christ provides bread for the people. The scene can also be interpreted as a sacramental image emphasizing the ritual of the Eucharist, often performed in a funerary environment such as a catacomb setting.[15]

In a separate cubiculum at the catacomb of Peter and Marcellinus, the miracle at Cana is depicted, flanked by scenes of Christ being baptized and Moses striking the rock (Figure 37). In a portrayal resembling the division of the loaves, Jesus is touching the jars of wine with his staff. He performs his miracle in front of gatherers at a sigma-shaped table. The scene recalls other banquet scenes at the same catacomb, in which captions indicate that the dinner guests are issuing orders for more wine to the servants Irene and Agape. This image appears to show Christ in the act of supplying the wine for the party. The eucharistic implications are more pronounced in this scene, as the meal recalls the Last Supper. The eucharistic overtones in the division of the loaves and the Cana miracle are apparent. In a funerary environment where people either dined with the dead or celebrated the Eucharist, the nature miracles of Christ mirrored the sacramental action taking place within the sacred space.[16] The image of Christ the Miracle Worker not only defined the person of Christ, it also defined the identity of the Christians by illustrating the liturgical actions that made them Christians.[17]

---

15. See Prudentius, *Peristephanon* 11.175-190, who emphasizes the benefit of enjoying the Eucharist in the catacombs.

16. For further reading, see Andrew McGowan, *Ascetic Eucharists: Food and Drink in Early Christian Ritual Meals* (New York: Oxford University Press, 1998); and Robin M. Jensen, "Dining with the Dead: From the Mensa to the Altar in Christian Late Antiquity," *Commemorating the Dead: Texts and Artifacts in Context* (Berlin: Walter De Gruyter, 2008).

17. See Cyprian, *Ep.* 63; and Augustine, *Confessions* 6.2.2; and Augustine's mention here of Monica's sober and delicate use of wine. Drinking at the tombs of the saints is a problem Ambrose and Augustine had to address as well. Augustine writes to Aurelius of Carthage in *Ep.* 22, exhorting congregations to

The Cana miracle scene also should be interpreted along with the cognate scenes in the arcosolium of the baptism of Christ and Moses striking the rock. It is a unique cubiculum that includes several images filled with a sacramental flavor. The baptismal connection between Moses and Jesus is also made clear by Origen: "You daily devote yourself to hearing the law of God and to looking upon the face of Moses, through which the glory of the Lord is revealed. But if you also have entered the mystic font of baptism . . . then when the Jordan parted, you will enter the land of promise by the services of the priests. In this land, Jesus receives you after Moses, and becomes for you the leader of a new way."[18] Origen viewed Moses's works as typological prefigurements of the Christian sacraments: just as the Israelites crossed the Jordan with Moses, so Christians pass through the baptismal font with Christ. Christ is thus further connected to Moses in such nature miracle images, and in Origen's words, Jesus is a successor to Moses as a patriarchal leader. Origen's attempt to compare Jesus and Moses in his homily is reflected in the visual art of the catacombs. Nearly a century after Origen's homily, at the catacomb of Peter and Marcellinus, paintings of the striking of the rock and the baptism of Christ face each other in a cubiculum, while the miracle at Cana is the central work. With the miraculous release of water juxtaposed with Christ's baptism and the changing of water into wine, the sacraments of the church are visually accentuated in this setting. Thus, the nature miracles of Christ in the canon of early Christian art are united in emphasizing the sacraments and in endorsing the power of the miracle-working Jesus.

Outside of the images of Christ raising the dead, the instances of Jesus using his staff in catacomb representations are limited to the nature miracles. Even with so few examples in comparison with the Lazarus paintings, the staff is a fairly key stylistic element that symbolizes Jesus' ability to work miracles. It is not accidental that Jesus' staff is often juxtaposed with the staff of Moses. At the catacombs of Peter and Marcellinus, Via Latina, Domitilla, and Vigna Massimo, images of Christ performing his miracles are housed in rooms that also contain a representation of Moses wielding his staff.[19] Nature miracles, chiefly the Cana miracle and the division of loaves, are also popular subjects in Christian relief sculpture.[20] Christ's wonder-working staff is featured in the depiction of the Cana miracle. Christ points the staff toward several small jars

abandon customs of drunkenness and riotousness. Augustine could not control events in private homes, but he was determined to eradicate such practices in churches. Also see Paulinus of Nola, *Ep.* 32; *Carm.* 27, 28; and Jensen, "Dining with the Dead."

18. Origen, *Homily on Joshua* 4.1 (Bruce).

19. See Wilpert's plates in *Die Malereien* for the representations in Domitilla, among others.

at his feet, indicating the miraculous transformative action that is occurring (Figures 4 and 5). In the representation of the division of the loaves, a tool is not usually depicted. Instead, Christ is portrayed with both hands extended, blessing two loaves held by flanking figures (Figure 38). At his feet are baskets of bread ready to be shared among the people. It is important to note that many of the extant sarcophagi were discovered within the catacombs. As in the catacombs, representations of the Cana miracle and the division of the loaves on funerary relief sculpture likely reflect the sacramental action taking place in the immediate space, be it a catacomb or another environment.

FOURTH-CENTURY CHRISTOLOGICAL SIGNIFICANCE

In Christian art of the fourth and fifth centuries, the miracles of Christ exhibit a divergence from the earlier representations. The art of the fourth century depicts the miracles and healings of Christ as before, but certain traits reveal a more robust Christology that is reflective of a fourth-century context. One may even argue that the miracles of Jesus depicted upon fourth-century Roman sarcophagi draw heavily from the Gospel of John. Each entry in the tableau of images in Christian relief sculpture possibly bears a connection to John's gospel. While the raising of the widow's son, the raising of Jairus's daughter, and the healing of the woman with the issue of blood might be cited as evidence against this argument, those instances pale in comparison to the large number of images that rely upon John's gospel, particularly the raising of Lazarus and the nature miracles. The sheer number of occurrences of such scenes leads one to believe that the Christian art of this era was greatly reliant upon the Fourth Gospel and its specific Christology.[21]

20. In the Roman body of evidence, the Cana miracle appears over forty-four times; in the Gallic and North African evidence, it appears over twenty-one times. See Bovini and Brandenburg, *Repertorium der Christlich-Antiken Sarkophage*, Band 1, *Rom und Ostia*, ed. F. W. Deichmann (Wiesbaden: F. Steiner, 1967), pt. 3, 122; and see Brigitte Christern-Briesenick, *Repertorium der Christlich-Antiken Sarkophage*, Band 3, *Frankreich, Algerien, Tunesien*, ed. T. Ulbert (Wiesbaden: F. Steiner, 2003), 303. For the division of loaves, the miracle appears in the Roman evidence over eight-four times; in the Gallic and North African evidence, over twelve times. Band I, 122; Band III, 299.

21. Consider the catalogued scenes of the Cana miracle (forty-four), the division of loaves (eight-four), and the raising of Lazarus (sixty-seven) in U. Lange, *Ikonographisches Register für das Repertorium der christlich-antiken Sarkophage* F.W. Deichmann, ed. (Dettelbach: Röll, 1996), Band I, 122; Band III, 303; Band I, 122; Band III, 299; Band I, 123; Band III, 302. Compare the number of Lazarus occurrences to the sixteen examples of the widow's son and Jairus's daughter in the Roman material, and the eight examples from Gaul and North Africa. See Band I, 123; Band III, 301–302.

The Gospel of John begins Jesus' ministry with the Cana miracle, a scene that is repeatedly carved in relief sculpture of the fourth and fifth centuries. The Cana miracle in John inaugurates the "signs" of Christ's miracle-working ability. In the text, Jesus heals an official's son upon his return to Cana. Then John details the healing of variously afflicted people at Bethesda, including the blind, the lame, and the paralyzed, all of whom are subjects in the relief sculpture (4:46; 5:2-4). The feeding of the five thousand in John 6 is possibly reflected in the scenes of Jesus dividing the loaves. This is an interpretive leap, as representations of the division of loaves could arguably recall the scene from any of the gospels. However, the story in John is a significant sign of Jesus' divine authority. As mentioned earlier in this chapter the sacramental interpretation in the imagery is overt. Underlying the image of the division of the loaves could be John's emphasis on the authority of Jesus, that all who desire salvation must go through Jesus (6:37).

The healing of the blind man and the healing of the paralytic in John 5 and John 9 are also scenes that John shares in common with Matthew, Mark, and Luke. While they occur in the Synoptic Gospels, however, their usage can still point toward a consistent attention to the Gospel of John. The narrative of the paralytic in John emphasizes the paralytic's "mat" and Jesus' command to "take it up and walk." [22] The prominence of the image of the mat in relief sculpture may indicate that it draws from the reading from John. While the scene in the Synoptic Gospels is meant to highlight Christ's authority in his ministry on earth, only John includes an extended passage following the event describing the authority of the Son of Man, a feature that is also indicative of the long dialogues that John attributed to Jesus. It is difficult to discern whether the scenes that overlap with the synoptic accounts are derivative of John. Nevertheless, when coupled with scenes that are exclusive to John, such as the Cana miracle and the raising of Lazarus, it seems likely that the art does indeed reflect John's narrative.

The scenes of Christ's miracles in relief sculpture are not usually presented in isolation from one another. The raising of Lazarus is balanced with other scenes of Christ's miracles, particularly the nature miracles (Figure 39). Resurrection and the new covenant are not the only themes being reflected in this funerary medium. The frequent portrayals of Christ's miracles in relief sculpture reveal a different Jesus than the one depicted in catacomb wall paintings. The repeated inclusion of the raising of Lazarus and the nature miracles reminds the viewer of the authority of Jesus that is apparent in John's

---

22. For example, the Matt. 9:2 story includes the edict to stand and walk, although it does not mention the mat nearly as much as John's account.

gospel. In John, the raising of Lazarus (John 11:28) served an important purpose: it showed Jesus' unique power over death and included the image of Lazarus emerging in his burial clothes, the very clothes Christ will leave behind when he emerges from the tomb (John 20:5). Thus, Christ is not bound by death, as personified by the burial wrappings. John uses the raising of Lazarus to illustrate Jesus' divine sonship and authority. John portrays Jesus as something different, something new. From the prologue through Lazarus, the Fourth Gospel characterizes Jesus as the Divine Logos, and his ability to raise the dead exhibits this identity. A key difference between the Jesus portrayed in the raising of Lazarus and the Jesus raising the dead in the Synoptic Gospels is captured by Luke. In Luke's narrative of the widow's son at Nain, upon the completion of the miraculous event, the crowd calls Jesus a "great prophet." In John's account of the raising of Lazarus, witnesses recognize Jesus not as a prophet as in Luke, but as the Messiah. Martha says, "I believe that you are the Messiah, the Son of God, the one coming into the world" (John 11:27).

The raising of Lazarus embodies a transitional moment in John's gospel. It is the final sign in what Raymond Brown memorably called the "Book of Signs" as the text moves into the passion narrative and ultimate resurrection of Christ.[23] The scene of the raising of Lazarus similarly indicates a transition in depictions of Jesus in Christian imagery. The scene's frequent inclusion in relief sculpture reveals what specific source material the artists were relying upon. The art serves as the able witness for John's Jesus, "the very works that I am doing testify on my behalf that the Father has sent me" (John 5:36). The increase in scenes of Lazarus's resurrection and the Cana miracle that are purely Johannine, combined with other scenes of healings and miracles that John shares with the Synoptic Gospels, lend weight to the argument that images of Christ's miracles in fourth-century Christian relief sculpture had John's Jesus in mind.

While the argument is persuasive, one simply cannot prove that early Christian art of the fourth century was derived from John. Lazarus was a popular theme in the third-century catacombs that also featured miracles from the Synoptic Gospels. Roman sarcophagi frontals such as those previously mentioned include images from Luke–Acts and the apocryphal *Acts of Peter* that involve the apostle, such as Peter's arrest at Acts 12 and his miraculous striking of the rock.[24] The persistence of the Lazarus image arguably lends credence to a strong interest in John. The argument regarding Johannine reliance offers an

23. See Raymond E. Brown, *An Introduction to the Gospel of John* (New York: Doubleday, 2003).

24. The episode of striking the rock occurs in the apocryphal *Acts of Peter*, a text that has a complicated provenance. For the text, see *Acta Apostolorum Apocrypha*, vol. 1 and 2. Ed. by Richard Lipsius (Hildesheim: G. Olms, 1959), 1–22. Also see chapter 7.

opportunity for a deeper discussion of the function of early Christian art. Art such as Christian relief sculpture exhibits more of a blended reading of John and other elements from Scripture. Lazarus and the Cana miracle are featured, as well as the noted emphasis on depicting Jesus as a miracle worker akin to Moses. Portraying Jesus as a New Moses derives more from the Gospel of Matthew than from John, as evidenced in Matthew's infancy narrative with the reflections of Exodus such as the massacre of the innocents and the flight into Egypt. Matthew places the holy family in Egypt so that his readers will connect Jesus to Moses.

What the fourth-century Christian art does indicate is the ability to convey theological traits regarding Jesus to its audience. This is no easy feat. How does art show a trait like "divinity," or even more difficult, "divinity" and "humanity" in one figure? To achieve this, the figure of Jesus cannot look like other ordinary figures; he must appear extraordinary. Portraying the human figure of Jesus performing feats of wonder achieves a rendering of divine qualities. The miracles of Jesus that are consistently featured attest to his divine status that inspires awe, wonder, and faith. The miracles portray the divine power of Jesus during his earthly ministry. They show the human Jesus and the divine Christ.

In the prologue of John 1:17, the author states, "The law indeed was given through Moses; grace and truth came through Jesus Christ." For John, Christ is above and beyond the law.[25] John's Jesus is the Divine Logos, preexistent to the law. Instead of miracles providing evidence of his divine status or inspiring faith, as in Luke, the miracles of John's Jesus require the apprehension and respect of the people. In this endeavor, the evangelist succeeds admirably, and the art reflects that success. Jesus' miracles are meant to testify to his supreme authority and that he is "above all," especially his competitors.

Christians drew upon existing traditions in non-Christian art and in effect transcended them by portraying a dominant Christ. *Post-pacem* (after Constantine) Christian art notoriously features elements of the imperial cult, including an enthroned Jesus. Sarcophagi such as the Sarcophagus of Junius Bassus (now in the Museo Pio Cristiano), which dates from 359 CE, show Jesus giving the law to Peter and Paul, seated in a throne above a representation

---

25. In the post-resurrection story of the Gospel of John, Mary Magdalene mistakes Jesus for "the gardener." Jaime Clark-Soles argues that this may be a significant sign that the evangelist had the school of Epicurus in mind in the composition of the gospel. Instead of "a gardener," it is "the gardener," possibly recalling the "garden of Epicurus," a noteworthy symbol of Epicurean philosophy. John may be in competition with Epicurean philosophy, but his gospel makes a great effort to surpass any similarity with Epicureanism. Jaime Clark-Soles, *Death and Afterlife in the New Testament* (New York: T&T Clark, 2006), 149.

of Caelus, a symbol of the heavens (Figure 40). In such an image, Jesus is denoted as separate, the "stranger from heaven" who is above the firmament of the world, ensconced in divine authority. The *traditio legis* scene would be oft repeated in Late Antiquity, and embellishments of the divinity of Jesus would appear in even grander locations than a sarcophagus such as the Mausoleum of Constanza, Constantine's sister, dating from the mid-fourth century.[26]

The miracle scenes that were repeatedly depicted on funerary monuments of the fourth century may conceivably reflect a reading of the Gospel of John, but they certainly reveal a developing Christology. Jesus' eternal nature can be perceived in scenes such as the *traditio legis*, but with the miracle images, Jesus is depicted in his earthly ministry. The miracles reflect the "signs" of John; the enthroned Jesus reflects the glory. The Christian art of the fourth century emphasizes Christ's divine status as well as his earthly ministry, featuring his miracles. In his sermons on the Gospel of John, Augustine showed an understanding of how powerful the miracle stories were for his audience. He urged his listeners to look behind the miracles and healings at the power and authority demonstrated by Jesus that will occur in the final resurrection, a moment that is greater "than healings of bodies. We have treated of this already, and must not linger upon it now. Greater is the resurrection of the body unto eternity than this healing of the body, wrought in that impotent man, to last only for a time. And greater works than these he will show him, that you may marvel."[27]

CONCLUSION

Fourth-century Christian art used images of the healings and miracles to underscore the authority of Jesus and of the church. At a moment when the church was just becoming established following Constantine, such an emphasis might have been necessary to drive home the message that Christ was the final authority above all rivals, Christian and non-Christian. An image of an enthroned Jesus could accomplish this goal admirably, as in the *traditio legis*. However, the imagery of the enthroned Christ did not visually embellish the traits and abilities that made Christ greater than his competitors.[28] The image of

26. Jesus above the four rivers of creation can notably be seen in the apse mosaics of the Basilica of Cosmas and Damien in Rome, and the apse mosaic of San Vitale, Ravenna.

27. Augustine, *Tractates on the Gospel of John* 23.12 (*NPNF* 1.7.156).

28. It is also possible the enthroned Jesus is more indicative of the imperial cult than other figures of pagan religion; however, this is a tendentious argument. See Hans Belting, *Likeness and Presence: A History of the Image before the Era of Art* (Chicago: University of Chicago Press, 1994); and Mathews' position beginning in *Clash of Gods* (Princeton, NJ: Princeton University Press, 1993), 3.

Christ the Miracle Worker showed an active Jesus demonstrating his superior abilities, not a seated and passive Jesus. More importantly, Christ the Miracle Worker exhibited a unique Jesus, a Jesus who is the resurrection and the life. Given the large number of these scenes on relief sculpture, it is obvious that Christians of Late Antiquity found it meaningful to view their savior performing these feats.

In light of previous studies, it is apparent that this emphasis on healings and miracles also borrowed from the available visual prototypes of Roman culture.[29] The emphasis is more than just an appropriation of pagan symbols and themes. It reflects that Jesus had to contend with serious threats to his status, and it demonstrates a patristic influence. The emphasis on Christ's status as a supreme physician and miracle worker came from treatises as well as the Christian pulpit. The message duly reached patrons and artists as it was painted and carved upon Christian walls and artifacts. The images of Christ's healings and miracles indicate not only outside threats but also a great internal anxiety regarding church establishment. This anxiety is apparent in the Christian relief sculpture after Constantine. In *post-pacem* relief sculpture, Moses is often replaced with the figure of Peter in an attempt to underscore who was the patriarch of the church. Moses and the Jews were not exactly a serious outside threat that had to be addressed in the visual art. The relief sculpture scenes of Peter appropriating the person of Moses, including the wonder-working staff, reveal the intent to exude a sense of church authority at a time when the ecclesial body was taking its infant steps toward becoming firmly established. Emphasizing the authority of the church through the sacrament of initiation, the sacrament of baptism, was a way to bolster that establishment. Scenes of Moses striking the rock, and subsequently of Peter striking the rock constitute an obvious baptismal reference.

Early Christians depicted Jesus performing miracles from Scripture that demonstrated his power over the natural world. Jesus divides loaves and changes water to wine, recalling the Johannine narrative. Jesus was intentionally portrayed as a more powerful figure than gods of the Roman pantheon such as Asclepius. But early Christians also exhibited an intentional desire to show Jesus as a New Moses—a wonder worker like Moses but also greater than Moses. In visual art, symbols were powerful ways to cast Jesus as a figure like Moses. The staff of Moses, a memorable element from the scriptural narrative, was a way early Christians could demonstrate Jesus as a miracle worker like Moses. Of course, in Scripture, Jesus never uses a staff to perform miracles, but Moses does. Up to the fourth century, the stylistic inclusion of Christ's staff in the performance of his miracles is a pertinent clue that illustrates Christ as the prophetic fulfillment to the patriarch Moses. By the fourth century, Christ's staff is also wielded by Peter in relief sculpture of that era. Visual art attached all three—Christ, Moses, and Peter—to the wonder-working staff, and that staff is the next subject to which this book turns.

7

The Staff of Jesus

From its inception, Christian art captured Jesus performing miracles and healings with the peculiar inclusion of what has been called a scepter, a staff, or a wand. In catacomb paintings of the third and fourth centuries and the relief sculpture of the fourth and fifth centuries, Christ the Miracle Worker is rarely portrayed without this enigmatic iconographic inclusion (Figures 25–29). As perplexing as the instrument is, it tends to be misconstrued and misunderstood by contemporary audiences. Theologians and art historians have interpreted Christ's miracle-working implement as a symbol denoting Jesus as a philosopher or a magician. However, the most reasonable interpretation of the staff can be realized by examining two other miracle-working figures that appear in Christian art bearing staffs: Moses and Peter.

Miracles and the figures who wrought them were greatly esteemed in antiquity. Eusebius of Caesarea, in the third book of his tract *Proof of the Gospel*, cited the miracles of Christ as the proof.[1] The healings and miracles of Christ "were the proofs of his divinity," legitimating his identity as Son of God. To rebut critics who challenged the veracity of Christ's miracles, Eusebius argued that the disciples of Christ were eyewitnesses and spoke truly of Jesus' miracle-working ability. In his defense of Christ's miracles, Eusebius not only touted the infallibility of Peter, "the apostle and disciple who was chief of them all," but also described Jesus' commission of the disciples as an order to "aim higher than the Jews under Moses' commandments."[2]

Akin to church billboards on a highway, the miraculous works of Jesus and his subsequent disciples were powerful signs that drew attention and inculcated faith.[3] Miracles were components of Jewish and Christian beliefs reaching back

---

1. Eusebius, *Proof of the Gospel* 3.4.109b. See the translation by W. J. Ferrar, *The Proof of the Gospel, Being the* Demonstratio Evangelica *of Eusebius of Caesarea*, vols. 1–2 (London: SPCK, 1920).

2. Eusebius, *Proof of the Gospel* 3.5.123; 3.5.109 (Ferrar). Eusebius found that the aforementioned "critics" of Christ's miracles included Porphyry.

3. For instance, see Augustine, *The Usefulness of Belief* 15.33 (CSEL 25.41).

to Moses, witnessed in Jesus, and passed on to Jesus' disciples, Peter foremost among them. Eusebius's text reveals that such an emphasis on miracles and miracle workers was apparent in early church documents. I will demonstrate how this emphasis manifested itself in early Christian art, accentuated by the appearance of a peculiar iconographic feature: the enigmatic miracle-working staff. I will explain the significance of the staff in early Christian art by highlighting key artistic examples from the third and fourth centuries and argue that the staffs of Jesus and Peter directly recall the staff of the miracle-working Moses. Examining the miracles of Moses and Jesus in Scripture and in early church texts will make evident the representation of Jesus and Peter as the "New Moses" in early Christian art.

Moses, Jesus, and Peter are the only miracle workers who appear with staffs in early Christian art. Dating from as early as the third century, the image of Christ performing healings and miracles appears quite frequently, mostly in a funerary context. Prior to images of Christ enthroned or Christ suffering that were normative after the fifth century, there was the image of Christ the Miracle Worker. Within the Roman and Gallic corpus of Christian images, Christ is often portrayed holding what appears to be a tool used in the performance of his miracles. Jesus' miracle-working apparatus is not depicted consistently in the same way. At times, the staff appears wand-like, rendered thin and slender in catacomb representations. And in funerary relief sculptures, the staff appears thicker and tapered (Figures 25, 27, 39). Even with this variety, however, the tool wielded by the miracle-working Christ consistently resembles the instrument wielded by the miracle-working Moses in cognate scenes. In funerary relief sculptures, this same emblematic staff is also brandished by Peter performing his water miracle. Thus, the staff was meant to associate Christ and Peter with another miracle worker, Moses, rather than to suggest Jesus was a philosopher or a magician.

In the "Red Cubiculum" of the catacomb of Domitilla, the raising of Lazarus is balanced by an image of Moses striking the rock (Figure 29). At the catacomb under the Vigna Massimo, a series of images including Daniel, Noah, and the visitation of the magi correlate to scenes on the upper and lower registers of Moses striking the rock and Jesus raising Lazarus to life (Figure 3). Two funerary relief sculptures that now reside in the Museo Pio Cristiano of the Vatican and the sarcophagus of Marcus Claudianus housed in the Museo Nazionale Romano show the staff attached to the figures of Jesus and Peter in the execution of their miracles (Figures 39, 41, and 42). And on the doors of the Church of Santa Sabina in Rome, a carving that portrays Jesus using a staff to perform miracles appears above a panel whose carving depicts Moses performing a miracle with his staff (Figures 43–44).

When examined closely, the staff of Jesus in early Christian art exhibits an intentional connection to Moses. The staff's presence indicates that it was an important symbol and contributed to an overall image of Christ that was greatly significant. From the catacomb representations of Moses' miracles to the funerary reliefs exhibiting Peter striking the rock, the artistic examples illustrate an insistent desire to connect Jesus and Peter to Moses in paint and stone and in the minds of their viewers. The staff is also a perfect example to illustrate the polyvalent quality of early Christian art, and of the miracle images in particular. The staff is a symbol, and while it connects Jesus and Peter to Moses, the context of the images of striking the rock provides sacramental implications—specifically, a reference to baptism. Just as the healing images of Jesus arguably suggest overtures of the Asclepius cult, due to their context, so the striking of the rock echoes Moses and baptism to highlight the power of the nascent church.

THE APPEARANCE OF THE STAFF

Staffs have a long history as a symbol in literature and in art. There are various terms in Greek and Latin that refer to some type of staff or wand that projects otherworldly power in the minds of a Late Antique audience. The staff of Jesus in Christian art has been considered a wand meant to exhibit Jesus as a magician. This section surveys the arguments that propose such an interpretation, an interpretation that ultimately is erroneous.

THE PROBLEM OF THE "MAGIC WAND"

The staff of Jesus has been explained as a relic of pagan influence or as evidence that early Christians considered Jesus to be a type of magician.[4] Viewers may find it irresistible to quickly assume that Christ wielding a wand-like staff is an intentional evocation of Jesus as a magician.[5] Morton Smith famously associated Jesus with magic, drawing connections between Jesus and Apollonius of Tyana. Smith argued that the gospel writers attempted to minimize Jesus' magical attributes; however, the miracles were the marks of the magician.[6]

---

4. See Jás Elsner, *Imperial Rome and Christian Triumph: The Art of the Roman Empire, ad 100–450* (New York: Oxford University Press, 1998), 153; and Thomas Mathews, *The Clash of Gods* (Princeton, NJ: Princeton University Press, 1993), 54–89.

5. A leap that Thomas Mathews takes. See Mathews, *Clash of Gods*, 54–89.

6. Morton Smith, *Jesus the Magician* (San Francisco: Harper and Row, 1978), 87–93.

More recently, John Dominic Crossan utilizes rabbinical material to argue that "Elijah and Elisha, Honi and Haninah were magicians and so was Jesus of Nazareth."[7] For a variety of reasons, any argument that suggests Jesus as a magician is unpersuasive. Smith was criticized for manipulating gospel citations to his advantage and disregarding the eschatological implications of his argument, as well as neglecting the difference between Jesus' formulae and magical incantations.[8] Not only do the gospel accounts differ from the magical papyri in the use of spells, a magician in Late Antiquity was expected to call upon gods or demons in the employment of magic, something Jesus does not do in the performance of his miracles.[9]

The chief reason any portrait of Jesus as a magician fails is that magic was greatly maligned by Christians in Late Antiquity. Magic, like the Asclepius cult, offered a viable alternative for convalescence in a world where there were few options. Magical incantations were used by people in Late Antiquity, much to the consternation of ecclesial leaders. The church fathers attacked the use of magic and any characterization of Jesus as a magician. Origen's rebuttal against Celsus, pointing out that Jesus did not use magical incantations, could work just as well against Smith.[10] Origen, Augustine, and Chrysostom all advocated for magic's banishment but found it persistent in Christian communities despite their vociferous attacks.[11] From the comments of the church fathers, it appears that the hatred of magic and refusal to distinguish among levels of magic comes

7. John Dominic Crossan, *The Historical Jesus: The Life of a Mediterranean Jewish Peasant* (Edinburgh: T. & T. Clark, 1991), 315; Crossan, *Jesus: A Revolutionary Biography* (San Francisco: Harper Collins, 1994), 104.

8. Graham Twelftree, *Jesus the Exorcist* (Tübingen: Mohr Siebeck, 1993), 153. Howard Clark Kee points out Smith's inconsistent use of the gospel accounts, such as leaving out the eschatological implications, and ridicules his argument as based upon his "eclectic personal preferences." Kee, *Medicine, Miracle, and Magic in New Testament Times* (New York: Cambridge University Press, 1986), 114. Spells were usually spoken softly and guarded securely to prevent theft. See Theissen, *The Miracle Stories of the Early Christian Tradition*, trans. Francis McDonagh (Philadelphia: Fortress Press, 1974), 64. Bernd Kollmann catalogs the various viewpoints on Jesus the Magician in *Jesus und die Christen als Wundertäter: Studien zu Magie, Medizin und Schamanismus in Antike und Christentum*. (Göttingen: Vandenhoeck and Ruprecht, 1996), 36–38.

9. See Michael Mach, "Jesus' Miracles in Context," in *The Beginnings of Christianity: A Collection of Articles*, ed. Jack Pastor and Menachem Mor (Jerusalem: Yad Ben-Zvi, 2005), 173–204.

10. Origen, *Cels.* 68.

11. Chrysostom among other things ridiculed the wearing of amulets to little avail; see *Homily on Colossians* 8.5. See N. Brox, "Magie und Aberglaube an den Anfängen des Christentums," *Trierer theologische Zeitschrift*, 83 (1974): 157–80; A. A. Barb, "The Survival of Magical Arts," in *The Conflict between Paganism and Christianity in the Fourth Century*, ed. A. Momigliano (Oxford: Clarendon, 1963), 100–25.

from the top down, not the ground up.[12] Publicly, Christian leaders denounced magic, but privately, magic was likely practiced by individuals who felt it was their only alternative to meet certain ends.

Thomas Mathews claims in his noteworthy text *The Clash of the Gods* that showing Jesus with a "wand" indicates he was clearly understood as a magician. In the context of healing and performing miracles while carrying a wand, Jesus has been intentionally transformed into a magician in visual art.[13] Such an argument is easily absorbed when approaching these images. The wand brands Jesus as a magician; hence, if Jesus looks like a magician, he is a magician.

Mathews's approach is problematic, since it reads current understandings of magic and magicians into the iconography. In addition, the term *wand* is a regrettable, distracting choice. "Wand" obviously implies magic and offers little in determining the stylistic element's origin and inclusion in visual art of this era. Observers are unavoidably influenced by the exploits of popular magicians waving wands and pulling rabbits out of hats or even by the more widespread visibility of the boy wizard Harry Potter in books and films. Christ pointing his staff and working wonders naturally suggests an image of a magician or wizard wielding a wand. Since these images show Christ performing miracles and supernatural feats, magical practice is a natural explanation for the wand's presence.[14] However, any argument involving magic is a red herring. *Magic* and *magician* were terms of slander and ridicule in Late Antiquity, and early Christians would not likely associate their savior with such a negative designation.[15] Moreover, Paul Corby Finney points out that there are no artistic

12. There likely is a class element to the message expressed in the art. Patrons who could afford sarcophagi were likely middle- to upper-middle-class citizens, while adherents to magic were among the lower, uneducated classes. See Paul Corby Finney, "Do You Think God Is a Magician?," in *Akten des Symposiums früchristliche Sarkophage* (Marburg: Deutches Archäologisches Institut, 1999), 107. It seems logical that magical use would be associated with the poor. The relative accessibility of spells made magic a viable alternative. Pliny noted the use of herbal remedies by the magi, claiming Pythagoras and Democritus borrowed from their treatments. *Natural History* 24.99-10; and in Christian Late Antiquity, see Jerome, *Life of Hilarion* 21, for the use of a love spell. Sarcophagus art is also a genre that allows the patron to express outwardly noble qualities and beliefs, religious and self-serving, and magic would not fit into that sphere.

13. Mathews, *Clash of Gods*, 59.

14. For opposing viewpoints, see Howard Clark Kee, *Medicine, Miracle and Magic in New Testament Times* (New York: Cambridge University Press, 1986), 112; Graham Twelftree, *Jesus the Exorcist* (Tübingen: Mohr Siebeck, 1993), 153.

15. The early church evidence ridiculing magic is fairly considerable. See Justin, *1 Apol.* 26 (critical edition: *Iustini Martyris Apologiae Pro Christianis* and *Dialogus cum Tryphone*, ed. M. Marcovich [Berlin: De Gruyter, 2005], 69–71); Irenaeus, *Against Heresies* 1.13, 2.31.2; Origen, *Cels.* 1.68. For magic as the

renderings of magicians in existence from Late Antiquity.[16] Images of purported magicians possibly existed; however, there were no known images of a magician in the act of exercising his trade.[17] There was no precedent for such an image in Late Antique art.

If Jesus actually were being portrayed as a magician, he would be performing exorcisms or providing love spells and incantations. None of these images, even gospel scenes of Jesus performing exorcisms, were in widespread existence.[18] Additionally, there is no convincing evidence in any remnant of the papyri that indicates a Late Antique magician would use a wand as a contemporary viewer would envision it. Late Antique magicians were not akin to popular iterations of magicians today, with an emphasis on wand use. Instead, exorcisms, certain healings, and love spells were the tasks of the day for the ordinary magician. These tasks focused on proper vocalization and technique, not the use of an external tool like a wand. Thus, the wand does not reveal Jesus as a magician, since the wand was not primary for the magician in Late Antiquity. Wand-like instruments are mentioned in the papyri. Certain spells in the papyri prescribed holding sprigs of laurel or an ebony staff; however, the laurel must be leafy, and the staff must be shifted from hand to hand while properly saying the spell.[19] Even when sprigs or accessories are mentioned in the papyri, they are not tools that procure the magical effect.[20] The instruments do not seem to play a primary role. Magicians relied upon the proper vocalization

work of demons, see Tertullian, *The Soul* 57.7; Eusebius, *Against Hierocles* 26. Chrysostom ridiculed the wearing of amulets to little avail in *Homily on Colossians* 8.5. Also see Harold Remus, *Pagan-Christian Conflict over Miracle in the Second Century* (Cambridge, MA: Philadelphia Patristic Foundation, 1983), 56; N. Brox, "Magie und Aberglaube an den Anfängen des Christentums," *Trierer theologische Zeitschrift* 83 (1974): 157–80.

16. Paul Corby Finney rebuts Mathews in "Do You Think God Is a Magician?," 106. Finney simply answers that Late Antique art does not include a tradition of depicting a magician doing his job.

17. One possible image of a magician is Alexander Severus's bust of Apollonius in his domestic shrine, although the *Historia Augusta* is a widely criticized source. However, even this mention warrants some consideration, since it treats the existence of imagery. *Life of Severus Alexander* 29 (*Historia Augusta* LCL vol. 140, trans. David Magie (Cambridge, MA: Harvard University Press, 1924).

18. The nearest example is a fifth-century ivory in the Louvre depicting Jesus casting the evil spirit into the pigs from Mark 5. See Finney, "Do You Think God Is a Magician?," fig. 40.2.

19. *PGM* I.262-347. For a collection of spells in translation, see Hans Dieter Betz, ed. and trans., *The Greek Magical Papyri in Translation, Including the Demotic Spells* (Chicago: University of Chicago Press, 1986);. Similarly, Philostratus rebutted any accusation of magic against Apollonius by listing the charges against him, revealing no indication of wand use (Philostratus, *Life* 1.2). See Lucian's description of a proper incantation in *Lover of Lies* 16. The "Syrian" is not Christ, but likely a contemporary of Lucian's. Also see Fritz Graf, *Magic in the Ancient World*, trans. Franklin Philip (Cambridge, MA: Harvard University Press, 1997), 78–79.

and physical execution mandated by the spell in order to procure the desired effect, not the use of an external tool like a wand.[21]

The lack of evidence in ancient sources may lead one to conclude that the staff in Christian art bears no association with magic. However, that distinction cannot be so strongly presented regarding the visual art. The presence of this stylistic attribute suggests some type of "power" that Christ is performing.

When I present these images to students, they instantly make the connection to the popular Harry Potter series of books, where the boy wizard and his friends utilize wands. Perhaps an early Christian audience would make a similar connection that the wand is an indication of power—not the power of a street magician in antiquity, but power nonetheless. Moses was certainly understood as a worker of wonders, of miracles, and in these images, Jesus is in line with Moses. The distinction between magic and miracle was not so disconnected; the fact that second-century apologists so vehemently distinguished Jesus' wonders as something other than magic suggests that understanding.[22] While the wand may not reveal Jesus as a magician specifically, it does resonate in the imagination of the viewer. And the tool Jesus uses symbolizes his divine power and his connection to the wonders of Moses.

THE STAFF IN THE ICONOGRAPHY

In text and image, Christ's use of the staff is always in the performance of healings or miracles. There is no scriptural evidence in the gospels of Christ making use of such a staff in any of his miracles or healings. Instead, Christ heals through physical touch or verbal command. In early Christian art, Christ was portrayed as healing and working miracles through physical touch with his hands or with his staff. The staff is utilized in images of Christ raising the dead, most prominently in the raising of Lazarus, the widow's son at Nain, Jairus's daughter, and Christ as Ezekiel in the Valley of the Dry Bones.[23] In the nature

20. Wormwood or myrtle branches are also mentioned in the papyri (PGM II.22; I.73), but they are recipes of the spell either ground up or shaken, and are not similar to the wand use attached to Circe or captured in the Christian art.

21. PGM I.262-347.

22. See note 15 above.

23. Lazarus occurs on sixty-five examples of Roman sarcophagi (1,042 pieces) and twenty-three times on examples from Gaul and North Africa (649 pieces). See G. Bovini and Hugo Brandenburg, *Reportorium der Christlich-Antiken Sarkophage*, Band I, *Rom und Ostia*, ed. F. W. Deichmann (Wiesbaden: F. Steiner, 1967), pt. 3, 123; Brigitte Christern-Briesenick, *Reportorium der Christlich-Antiken Sarkophage*, Band III, *Frankreich, Algerien, Tunesien*, ed. T. Ulbert (Wiesbaden: F. Steiner, 2003), 302. The widow's son and Jairus's daughter occur in sixteen examples in the Roman material and in eight examples from Gaul

miracles, images of the wedding at Cana prominently feature the use of Christ's staff. In some examples, the images of Christ and the staff have been damaged; however, these images all display some type of staff use in the performance of the miracle.

The staff is recognizable as Christ's miracle-working tool in catacomb scenes of the raising of Lazarus (Figures 3 and 28–29). In third- and fourth-century catacomb images of Christ raising Lazarus, the staff appears in a majority of the scenes.[24] In the "Red Cubiculum" of the catacomb of Domitilla, the staff is visibly perceptible in the Lazarus scene. In this instance, Lazarus is housed within a carved *aediculum*, mummified without any discernible facial features. Christ, using his staff, touches the *aediculum* of Lazarus, beckoning him to renewed life. On the opposite arch of the arcosolium is a representation of Moses striking the rock, recreating the miracle performed in Exod. 17:1-7. Moses is depicted quite like Jesus in dress and style as he touches the rock with his miracle-working staff, a mirror image of Jesus' instrument.

These same two images are incorporated in a wall painting in the fourth-century catacomb painting under the Vigna Massimo (Figure 3). Moses striking the rock and Jesus touching the *aediculum* of Lazarus appear dressed in similar guise. The two images are not as balanced as in Domitilla. Daniel, Noah, and the magi are included in the wall painting along with Moses and Jesus. In addition, directly next to Moses striking the rock is a representation of Jesus dividing the loaves, touching the baskets with his staff. In the catacombs, the image of Moses striking the rock is not the only one of Moses' miracles that

---

and North Africa. See Bovini and Brandenburg, *Repertorium*, Band I, pt. 3, 123; Christern-Briesenick, *Repertorium*, Band III, 301–302. Cana appears forty-four times in the Roman body of evidence, and in the Gallic and North African evidence, the miracle appears twenty-one times. See Bovini and Brandenburg, *Repertorium*, Band I, pt. 3, 122; and Christern-Briesenick, *Repertorium*, Band III, 303. There are two rare exceptions of the Lazarus scene on relief sculpture that eschew staff use: First, on a sarcophagus frontal in the Vatican Museo Pio Cristiano (inv. 31546), Christ grasps Lazarus from the tomb in a similar manner as the image of Prometheus shaping man on a sarcophagus in Naples. See Robin M. Jensen, "The Trinity and the Economy of Salvation on Two Fourth-Century Sarcophagi," *JECS* 7, no. 4 (Winter 1999): 529–49. The other example is from Aire-sur-L'adour; the early-fourth-century relief features Christ gesturing toward the mummified Lazarus. See Christern-Briesenick, *Repertorium*, Band III, 6.

24. J. Partyka speaks specifically to the prominence of the *virga* in the catacomb representations in the third and fourth centuries. See J. Partyka, *La résurrection de Lazare dans les monuments funéraires des nécropolis Chrétiennes à Rome* (Warsaw: Zakland Archeologi Sródzimnomorskiej, 1993), 42–46, 106. While this article refers to two specific fourth-century catacomb examples, other third-century examples include the raising of Lazarus in the catacomb of Callistus and the catacomb of Priscilla. See ibid., 115, 171.

is rendered to foreshadow Jesus. In the Via Latina Catacomb, the crossing of the Red Sea with Moses utilizing his staff is featured twice, with each image corresponding to an image of Jesus raising Lazarus.[25]

Cognate representations of Christ on relief sculpture depict a similarly clad Jesus performing his miracles. On the sarcophagus of Marcus Claudianus, Christ the Miracle Worker is on full display. Christ is portrayed performing the Cana miracle, dividing loaves, healing the blind man, and raising Lazarus. On this particular sarcophagus, the scene of raising Lazarus diverges from the catacomb examples, as Jesus is depicted with a woman (possibly Martha) at his feet (Figure 39). On the Vatican relief sculptures, Christ is seen using the staff to raise Lazarus, change water to wine, and raise a prone figure to life, perhaps the widow's son at Nain (Figures 41–42). Christ is consistently portrayed as youthful, clean-shaven with short, curly hair, and dressed in a robe. In these portrayals, Jesus utilizes the staff as in the catacomb scenes to perform his miracles, particularly in scenes of raising the dead and the nature miracles such as the wedding at Cana. Christ's distinctive use of the staff is even more apparent on the funerary reliefs. With multiple miracle scenes carved onto a large piece of marble or travertine, it is apparent that the staff is not a symbol but an important element in the unfolding action. Whether the relief sculpture shows him raising the dead or enacting a nature miracle, Christ grasps the staff, points and touches its intended object.

As omnipresent as the staff is in scenes of raising the dead, it is absent in most representations of Christ healing the blind man, the woman with the issue of blood, and the paralytic. In the healing scenes, Christ heals through vocal command or physical touch. The evidence of Christian relief sculpture demonstrates that the staff is most often employed in the raising of the dead and the nature miracles.[26] With the artistic evidence in mind, it is difficult to make any firm conclusions differentiating miracle scenes involving Christ's

25. In the Via Latina Catacomb, the images reside in Cubiculum C and Cubiculum O. See Antonia Ferrua, *The Unknown Catacomb: A Unique Discovery of Early Christian Art* (Florence: Geddes and Grosset, 1990), 170; and see Ferrua, *Le Pitture della Nuova Catacombs di Via Latina*, Monumenti di antichita cristiana, ser. 2, vol. 8 (Vatican City: Pontifical Commission of Sacred Archeology, 1960). William Tronzo argued that since Moses is depicted adjacent to the image of Lazarus, the scene of Jesus raising Lazarus in Cubiculum C was an alteration of a scene depicting Joshua entering Israel with the twelve tribes. This seems unlikely, given that the instrument Christ bears was also wielded by Moses, not Joshua, in cognate scenes. Regardless, the motivation behind such an alteration reveals the close connection in Christian art between the figures of Jesus and Moses. Tronzo, *The Via Latina Catacomb: Imitation and Discontinuity in Fourth-Century Roman Painting* (University Park: Penn State University Press, 1986), 53–56; and see Enrico Josi, "Découverte d'une série de peintures dans un hypogée de la voie Latine," *Comptes rendus de l'Académie des Inscriptions et Belles-Lettres* (1956): 275–79.

hands from those where he uses his staff. Raising the dead was not something that physicians or healing cults routinely performed, which set Jesus apart from these groups.[27] In early Christian art, showing Jesus as unique was a likely aim whether he was portrayed performing miracles using his hands or his staff.

THE STAFF IN CLASSICAL AND EARLY CHURCH WRITINGS

Staffs and staff-like instruments are well documented in classical and early church texts. A "wand" or "staff" was called a *rabdos* in Greek or a *lituus, baculum,* or *virga* in Latin. The word *rabdos* initially referred to a supple or pliant twig, while a *lituus* suggested a more rigid implement.[28] The Roman *lituus* was connected to religion and religious performances, as it was specifically used by the college of priests, the augurs, in the operation of their rituals. Livy spoke of a ritual involving a *lituus*: "The augur seated himself on Numa's left; his head covered and in his right hand he held a crooked staff without a knot which they called a *lituus*. . . . Then, transferring the crook to his left hand and placing his head on Numa's head he prayed."[29] The curved *lituus* that the augurs utilized in their rituals is still evident in Christianity today, witnessed by the curved head of the bishop's crosier (occasionally still called by its Latin name). A *baculum,* another term for a walking staff, referred to the ever-present staff that symbolized the itinerant Cynic philosophers.[30] Both the *lituus* and the *baculum* became symbols of their bearers, the augurs and the philosophers. However

26. See note 12 above. For the division of loaves, the miracle appears in the Roman evidence eighty-four times; in the Gallic and North African evidence, twelve times. Bovini and Brandenburg, *Repertorium,* Band I, pt. 3, 122; Christern-Briesenick, *Repertorium,* Band III, 299. In the miracle of the division of the loaves, the staff is not as uniformly depicted as in the Cana miracle, instead exhibiting the miracle-working quality of Christ's physical touch through his hands.

27. Christ raising the dead recalls his competition with the healing cult of Asclepius, as it has more to do with divine authority than with healing. Asclepius was also known for raising the dead. However, Asclepius was killed by Zeus for his act of resurrection; he did not have authority over life and death. Early church writers knew this quite well, as this lack of authority was the tactic of choice when deriding Asclepius. Justin, Clement, Origen, and Tertullian all point out that Asclepius's downfall was due to his lack of authority, since he was not really a divine agent. Justin, *1 Apol.* 21 (Marcovich, 63.2-6); Clement, *Ex.* 2.24; Origen, *Cels.* 3.22 (PG 11, 944C); Tertullian, *To the Heathen* 2.14.45 (CSEL 20.127). Also in Arnobius, *Against the Pagans* 4.24 (CSEL 4.161); and Lactantius, *Inst.* 1.19.3 (CSEL 19.71).

28. See F. J. M. De Waele, *The Magic Staff or Rod in Greco-Italian Antiquity* (The Hague: Drukkerij Erasmus, 1927), 21.

29. Livy, *History of Rome* 1.18.6-10, in *Roman Religion: A Sourcebook,* ed. Valerie Warrior (Newburyport, MA:Focus, 2002), 18–19.

30. Zanker calls the Cynic *baculum* a "club," and points out that it reflected their patron Herakles, whose strength, endurance, and travels mimic their own, and the Cynics often needed it for protection.

the *lituus* and the *baculum* were not instrumental in the performance of their divination, rituals, or teachings. They were accessories, while the staff of Christ appears to be an integral tool. In Christian art, it does not appear that the staff of Christ intends to recall the *lituus* or the *baculum*; however, the mind of an early Christian viewer may leap to such an association.

Staffs or wands also appear as attributes of mythical characters in the Greco-Roman pantheon. In Pausanias's book on his travels to Corinth, he describes the statue of Asclepius in the temple as holding a *bakteria*, a lesser-used Greek term for "staff."[31] Asclepius's staff is readily noticeable in imagery, as it is most often entwined with a serpent. Even in the rare cases that Asclepius's staff does not include a wrapped serpent, it appears as a ruddy walking staff.[32] As in the cases of the Cynic *baculum* and the augurs' *lituus*, Asclepius never utilized his staff in the same manner as Christ in the healing and miracle images. Christ is physical with his staff, touching his recipients directly. Thus, the staff of Asclepius bears no relation to the staff of Christ.[33]

Homer's *Odyssey* introduced the story of Circe's transformation of men into pigs, connecting an act of magic to the use of a type of wand: "And when they had drunk she turned them into pigs by a stroke of her wand (*rabdos*)."[34] It was a popular story, as not only Vergil but Ovid's *Metamorphoses* described Circe's use of a wand (*virga*) to transform Odysseus's soldiers into pigs. However, in both Homer and Vergil, the wand is not actually connected to magical practice; rather, both authors stress that "drugs" were the catalyst for Circe's magic.[35] Given this emphasis, it seems unlikely that Christ's miracle-working staff reflects Circe's wand.

See Paul Zanker, *The Mask of Socrates: The Image of the Intellectual in Antiquity* (Berkeley: University of California Press,1996), 265–66.

31. Pausanias, *Description of Greece* 2.27.2.

32. John Boardman et al., eds., *Lexicon iconographicum mythologiae classicae* (Zürich: Artemis, 1981–97). See the section by B. Holzmann on "Asklepios," 2:863–97, pls. 631–68.

33. Hermes is another mythical character who employs a type of wand. Homer refers to the *rabdos* of Hermes. *Iliad* 24.343; *Odyssey* 5.47; 24.2. The *caduceus* of Hermes, expressed in art as a scepter marked by two intertwined serpents, appears to be more of an accessory than a tool of the god. Hermes's instrument was occasionally noted as a *kerukeion* in Greek, deriving from the word for "herald" (*kerux*), denoting his vocation. See De Waele, *The Magic Staff*, 29–75; and for an early church reference, see Prudentius, *Against Symmachus* 1.89-91. See Emma J. Edelstein and Ludwig Edelstein, *Asclepius: A Collection and Interpretation of the Testimonies* (Baltimore: Johns Hopkins Press, 1945), 2:113, n. 10; O. Kern, *Die Religion der Greichen* (Berlin: Weidmannsche Buchhandlung, 1926–38), 2:19. See also Philip Esler and Ronald Piper, *Lazarus, Mary and Martha: Social Scientific Approaches to the Gospel of John* (Minneapolis: Fortress Press, 2006), 138–41, who argue that the staff recalls Hermes, albeit without much support.

34. Homer, *The Odyssey* 10.293.

In early church documents, the *virga* is mentioned as an attribute denoting power and authority. In the *Passion of the Holy Martyrs Perpetua and Felicity*, Perpetua mentions a vision in which a huge man approaches her, bearing a "wand like an athletic trainer" (*et ferens virgam quasi lanista*).[36] A *virga* was memorably referenced in terms of protection and comfort in Psalm 23: "Your rod (*virga*) and your staff, they comfort me." Augustine commented on this Psalm that the "rod" was more for discipline and the "staff" mentioned in the Psalm was for protection.[37] In a sermon on Psalm 45, Augustine compared the scepter wielded by an enthroned God to a "rod of direction," as he tells his listeners that it is Christ who rules with an iron and inflexible rod.[38] To further confuse the philological issue, there is not much uniformity in translating *virga* as a "staff," "wand," or "rod."[39] Augustine's mentor Ambrose compared the use of the rod of Moses in Exodus to the power of Christ's words in the institution of the Lord's Supper.[40] Regardless of the terminology, early church authors believed the *virga* likely represented power, authority, and even divine authority.[41] The more important question is what artists intended Christ to

35. Vergil, *Aeneid* 7.185-190; Ovid, *Metamorphoses* 14.278. This is consistent with the actual practice of magic.

36. *Passion of the Holy Martyrs Perpetua and Felicity* 10.8. Hilarianus also orders Perpetua's father to be beaten with a rod (*et virga percussus est*; 6.5). Critical edition: W. H. Shewring, *The Passion of SS. Perpetua and Felicity: A New Edition and Translation of the Latin Text together with the Sermons of S. Augustine upon These Saints* (London: Sheed and Ward, 1931). Latin text and English translation: Herbert Musurillo, *Acts of the Christian Martyrs* (Oxford: Clarendon, 1972), xxv–xxvii, 106–31.

37. Augustine, *Sermons on the Psalms* 23.4 (trans. author). Note Augustine's use of *virga*: "*Virga* tua et *baculus* tuus, ipsa me consulate sunt. Disciplina tua tamquam *virga* ad gregem ouium, et tamquam *baculus* iam ad grandiores filios" (CSEL 93.332-333).

38. Augustine, *Serm. Ps.* 44.18 (CCSL 38.506). Augustine used the term *virga*; Gregory of Nyssa also mentioned the staff of Moses in *Life of Moses* 2.36; 2.124.

39. Earlier historians and scholars have interpreted the staff in art with some degree of divergence. Josef Wilpert simply identified the staff with its Latin title as *virga virtutis*, the mark of a wonder worker, while Bovini and Brandenburg referred to the staff simply as a "wand." Josef Wilpert, *Le pitture delle catacombe romane*, Testo I (Rome: Pontificio istituto di archaeologica Cristiana, 1903), 41; *I Sarcophagi cristiani antichi*, Testo I (Rome: Pontificio istituto di archaeologica cristiana, 1929), 41; and see Christern-Briesenick, *Reportorium*, Band III, 53. Martine Dulaey believes that the Christians appropriated the *virga* as a symbol denoting power, see Dulaey, "Le symbole de la baguette dans l'art paléochrétien," *Revue des études augustiniennes* 19, nos. 1–2 (1973): 12. L. de Bruyne also reflects upon the numerous instances of the "baguette" and its significance with other symbols in "Les 'lois' de l'art paléochrétien," *RAC* 39, nos. 1–2 (1963): 27.

40. Ambrose, *On the Mysteries* 9.51.

41. L. de Bruyne, "L'imposition des mains dans l'art chrétien ancien," *RAC* 20, nos. 1–4 (1943): 129–30, 196, where he calls the instrument "*virga thaumaturga*." He directly related the use of the *virga* to

represent whey they depicted him working healings and miracles with such an instrument.

Jesus the Philosopher

Most recently, in the papal encyclical *Spe Salvi* (Saved in Hope) Pope Benedict XVI refers to the staff in early Christian relief sculpture. Benedict identifies two consistent themes that appear in Christian sarcophagi: the Good Shepherd and, in his words, the philosopher:

> The figure of Christ is interpreted on ancient sarcophagi principally by two images: the philosopher and the shepherd. . . . Towards the end of the third century, on the sarcophagus of a child in Rome, we find for the first time, in the context of the resurrection of Lazarus, the figure of Christ as the true philosopher, holding the Gospel in one hand and the philosopher's traveling staff in the other. With his staff, he conquers death; the Gospel brings the truth that itinerant philosophers had searched for in vain. In this image, which then became a common feature of sarcophagus art for a long time, we see clearly what both educated and simple people found in Christ: he tells us who man truly is and what a man must do in order to be truly human. He shows us the way, and this way is the truth. He himself is both the way and the truth, and therefore he is also the life which all of us are seeking. He also shows us the way beyond death; only someone able to do this is a true teacher of life.[42]

Benedict classifies the staff in these early depictions of Christ as the "staff" of the philosopher. Christ is therefore represented as the true philosopher, exhibiting the proper mode of life, and is the teacher of the future resurrection.

Benedict's statement surmises that the early images of Christ were influenced by the iconography and the importance of philosophers in Late Antiquity.[43] There was a tradition within early Christian art of depicting Christ

the miracles Christ wrought by hand. Bruyne centers his argument on pertinent scenes such as the healing of the paralytic. However, for his argument on the significance of the imposition of hands, he focuses on the Terme fragment of Jesus (Figure 35 noting its emphasis on touch, without commenting on the connection between Jesus and Asclepius that Mathews exploits. See Mathews, *Clash of Gods*, 69–70.

42. Benedict XVI, *Spe Salvi*, 6 (November 30, 2007).

43. The stick indicates the peripatetic lifestyle of the philosopher, but it does not clearly represent what school the figure is mean to evoke. In fact, on philosophers' sarcophagi, it is not uncommon to find

as a philosopher, thereby placing Christianity and its chief deity in an honored tradition, and thus legitimizing Christianity as a philosophy instead of a maligned superstition. Images of Christ seated while surrounded by disciples or of Christ standing while holding a scroll in the gesture of speech are meant to portray Christ as a teacher of wisdom.[44] In the scenes of Christ's miracles, however, the actions of this "philosopher" are not those of a rudimentary philosopher, but a very special type of philosopher. Jesus exemplifies Pope Benedict's understanding of Jesus as a philosopher unlike ordinary philosophers since he teaches humans the truth about life and death. Benedict calls the staff that Christ uses a "philosopher's staff" with which he conquers death. From examining the imagery, the figure of Christ is defeating death with the staff in the raising of the dead, but he is performing other tasks as well. If Christ is to be interpreted as a philosopher, then the images of his healings and miracles exhibit him as a philosopher far from ordinary.

Christ is thus being portrayed not just as any philosopher, as on earlier Roman sarcophagi, but as an extraordinary philosopher, a figure with special power. Christ is no average philosopher. Philosophers were earthly wisdom teachers, but a teacher like Christ performs actions that reveal his attunement with the divine. Origen commented on this matter in his remarks against Celsus: "Even philosophers who have sometimes been taken in by it [magic] may read what has been written by Moiragenes of the memoirs of Apollonius of Tyana, the magician and philosopher. In them the author, who is not a Christian but a philosopher, observed that some not undistinguished philosophers were convinced by the magic of Apollonius, although when they went to him they regarded him merely as a charlatan."[45]

Origen was recalling the work of Moiragenes, who regarded Apollonius as a magician, and Philostratus's third-century biography that depicted Apollonius as a wonder worker and philosopher, not a common magician but a theurgist.[46] Origen pointed out that it was not uncommon for philosophers to recognize magicians such as Apollonius as figures who walk the line between philosophy and magic. In fact, Origen claimed philosophers found Apollonius's tricks to

---

several schools represented on the same sarcophagus, sending a message of respect and admiration of all schools, rather than specific association. Zanker, *Mask of Socrates*, 273, where he cites the sarcophagus of the soldier Peregrinus, fig. 147.

44. See Robin M. Jensen, *Understanding Early Christian Art* (New York: Routledge, 2000), 44–46; and Robin M. Jensen, *Face to Face: Portraits of the Divine in Early Christianity* (Minneapolis: Fortress Press, 2005), 44.

45. Origen, *Cels.* 6.41 (Chadwick).

46. Philostratus attacks Moiragenes's characterization of Apollonius in *Life* 1.3; 3.41.

be the work of a charlatan.[47] Philostratus attempted to brand Apollonius as a philosopher, at one point utilizing the words of Vespasian, who referred to Apollonius as an esteemed philosopher.[48] There seems to be a distinction between the works of wonder performed by a described "philosopher," as Philostratus deems Apollonius or as the early Christians labeled Christ, and the incantations of a common magician.[49]

Apollonius and Christ were philosophers no doubt, but it was not their most defining characteristic. Their ability to heal and work miracles was. The designation of miracle worker occupied a place in the hierarchy above magicians and at least commingling with philosophers. Miracle working contained elements of philosophy and described other Christian figures such as Martin of Tours and Gregory Thaumaturgus, whose legends included miracles and healings. In the fourth century, Severus's *Life of Martin* and Nyssa's *Life of Gregory Thaumaturgus* make it apparent that these figures who worked miracles and healings were distinct miracle men, connected with Christian philosophy, yet in a category that distinguished them from any ordinary teachers. Nyssa called Gregory the "Teacher," as his ability as a philosopher was consistently recorded, and his name Thaumaturgus is a derivative of *theurgy* and translates as "wonder worker." Gregory is not described as an ordinary philosopher; he is directly compared to Moses, whose philosophy included works of miracles.[50] Nyssa also does not include a staff among Gregory's attributes as a philosopher, except when he is emphatically comparing Gregory to Moses, implying that the staff is more indicative of Moses's rod than a philosopher's staff.

In certain pieces of art the sole correlation between the staff bearer figure and a philosopher is the occasional depiction of a listening audience.[51] In Roman iconography, philosophers were depicted among students but usually

47. True philosophers were deemed immune to magic, as Plotinus stated that the wise man is "incapable of being affected in his soul by enchantment, and his rational part would not be affected." Plotinus, *Enneads* 4.4.43.

48. Philostratus, *Life* 8.7.

49. Philostratus's efforts to cloak Apollonius as a philosopher were largely unsuccessful. Apollonius was thought of as a magician by other magicians, and as a wonder worker, but not as a definitive philosopher. The papyri indicated that magicians invoked Apollonius. *PGM* XIa.

50. See Gregory of Nyssa, *Life of St. Gregory Thaumaturgus*, PG 46.908D. Theurgy as a category of distinction also applies to Gregory. Nyssa calls him the "Great One" or "Teacher," Sozomen's *Hist. eccl.* 7.27, written in the early fifth century, also mentions Gregory.

51. See the unique piece of relief sculpture residing in the Museo Nazionale Romano delle Terme that portrays not just any philosopher but Christ as a philosopher, preaching to his followers. John Dominic Crossan has insisted that the fact Jesus holds the scroll in his hand and is dressed in such a way intentionally recalls Cynic philosophers. The bare chest and clutched scroll do not necessarily support

with a scroll or codex indicating the contemplative life, and they were often seated.[52] In one sarcophagus fragment from the fourth century now at the Vatican, a figure is depicted as a philosopher seated and studying, flanked by students (Figure 45). On another early Christian sarcophagus fragment now at Arles, Christ is depicted as a philosopher seated with a scroll surrounded on either side with his disciples (Figure 46). It was not uncommon to have Christ appear as a philosopher, indicating Christianity as the "true" philosophy.[53] However, there are no examples in iconography of a philosopher healing or performing miracles, and for good reason. Philosophers in Late Antiquity were not in the business of healing or performing miraculous works, especially resuscitating the dead. Thus, any connection of the miracle-working staff to philosophy is a leap.

The only link that can be drawn between the philosopher's staff and Christ's staff is that they are similar in appearance, but they are not similar in the way they are used. The staff of the philosopher is a symbol of knowledge and wisdom. In the Christian imagery, Christ's staff is a tool used to perform his healing and miracles.[54] Christ healing and performing miracles with the staff may recall Apollonius, but this is not the primary intention of the inclusion of the staff. In Philostratus's fervent desire to cast Apollonius as a miracle-working philosopher, he describes no type of staff or similar instrument in the action of Apollonius's miracles.

The Staff of Moses

The staff is the symbol that can be used to unlock the special significance of these images and answer what type of message the early Christians desired to transmit. Part of the answer can be found in pursuing the miracle worker who

such a conclusion. See Mathews, *Clash of Gods*, figs. 48–49 for the image; Crossan, *Jesus: A Revolutionary Biography*, v.

52. See Jensen, *Face to Face*, 44. As support, Jensen cites other visual evidence of philosophers depicted seated.

53. For example, a statue of Christ seated at the Palazzo Massimo alle Terme, Rome, dated 350–375 CE is the "philosopher" type. Also see Justin, *1 Apol.* 5, 44, 46, referring to Greek philosophers such as Socrates as pre-Christian (Marcovich, 38-9; 94-5; 97).

54. However, the staff can also be understood as a symbol of power and authority. The longer version of the staff is also utilized in several portrayals of the gods. Included in several depictions of Zeus/Jupiter enthroned, the staff appears to be a symbol of divine power, especially in an enthronement context. In a fifth-century representation from Vergil's *Aeneid* that now resides at the Vatican Museum, several gods are depicted holding a long, narrow staff. See Mathews, *Clash of Gods*, fig. 75.

did use such an instrument in his miracles. The images of Christ wielding the staff bear a direct correlation with the theurgist Moses.

SCRIPTURAL EVIDENCE

The catacomb paintings in Domitilla and under the Vigna Massimo depict Jesus as a wonder worker like Moses in dress and style, and the two men use similar tools to perform their miracles (Figures 3, 29). Juxtaposing Moses with Jesus was a well-established theme in Scripture. The infancy narratives in the gospels of Matthew and Luke both establish the prophetic connection from the Old Testament to Jesus. The Gospel of Matthew in particular uses familiar elements from the Exodus story to link Jesus to Moses.[55] In the first chapter of the gospel, the author presents his genealogy exhibiting Jesus as a descendent of Abraham and David, as well as connecting Isaiah's Emmanuel prophecy to Jesus.[56] The second chapter of Matthew's narrative illustrates the connection between Moses and Jesus by attaching motifs from Exodus to the holy family. Matthew presents Herod's slaughter of the innocents as parallel to the circumstances of Moses's birth in Exodus.[57] Matthew's flight of the holy family places Jesus within Egypt in order to demonstrate the child as fulfilling the prophecy from Exod. 4:22: "Out of Egypt I have called my son." Matthew also states that, following Herod's death, the family went to live in Nazareth. This forges a possible connection to Moses coming of age in Midian, because Moses and Jesus are figures who mature safely in obscurity until their divine calling urges them into action.

There appears to be a strong desire to depict Jesus as a New Moses in Scripture. Matthew's gospel couches Jesus as Moses by peppering his infancy narrative with Exodus references.[58] In addition, actions such as signs, wonders, and miracles helped make this connection more resolute. In Deut. 34:11, after the death of Moses, that narrator provides a type of eulogy, saying, "Never since

---

55. For more detail on this, see Dale Allison, *The New Moses: A Matthean Typology* (Minneapolis: Fortress Press, 1993), 141–65. Allison also cites the doors of Santa Sabina as evidence of juxtaposing Jesus and Moses artistically. Ibid., 105. And see John Lierman, *The New Testament Moses: Christian Perceptions of Moses and Israel in the Setting of Jewish Religion* (Tübingen: Mohr Siebeck, 2004), 55.

56. Matt. 1:18; Isa. 7:14.

57. Exod. 1:22.

58. The connections do not end in Matthew's infancy narrative. In Matthew 8–9, Jesus performs ten miracles, akin to the ten plagues of Exodus 7–12. And Moses's name is offered in Matt. 8:4: "Offer the gift that Moses commanded." In Matthew's chapters the wonders of Jesus are displayed, recalling the wonders of Moses. See John Gager, *Moses in Greco-Roman Paganism* (Nashville: Abingdon, 1972), 134; Allison, *New Moses*, 208–209.

has there arisen a prophet in Israel like Moses, whom the Lord knew face-to-face. He was unequaled for all the signs and wonders that the Lord sent him to perform in the land of Egypt."[59]

Moses was clearly regarded as the preeminent worker of signs and wonders from Scripture. Arguably, Moses and Aaron use a staff to perform magic in his competition with Pharaoh's magicians in Exodus 7. But even in the examples from Exodus, Moses's actions were indicative of his divine authority (as in Exodus 4), greater than any earthly magic. And early church authors including Origen understood Moses as a wonder worker and connected to God, not as a magician. The gospel writers stressed the vocation of Jesus as a miracle worker like Moses in their texts. In the gospels, the advent of Jesus' ministry is usually marked by a wondrous act.[60] From the time of Deuteronomy, there would be no one like Moses until Christ arrives.

However, the authors of Matthew and Luke–Acts arguably establish a more perceptible connection between Moses and Jesus than the other gospels. The author of the Gospel of Luke and the Acts of the Apostles performed a similar mandate as Matthew in depicting Jesus as Moses. While Matthew's connection is made prominent in his infancy narrative, Luke–Acts paints a more ambiguous correlation in different places throughout the narrative, and the connection to Moses extends to apostles such as Peter. In Luke's account of the transfiguration of Jesus on the mountain with Peter, John, and James as witnesses (9:28-36), the appearance of Jesus' face was altered. Such an alteration recalls Moses's transformation in Exod. 34:29-35, when Moses converses with God face-to-face, resulting in his facial alteration. In Luke's transfiguration, Jesus convenes directly with God, meets God face-to-face, and his face is distorted by the light ("the appearance of his face changed") while Moses and Elijah interact with Jesus and oversee the proceedings. Luke reports that Moses apparently spoke with Jesus about the task at hand: "They were speaking about his departure, which he was about to accomplish at Jerusalem."[61] This episode is not an exact replica of Exodus 34; however, the similarities perhaps indicate Jesus as Moses, even including Moses as a witness to Christ, as Luke foreshadows the exodus that Jesus accomplishes for the people of God through the crucifixion and resurrection.[62]

---

59. All scripture quotes are taken from the NRSV.

60. In the Synoptics, healings and miracles follow Jesus' baptism and calling of the first disciples. See Mark 1:29-31 for Peter's mother-in-law; Matt. 4:23; and Luke 4:38. In John following the prologue, Jesus begins his ministry with the Cana miracle in chapter 2.

61. Luke 9:30.

While Jesus is connected to Moses in the gospels, Acts continues the assertion by invoking Scripture. In Peter's address in Acts 3:22, he describes Jesus as a prophet like Moses, citing Deut. 18:15-19: "The Lord your God will raise up for you from your own people a prophet *like me* [Moses] (italics added). Thus, Jesus is Moses's successor, and by extension so are Peter and the apostles. Instead of deliverance to a promised land, Jesus the New Moses and subsequently Peter the New Moses offer deliverance to salvation. In Stephen's speech to the Sanhedrin in Acts 7:35-43, Jesus as the New Moses is again determined as Stephen recites the verse from Deuteronomy as well as several of the Exodus miracles involving Moses: "God will raise up a prophet for you from your own people." In this instance in Stephen's speech, the Moses connection is described through the lens of signs and wonders: "He led them out, having performed wonders and signs in Egypt, at the Red Sea, and in the wilderness for forty years." The proof of the Moses connection to Jesus was in the ability to perform miracles.

Moses' feats of wonder in Exodus were not the only miracles from Scripture that early Christians manipulated. The pericope of Num. 21:6-9 is referred to as the "brazen serpent" episode. In the text, Moses is leading the Israelites toward the Promised Land, but due to their persistent complaining, the Lord sent poisonous serpents among the people, and they bit the people, so that many Israelites died. The people came to Moses and said, "We have sinned by speaking against the Lord and against you; pray to the Lord to take away the serpents from us." So Moses prayed for the people. "And the Lord said to Moses, 'Make a poisonous serpent, and set it on a pole; and everyone who is bitten shall look at it and live.' So Moses made a serpent of bronze, and put it upon a pole; and whenever a serpent bit someone, that person would look at the serpent of bronze and live" (NRSV). In John's gospel, the author refers directly to the text in Numbers, connecting the serpent of Moses to the passion of Jesus: "And just as Moses lifted up the serpent in the wilderness, so must the Son of Man be lifted up, that whoever believes in him may have eternal life" (John 3:14-15).[63]

---

62. The Gospel of Luke may have Deuteronomy more in mind than Exodus when depicting a journeying Jesus who sacrifices himself on behalf of his people. This is akin to Deuteronomy's portrayal of Moses as one who delivers the people to the new land without seeing it for himself. See David P. Moessner, "Luke 9:1-50: Luke's Preview of the Journey of the Prophet Like Moses of Deuteronomy," *JBL* 102, no. 4 (1983): 575–605.

63. John's text provided the designation "the brazen serpent" to Moses' story. The serpent of Moses appears in many instances of early Christian art and becomes a popular theme in Renaissance painting, including a depiction in Michelangelo's Sistine Chapel. Tintoretto, Poussin, and Rubens all include representations of it in their repertoire.

In Christian art, the brazen serpent is represented often. The scene appears on a panel of the wooden doors of the church of Santa Sabina in Rome, erected around 432 CE. The relief panels include scenes from the Old and New Testaments, featuring one of the oldest known representations of the crucifixion. The doors of Santa Sabina have been restored, and not only have some panels been lost but the original order of the panels has been altered, given the obvious lack of chronology in the scenes represented.

One of the relief panels depicts scenes from Exodus, including the crossing of the Red Sea. At the bottom of the panel is an enigmatic image of Moses wielding the staff in front of another individual, with two snakes separating the figures (see Figure 43). This has been interpreted as a scene of the "brazen serpent" from Numbers; however, it could also be the scene of Moses and Aaron before pharaoh, and the rod turning into a serpent (Exod. 7:12). Remarkably, not far from this panel is an image of Christ performing the miracle at Cana, the division of the loaves, and the raising of Lazarus, all with a staff (Figure 44). The staff that Christ uses is the same instrument that Moses uses in his panel, and such a feature seemingly affirms their iconographic connection.[64] Whether the Santa Sabina panel depicts the brazen-serpent scene from Numbers or a miracle from Exodus does not detract from the strong link between the depiction of Jesus and Moses as miracle workers. The link between the two can be visually confirmed by observing the staff wielded by each figure. Still, the authors of such iconography were merely following the scriptural links between the two biblical icons.

Just as Moses performed signs and wonders (before Pharaoh, crossing the Red Sea, and in the wilderness such as the striking of the rock), so did Jesus. Early Christian art was following the emphatic connection between Jesus and Moses displayed in Scripture. Jesus and Peter brandishing their staffs, prominently featured in the Roman relief sculptures, were heirs to Moses. The gospel influence is illuminated in the ending of Luke's gospel with the appearance of the risen Jesus on the road to Emmaus. In Luke 24:27, Jesus

64. The brazen serpent appears on the reliquary casket of Brescia in a similar manner as on the doors of Santa Sabina (see figure 22). In this instance, the scene of Moses and the serpent is smaller than the scenes of Christ working miracles, but the staff they both utilize is unmistakably the same instrument. On the late-fourth-century casket, the serpent is entwined around a rod, while Moses is depicted next to it, gesturing toward the serpent with his staff. See Catherine Brown Tkacz, *The Key to the Brescia Casket: Typology and the Early Christian Imagination* (Paris: University of Notre Dame Press; Institut d'Etudes Augustiennes, 2001), 86. Her interpretation is influenced by W. F. Volbach, who reached the same conclusion in his *Early Christian Art* (New York: Abrams, 1962), 328. Interpreting it as a paradox to Christ' victory over death on the cross is far-fetched. There is no strong precedent for including this image from Daniel in Christian art.

reveals himself to his fellow travelers and begins to first-handedly connect the prophecies concerning his legitimacy: "Beginning with Moses and all the prophets, he interpreted to them the things about himself in all the scriptures." Thus, in Luke's version, Jesus begins talking about himself by invoking Moses. Jesus' miracles prove Moses's words in Deuteronomy true, and in early Christian art, the connection indubitably shows that Jesus is a "likeness" of Moses, down to the common attribute of the staff.

For the gospel writers, Scripture confirmed the connection between Moses and Jesus, such as the endangered child motif involving the birth of Moses in Exodus 1–2 and Matthew 2, and the claim in Deut. 18:15-19 that God will raise up another prophet after Moses. However, mere prophetic connections were not as convincing as working miracles. It seems the key element that confirmed Jesus or Peter as a New Moses was the ability to perform miracles, highlighted in all four gospels and Acts.[65] This is perhaps made clearer by patristic-era writers: "That Jesus was indeed he who, according to the prophecy of Moses, was expected to come; since, indeed, as Moses wrought signs and miracles, so also did Jesus."[66]

LATE ANTIQUE AND EARLY CHURCH EVIDENCE

Moses was certainly depicted as the preeminent Jewish leader in writings from Late Antiquity. Philo of Alexandria wrote a two-volume work devoted to Moses, *De Vita Mosis*, where he portrayed Moses as a divine king.[67] More importantly, Moses was known in Late Antiquity as a Jewish wonder worker, a status conferred on him by critics such as Pliny and Celsus. Eusebius even went so far as to call Moses a contributor to the Isis cult, emphasizing his wonder-working ability.[68] Moses was also referenced in several places in the magical papyri. In one incantation, the magician was supposed to take on the persona of

65. For starters (and in no way an exhaustive list), see Jesus healing the blind man in the Synoptics at Mark 10:46-52; Matt. 20:29-34; Luke 18:35-43; Jesus healing the woman with the issue of blood at Mark 5:21-34; Matt. 9:18-26; Luke 8:40-48; the division of loaves at Mark 6:41; 8:19; Matt. 14:20; 15:36; Luke 9:16; John 6:11; John's Cana miracle and raising of Lazarus from the dead in 11:1-46; and Peter's shadow healing people at Acts 4:7. See also Acts 5:12-16: "Now many signs and wonders were done among the people by the hands of the apostles."

66. Pseudo-Clement, *Rec.* 1:57 (*ANF* 7.92).

67. See Wayne Meeks, "The Prophet-King," in *Religions in Antiquity: In Memory of E. R. Goodenough*, ed. J. Neusner (Leiden: Brill, 1968), 354–71. Also Peder Borgen, "Moses, Jesus, and the Roman Emperor:Observations in Philo's Writings and the Revelation of John," *Novum Testamentum* 38, no. 2 (1996): 146.

68. See Pliny, *Natural History* 30.11. Origen cited Celsus's claim concerning the Jews: "They worship angels and are addicted to sorcery of which Moses was their teacher." *Cels.* 26, trans, Henry Chadwick

Moses, saying, "I am Moses your prophet to whom you have transmitted your mysteries, celebrated by Israel."[69] In another incantation, Moses is credited as an author of a secret book of spells, "The Eighth Book of Moses," exhibiting Moses as a model for all magicians.[70] Moses was considered a supernatural leader, as Origen claimed: "There have been two men who have come to visit the human race of whom supernatural miracles have been recorded; I mean Moses, your lawgiver . . . and Jesus."[71]

Comparing Jesus to Moses was fairly common in early church texts. Justin Martyr and the author of the *Epistle of Barnabas* employed an allegorical typology to demonstrate Moses as prefiguring Jesus.[72] In the case of Justin, it appears that the staff of Jesus was meant to recall the staff Moses utilized in the performance of his miracles. The iconography of the Roman relief sculptures confirms the intention by sight, and the textual references reveal the motivation to connect the wonders of Moses to the miracles of Jesus. Justin in his *Dialogue with Trypho* was perhaps the most explicit:

> When Moses was sent with a rod to deliver the people, he held it in his hands at their head, and he divided the sea in two. With this rod he touched the rock and saw water gush forth. And, by throwing a tree into the bitter waters of Marah, he made them sweet. By placing rods in their drinking-places, Jacob caused the sheep of his mother's brother to conceive. . . . Aaron's rod, by blossoming, proved him to be the high priest. Isaiah, indeed, foretold that Christ would come forth as a rod from the root of Jesse.[73]

According to Justin, Christ will come as a "rod." His miracle-working power is connected to the wonders of Moses.

The staff became a common element tying the two figures together. It is no accident in the artworks that the staff of Jesus is stylistically similar to the

(Cambridge: Cambridge University Press, 1965); Eusebius, *Preparation for the Gospel* 9.27.30. See G. Schroeder and É. des Places, eds., *La préparation évangélique*, SC (Paris: Éditions du Cerf, 1991).

69. *PGM* V.110 (Betz).

70. *PGM* XIII.1–343 (Betz).

71. Origen, *Cels.* 1.45 (Chadwick).

72. *Epistle of Barnabas* 12.5, reminding his audience of Moses and the brazen serpent.

73. Justin, *Dial.* 86.1-4 (Marcovich 219–20), trans. Thomas B. Falls (Washington, DC: Catholic University of America Press, 2003). Centuries later, John of Damascus calls the rod of Moses akin to the "cross" of Jesus. *Orth. Faith* 4.11. Moses is connected to Christ with the rod/tree as a common element, foreshadowing Christ's death on a "tree," and in the fourth to fifth centuries, the tree/true cross performed as many healings and wonders as Moses did.

staff of Moses. The motivation of depicting Christ wielding a staff is to depict him as a wonder worker similar yet superior to Moses. The staff marks him as a prophecy fulfilled: He is the rod from the root of Jesse, and his staff and effective miracles prove it to be so. The staff of Moses was a remarkable and tangible attribute that was useful for endowing Christian figures with the traits of Moses and reminding viewers of the Christian fulfillment of Old Testament prophecies.

Eusebius provided an even clearer and more straightforward comparison between Moses and Jesus in book 3 of his *Proof of the Gospel*. There is no typology in Eusebius's text; instead, he offered more direct parallels.[74] Eusebius established Moses as unique, unlike any successive prophet or leader, and the liberator and lawgiver of the people. Eusebius contrasted Moses's accomplishments with the slightly greater accomplishments of Christ: "Moses may be called the first and only lawgiver of religion to the Jews, and Jesus Christ the same to all nations. . . . Moses again by wonderful works and miracles authenticated the religion that he proclaimed; Christ likewise. . . . Moses again transferred the Jewish race from the bitterness of slavery to freedom; while Jesus Christ summoned the whole human race to freedom."[75] Moses performed great deeds such as the liberation of an enslaved people, but Christ liberated all of humanity to the kingdom of heaven. Eusebius stated, "And you will find other works done by our Savior with greater power than those of Moses, and yet resembling the works which Moses did."[76] Moses cleansed a leper (Miriam) by crying out to God, but Jesus cleansed a leper "with more superb power," by performing it directly without any intermediary.[77] Jesus was like Moses yet greater than Moses. Moses was unique; he knew God face-to-face. However, Jesus was the face of God.

In *Ep.* 137, Augustine revealed the popular sentiment surrounding the wonder working of Moses.[78] Augustine stated in his letter that it was natural for Christ to perform similar miracles as Moses did before him: "We read that

74. There likely was a reason for this. Eusebius was attempting to rebut the work of Porphyry and moreover may have been paraphrasing the lost work of Ammonius, *On the Agreement between Moses and Jesus*. Whatever Eusebius's intentions, the comparison exhibits a clear interest in juxtaposing Moses and Jesus. See J. Edgar Bruns, "The *Agreement of Moses and Jesus* in the *Demontratio Evangelica* of Eusebius," *VChr* 31, no. 2 (June 1977): 117–25.

75. Eusebius, *Proof of the Gospel* 3.2.91d (Ferrar).

76. Eusebius, *Proof of the Gospel* 3.2.92a.

77. Eusebius, *Proof of the Gospel* 3.2.93b.

78. Augustine, *Ep.* 136.1. Marcellinus forwards Volusian's queries to Augustine in this letter, requesting a lengthy response.

the magicians of the Egyptians, men most skilled in these arts, were surpassed by Moses, the servant of God. . . . But Moses himself and the rest of the most truthful prophets foretold Christ the Lord and gave great glory to him. He [Jesus] himself afterwards chose to work such miracles so that it would not seem strange if he did not do in person what he had done through them."[79]

Jesus was not merely equal to Moses for early church exegetes. His exceptional abilities were touted. Jesus was unlike any other miracle man, for he was a true product of the divine, a mark that set him apart even if his actions resembled those of others. In his letter, Augustine stated that Jesus was superior in the realm of working wonders but distinct in his divinity and chose to work miracles to prove to eyewitnesses his connection to Moses and his special status. The real evidence of Christ's superiority was in the miracle of his virgin birth and his resurrection—in essence, the fact that he was the Son of God. Even in his letter, Augustine understandably did not want local congregations to raise any local magician or rival figure who could possibly threaten Christ.[80]

The task for early Christians was to illustrate Jesus effectively as a wonder worker similar to but superior to the previous wonder worker in the canon, Moses. Jesus raising Lazarus to life coupled with an image of Moses striking the rock exhibits Jesus performing a miracle Moses never accomplished (Figures 3, 30). Thus, in the iconography, Moses as the supreme miracle worker is superseded by Christ. Moreover, the selection of Moses striking the rock may have sacramental implications. The selection of the Moses scene possibly insinuated the sacrament of baptism symbolized by the release of the water. Paul in his letter to the Corinthians tells his audience they were all baptized "into Moses," and "they drank from the spiritual rock that accompanied them, and that rock was Christ" (1 Cor. 10:4). Juxtaposing Moses with Jesus through their miracles appears to be a primary intent that connects Jesus to Moses and suggests baptism. The works of Moses as well as his miracle-working instrument obviously struck a chord with Christians.[81] The fascination with

---

79. Augustine, *Ep.* 137.13 (CSEL 44.110), trans. R. Teske in *The Works of St. Augustine: A Translation for the 21st Century*, ed. John E. Rotelle (Hyde Park, NY: New City, 2003).

80. In *City of God*, Augustine noted the belief that magic and sorcery were illicit while theurgy was more honorable and its practitioners were more esteemed. See *City of God* 10.9 (CSEL 40.460).

81. Moses was a wonder worker of such esteem that early church authors attempted to connect important figures other than Jesus to Moses in order to appropriate his wondrous attributes. Nyssa's *Life of Gregory Thaumaturgus* accomplished the appropriation of Moses, as Gregory was depicted performing similar miracles, including a miracle using a staff in a direct attempt to replicate Moses. Nyssa recorded Gregory's miracle of curtailing the flow of a river by plunging his staff deep into the ground and leaving it there, where it sprung into a tree. *Life of Gregory* (PG 46.928A).

connecting Moses to Jesus in early church documents is easily recognizable in early Christian art. The association is made concrete through Jesus' appropriation of Moses' staff.

The staff of Moses is recognized as an important accessory that accentuates the miracle-working nature of the patriarch. In early Christian art, the most prominent scenes that depict Moses' use of the staff are the crossing of the Red Sea and the striking of the rock. In the catacomb representations, the staff of Moses is reed-like and flexible, as depicted in the striking of the rock. Moses touches the rock with his staff while representations of the Israelites kneel below to catch the water. What is notable in the painting under the Vigna Massimo is that Moses's miracle is coupled with several images of Christ's miracles. Directly to the right of the striking of the rock is Christ miraculously dividing loaves with his staff. On the far right of the painting is the ubiquitous image of the raising of Lazarus with the staff touching Lazarus's *aediculum*. It is apparent in text and art that the staff of Moses is an inextricable component of his wonder-working action in these scenes. Likewise, in the Vigna Massimo catacomb painting, the staff was visually attaching the wonders of Moses to the miracles of Christ.

THE STAFF OF PETER

The appropriation of Moses's staff is restricted to two characters in early Christian art: Jesus and Peter. Peter's staff is most notable on the funerary relief sculptures of the fourth century. Not only is Jesus represented on the same artwork performing miracles with the staff, but Peter brandishes a staff as well, performing a water miracle as Moses did (Figures 4, 5). The image of Peter striking the rock underscores the disciple as a New Moses, and the relief sculpture reinforces the argument that the staff itself in the hand of Jesus or Peter directly recalls Moses.

Peter wields the staff of Christ in multiple scenes on early Christian relief sculpture (Figures 39, 41, and 42).[82] In the sarcophagus of Marcus Claudianus as well as the Vatican examples, Peter is depicted releasing water from the rock. These scenes recall a legend of Peter baptizing his Roman jailers before his martyrdom.[83] The legend is not from the canonical gospels but from the

---

82. The scene of Moses striking the rock appears in twenty-two examples on Roman sarcophagi; Peter in cognate scenes occurs fifty-six times. See Bovini and Brandenburg, *Reportorium*, Band I, pt. 3, 124. The Gallic and North African material is similarly conflated; see Christern-Briesenick, *Reportorium*, Band III, 302. The problem is how to identify true Moses scenes and true Peter scenes. The evidence of the jailers and other symbols on the relief sculpture points towards a larger number of Peter scenes than Moses scenes.

apocryphal *Acts of Peter*. The story describes Peter striking the "rock" of his cell walls, which released water he used to baptize the Roman converts, Processus and Martinianus.[84]

The apocryphal *Acts of Peter* portray the apostle as a formidable miracle worker. The text including the story of Peter striking the rock is difficult to date. It was preserved in a Latin version narrated by Pseudo-Linus and inserted in the narrative before the episode of Peter's martyrdom.[85] The date of the text was likely in the late fourth century, but the story and legend of Peter striking the rock was probably much older, as it was transmitted through oral tradition. The stories of Peter's miracles and abilities, compiled in the *Acts of Peter*, were possibly well-told tales. In some memorable instances, Peter out-dueled Simon Magus, made a dog speak, and even brought smoked herring back to life.[86] All recorded instances of relief sculpture depicting Peter striking the rock began appearing in the second quarter of the fourth century.[87] The dating of the visual art suggests that Christians knew the story of Peter striking the rock well enough to portray it frequently.

In early Christian art, the way Peter is depicted in the water miracle scene is analogous to Moses striking the rock. Both figures are portrayed standing next to a rock and striking it with the staff as a stream of water rushes down the side. In the catacomb images, Moses is portrayed striking the rock for the Israelites, as Moses utilizes his staff to produce the water while one or more followers

83. *Acts of Peter* 5 (Linus text). For further reading, see Robin M. Jensen, "Moses Imagery in Jewish and Christian Art," SBLSP (1992): 395–98. The *Acts of Peter* is difficult to date, as it incorporates several strains. The text that includes the water miracle was narrated by Pseudo-Linus and dates from the mid-fourth century. For the Latin text, see Lipsius, *Acta Apostolorum Apocrypha* (Hildesheim: G. Olms, 1959), 1:1–22; for the text and transmission, see Wilhelm Schneemelcher, *New Testament Apocrypha* (London: SCM, 1975), 2:285.

84. *Acts of Peter* 5 (Linus text). The text certainly depicts Peter as a wonder worker. Processus and Martinianus are so grateful that they help Peter escape from jail. Upon his escape, Peter meets Christ on the road outside Rome and becomes aware of his destiny.

85. See Andrew Gregory, *The Reception of Luke and Acts in the Period before Irenaeus* (Tübingen: Mohr Siebeck, 2003) 347; and Jensen, "Moses Imagery," 395. The dating of the text is a problematic and complicated issue that can only be briefly noted here. The Linus text possibly dates as late as the sixth century; however, Thomas argues for a late-fourth-century date and also notes (as Jensen does) that the stories in the *Acts of Peter* were passed down through oral tradition and very well could be as early as the second century. See Christine Thomas, *The Acts of Peter, Gospel Literature, and the Ancient Novel: Rewriting the Past* (New York: Oxford University Press, 2003), 14 and 43. Also see C. Pietri, "Pierre-Moïse et sa communauté," *Roma Christiana* 1 (1976) : 336–40.

86. *Acts of Peter* 12-14.

87. This is confirmed in Bovini and Brandenburg, *Repertorium*, Band I, pt. 3, 86-7.

anxiously await its release. In Christian relief sculpture, Moses is still represented as a major character, but in the striking of the rock, he is often replaced with the figure of Peter.[88]

The conflation of Moses and Peter makes it difficult to interpret the identity of the main character whenever the striking of a rock appears on Christian relief sculpture: Is the staff wielder Moses, or is it Peter? Some clues aid in determining whether the person is Moses or Peter. When the striking of the rock occurs among other scenes, it is common for the image to appear at one end of the relief. This is perhaps due to carving techniques, as the "water" featured in the scene serves as a border encapsulating the carved scenes (Figure 42 and 47). On particular sarcophagi, next to the scene of the striking of the rock is a depiction of the arrest of Peter, a scene that is scripturally canonical, appearing in Acts 12. Peter is bearded and is grasped on either side by soldiers, denoted by their short tunics and head coverings (Figures 39, 41, 42, and 48). The cock standing at his feet, visible in the example at the Vatican, occasionally identifies Peter, reminding viewers of his betrayal of Christ (Figure 42). One or more of these Petrine scenes occurring in conjunction with the striking of the rock offers conclusive evidence that the person striking the rock is Peter. Once the staff is associated with Peter in the striking of the rock, the instrument does not go away. In surrounding scenes of the arrest of Peter and Peter's betrayal, the apostle is shown clutching the staff in his hand. Although the staff is not an integral part of the action, as in the striking of the rock, the art exhibits the Christian desire to associate Peter with Moses by including this visual attribute with Peter.[89]

It is curious why Christians would be interested in replacing a frequently depicted scene of Moses from the catacombs with a scene of Peter. Even if the story of Peter baptizing his jailers was popular, the Acts of the Apostles includes several examples of Peter baptizing that would seem more likely candidates for

88. For example, the Crossing of the Red Sea occurs eleven times in the Roman corpus and fifteen times in the Gallic and North African corpus. Bovini and Brandenburg, *Reportorium*, Band I, 121; Christern-Briesenick, *Reportorium*, Band III, 300; also see plates in Band III, 340, 356.

89. In nonfunerary art as in the apse mosaic of S. Constanza, Peter is handed the law from Christ, and Peter bears a strong resemblance to Moses and clutching a thin rod that is further meant to associate Peter with Moses. In the Mausoleum of Constanza, built for Constantine's sister in 350 CE, two opposing apses are decorated in mosaics featuring Peter. For further reading, see Johannes Deckers, "Constantine the Great and Early Christian Art," in *Picturing the Bible: The Earliest Christian Art*, ed. Jeffrey Spier (New Haven, CT: Yale University Press, 2007), 95; and Hugo Brandenburg, *Ancient Churches of Rome from the Fourth to the Seventh Century* (Turnhout: Brepols, 2005), 82–86. Also see Allison, *New Moses*, 106–109. Allison suggests that the artistic representations of the striking of the rock may have elicited the apocryphal story involving Peter baptizing his jailers.

early Christians to portray.[90] The apocryphal selection was chosen because it firmly places Peter in the guise of Moses. The staff is the key visual element that connects Peter to Moses, and by inserting Peter into the narrative, the artist assigns to Peter the place of Moses in Christian art. Not only is Peter the New Moses—the shepherd of the church, just as Moses was shepherd of the Israelites—Peter also is inserted into a scene connoting baptism. Peter is portrayed as the first bishop of the church, endowed to perform Christ's holy sacrament. The apocryphal text from the *Acts of Peter* was chosen due to its portrayal of Peter as Moses within the context of baptism. No other baptismal scene in Acts has the apostle wielding an instrument that releases water from a rock as in Exodus and appearing as the Jewish patriarch. Baptism is symbolized in the catacombs when Moses is the agent in the image; however, the Christian relief sculpture transfers to Peter the patriarchal role Moses occupied.

The catacomb images with Christ wielding an instrument similar to Moses's staff similarly insist upon Christ as the New Moses. On the sarcophagi frontals, Christ wields the staff as well; however, Peter is also associated with Moses due to his inclusion in the striking of the rock (Figures 39, 41, 42, 47, and 48). The Jewish patriarch becomes the Christian patriarch, as the inclusion of the apocryphal scene makes clear. Peter is a miracle worker and leader on par with Moses.

The baptismal stories involving Peter were not the only influential texts that exhibited Peter's wonder-working ability. There were also stories of Peter's remarkable ability as a healer. The first half of Acts includes several notable accounts of Peter's ability as a healer. He healed the lame with his touch and with his voice in the name of Jesus, and he even raised Tabitha/Dorcas back to life.[91] Peter healed not only directly but also indirectly. As Jesus healed the woman with the issue of blood indirectly, Peter's shadow healed: "so that they even carried out the sick into the streets, and laid them on cots and mats, in order that Peter's shadow might fall on some of them as he came by" (Acts 5:15). The Acts accounts involving Peter demonstrate the many options early Christians could consider when depicting Peter in art. Granted, carving an image of Peter's shadow healing men and women would be difficult. Instead of selecting from Acts, the early Christians relied upon an instance of Peter baptizing his jailers to decorate their funerary monuments and deliberately show Peter as Moses.

90. As in Acts 2:40 and 10:48 and his report on baptism to the church at Acts 11:15.

91. Peter heals a crippled beggar in Acts 3, heals Aeneas in the name of Jesus in Acts 9:32, and resurrects Tabitha/Dorcas in Acts 9:41.

While Christ is continually portrayed as a miracle worker, Peter's most frequent miracle depiction is the striking of the rock. Other miracles involving Peter are rare in early Christian art.[92] Moses's staff, mentioned in the texts and realized in art, was appropriated by Christ in the performance of his healings and miracles. In the examples of Roman relief sculpture, the staff is bequeathed to Peter (Figures 39, 41, 42, 47, and 48). This does not mean Christ is bereft of his staff completely in early Christian art. Christ is still shown performing miracles with the staff, often on the same frontals as Peter striking the rock with the staff (Figures 39, 41, 42, 47, and 48). The art indicates that the staff is in the act of being appropriated by Peter. In these examples that include both Jesus and Peter brandishing staffs, it seems that Christ is cast as the supreme miracle worker greater than Moses, while Peter is inaugurated as the New Moses, the Christian patriarch of the church.

Following the third century, there was certainly a Christian interest in comparing Peter to Moses. In the wake of the Decian persecution, Cyprian advocated the church as the sole gateway to salvation.[93] To push this image of the church and its episcopate as the only dispensers of grace, Cyprian utilized Peter: "A primacy is given to Peter, and it is made clear that there is but one Church and one Chair."[94] Subsequent early-church authors not only endorsed Cyprian's espousal of Petrine authority, they also profitably compared Peter to Moses. Augustine in his treatise *Against Faustus* compares Peter's volatile swordplay in Gethsemane to Moses killing the Egyptian.[95] Similarly, Maximus of Turin preached specifically that Jesus "sailed in the Red Sea" with Moses but eventually "He chooses Peter's boat and forsakes Moses'; that is to say, He spurns the faithless synagogue and takes the faithful Church."[96] Peter as representative

92. See Herbert Kessler, "Scenes from the Acts of the Apostles on Some Early Christian Ivories," *Gesta* 18, no. 1 (November 1977–Februrary 1978): 111–12. On a late-fourth-century ivory that is in the British Museum in London, below a depiction of Peter striking the rock is a scene of Peter raising Tabitha, which illustrates a story from Acts 9:36-42. On the Brescia Casket, a reliquary that shows Jesus raising Lazarus with the staff, Peter is included in a large frontal in a scene of Ananias and Sapphira. The scene of Ananias and Sapphira occurs more often after the fifth century, with Peter's role as heir to Christ and head of the church secure. The scene is included to emphasize the power Christ's scion had over life and death, and that Peter should be feared as God should be feared.

93. See Cyprian, *On the Unity of the Church* 4-5. For an excellent commentary on Cyprian's Carthage, see J. P. Burns, *Cyprian the Bishop* (New York: Routledge, 2002), 82.

94. Cyprian, *On the Unity of the Church* 4. See *Cyprian: De Lapsis and De Ecclesiae Catholicae Unitate*, trans. M. Bévenot (Oxford: Clarendon, 1971), 63.

95. Augustine, *Against Faustus* 22.70. (CSEL 25.666-67). Citing John 18:10 and Exod. 2:12.

96. Maximus of Turin, *Sermon* 49. See *The Sermons of Maximus of Turin*, trans. Boniface Ramsey; ACW(New York: Newman, 1989), 115.

of the church becomes identified as the "rock": the representative of the church and the leader and gate to salvation. Naturally, Christian art followed suit, discarding the Jewish Moses for the Christian one found in Peter. The staff is obviously enmeshed with the person and miracle-working action of Moses. The staff also recalls a particular miracle Moses wrought, releasing water from a rock. Thus, it seems that in early Christian art, the staff of Jesus and Peter recalls Moses as well as signifying the sacrament of baptism.

Conclusion

The staff's persistent inclusion in the art and imagery of the early Christians demands an explanation. The staff in Christ's hand is not an empty symbol, the mark of a magician, or an example of the influence of pagan artists and workshops. And the staff of Jesus is more than just a symbol of power; it is an indication of his miracle-working and restorative ability.

The staff's connection with Moses illustrates that early Christians were utilizing the visual medium to express the portrait of Christ as the superior wonder worker. The staff defines the consistent desire to portray Christ with a familiar stylistic accessory that places Moses in the minds of their viewers so Jesus will be viewed not only as the fulfillment of prophecy but also as greater than Moses. Moreover, it is possible that the staff suggests Jesus and Peter succeeding where Moses failed. In Numbers 20, Moses and Aaron are ordered by God to "speak" to the rock and release the water. However, Moses in his anger toward the mob-like Israelites strikes the rock with his staff. God tells Moses that since he did not follow the command, he will not be allowed into the promised land. Where Moses is punished by God and is not offered entrance due to his staff misuse, Jesus and Peter with their staffs offer entrance into eternal life. In the catacombs, the association between Moses and Christ is fairly clear, due to the images' proximity to one another. Jesus with the staff obviously recalls Moses's staff, which is portrayed nearby, as in the wall paintings at Domitilla and at the catacomb under the Vigna Massimo. In the fourth-century relief sculpture, Peter is included in the exclusive cast of staff bearers, effectively replacing Moses.

In the relief sculpture, Peter takes Moses's place, and the staff also takes on a different valence. The staff is endowed to Peter in the effort to cast him as the New Moses. The staff is still omnipresent in the miracles of Christ. With the inclusion of Peter in the imagery, Christ allows Peter, the leader of his church and feeder of his sheep, to inherit the symbol of his ability and carry the tradition forward.

The staff that occurs on numerous occasions in the fourth century does not entirely disappear, although its appearance certainly dissipates. The miracles and healings of Christ are portrayed with less frequency after the fifth century, with only the requisite miracles such as the raising of Lazarus remaining the most depicted in circulation.[97] When Jesus is depicted performing healings and miracles in art following the fifth century, he emphatically demonstrates his divine power without paraphernalia. The staff of Christ is left to the era when Christ's miracles and healings were deemed most important. Following the fifth century, the staff of Jesus is not usually depicted, for its depiction is not necessary. To repeatedly assert Jesus or Peter as the New Moses in art and imagery was inessential when that connection was already well established. For the nascent church the staff was an unnecessary accoutrement, written out of the art and replaced with a cross, a hand, or nothing at all.

This understanding of the staff is not necessarily an exclusive interpretation. The staff is a symbol, and viewers of the symbol may realize Jesus as a philosopher, see him as a New Moses, or provide their own import influenced by existing resources. The funerary context of the staff images strongly suggests that they imply the authority of the church, the institution that was beginning to be understood as the gatekeeper of salvation. Moreover, the scenes of striking the rock suggest the rite of baptism. During the fourth century, the rite of baptism was read in light of Paul's letter to the Romans, recalling baptism as a ritual where one participates in the death of Christ (Romans 6).[98] Just as Christ was raised from the dead, the newly baptized are raised to new life. This understanding makes the staff images perfect for a funerary atmosphere, and the staff itself is a powerful symbol of salvation as it releases baptismal water from the rock.

97. In later depictions, the staff of Jesus evolves into a cross. On the fifth-century Andrews diptych, the staff is still present; however, on an ivory diptych in Ravenna from just a century later, the staff has visibly transitioned into a cross, as Christ gesticulates with his hand toward the *aediculum* with a newly discernible Lazarus. See Volbach, *Early Christian Art*, pl. 223.

98. See Jensen, *Understanding Early Christian Art*, 87–88.

8

Conclusion

The image of Christ the Miracle Worker burned brightest for several centuries, but early Christians would eventually adopt different themes as their focus in creating art and imagery. Just as the author of Luke–Acts shifts attention to the miracles of the saints in Acts following the miracle stories of Christ in the gospel, early Christian art similarly transitioned. Images involving Jesus performing miracles began to fade, as fervent attention to material relics of the saints ascended. The image of Christ the Miracle Worker mirrored the attention to the miracles of Jesus by early church authors. The surviving art is significant in telling the story of Christian piety and practice in Late Antiquity. After discussing the transition from the images of Jesus performing miracles to the miracles of the saints, this conclusion will discuss the enduring and vital influence of the Christ the Miracle Worker in early Christian art.

THE MIRACULOUS HEALINGS OF THE SAINTS

After the fifth century, the focus in Christian material culture shifted from healing and miracle imagery to the relics of the saints. Healing and miracle imagery was still prevalent, but the person of Christ was not the pivotal actor in the drama. The miracle-working agency of the apostles and the saints was emphasized. Whether artists concentrated on Peter, Paul, Stephen, or local martyrs, they replaced Christ as the primary miracle worker in favor of the saints. The shift reflected the attention and devotion to the cult and relics of the saints. Chronic ailments and plagues continued in early medieval Europe, requiring the divine healing provided by the relics, which filled the role once occupied by the pagan healing cult.[1] On caskets, reliquary boxes, and other objects, images of the apostles signified the divine source of the miracles and their efficacy.

---

1. Katherine Park calls early medieval Europe a "universe of disease." Park, "Medicine and Society in Medieval Europe, 500–1500," in *Medicine in Society* (Cambridge: Cambridge University Press, 1992), 60.

The material culture of the period may also reflect a continuing competition with the practice of magic.[2] The work of the wonder worker continued to be distinguished from magic into the early medieval period. The great miracle worker in Christ, however, was not as omnipresent in text and art as in the third and fourth centuries. Martin of Tours, Gregory of Tours, and Gregory Thaumaturgus became renowned and beloved in the Christian West as miracle workers par excellence. The power of their miracle-working nature was divine, except not in the same way as Christ. Their miracle-working power was manifested through their material remains. The transference of power regarding relics has Acts 19:11 in mind: "And God did extraordinary miracles by the hands of Paul, so that handkerchiefs or aprons were carried away from his body to the sick, and diseases left them and the evil spirits came out of them."

Material objects that came in contact with the saints were thought to have the ability to work miracles. Augustine dealt with this burgeoning trend in Hippo with the arrival of Stephen's relics. In Gaul, the cult of Martin of Tours was undoubtedly the most prominent, although several others existed in Gaul, including the cult of Hilary in Poitiers and the cult of Julian in Brioude. Martin of Tours's popularity was unsurpassed, given that he was a miracle worker in his own lifetime. In the late fourth century, people would gather any object his hand might have graced and would use it as a healing relic. Although Martin died in 397, his hagiographer (and Paulinus of Nola's close friend) Sulpicius Severus completed a collection of his miracles in Martin's own lifetime.[3] Over a century later, Gregory of Tours continued Martin's legacy and chronicled his healings through the use of assorted paraphernalia. Gregory's brother was cured of an illness by dust at the tomb of Julian at Brioude, and Gregory himself was healed at the tomb of Martin. Gregory used Martin's relics for protection as well as curing various people in his episcopate.[4]

2. See Herbert L. Kessler, *Seeing Medieval Art* (Orchard Park, NY: Broadview, 2004), 116; and A. A. Barb, "The Survival of the Magic Arts," in *The Conflict between Paganism and Christianity in the Fourth Century*, ed. A. Momigliano (Oxford: Clarendon, 1963), 100.

3. See Clare Stancliffe, *St. Martin and His Hagiographer* (Oxford: Clarendon, 1983), 112; Peter Brown, *The Cult of the Saints* (Chicago: University of Chicago Press, 1981), 55. Brown does not underestimate Severus's or Paulinus's importance. He calls Paulinus a founder, along with Augustine, of Latin Christian piety. In the *Life of Martin*, a woman thought she was blinded because of her sins, and a man believed his paralysis was due to his own actions. Severus, *Life of Martin* 2.28; 2.40. Martin's sixth-century successor, Gregory of Tours, effectively marketed the life and relics of Martin as healing implements. See Raymond Van Dam, *Saints and Their Miracles in Late Antique Gaul* (Princeton, NJ: Princeton University Press, 1993), 50.

4. See Gregory, *Life of Martin* 1.32-33, 36; 2.2, in Van Dam, *Saints and Their Miracles*, 199.

Gregory Thaumaturgus's healings included the use of paraphernalia. In one account recorded by Nyssa, Gregory healed an afflicted boy by breathing on a linen cloth and throwing it over the boy.[5] Following the tradition of *brandea*, material relics, the object that comes into direct contact even with the living saint can produce miraculous cures. During the late-sixth-century pontificate of Gregory the Great, the prominence of *brandea* was firmly established and widely known. Gregory received requests from the Byzantine empress Constantina for the head of the apostle Paul or some part of Paul's body. Gregory rejected the empress's request and replied that the bodies of Paul and Peter were so powerful that "one cannot even go to pray there without great fear." He reported that the monks involved in an excavation project encountered the remains of St. Lawrence and died shortly afterward.[6] Relics were considered too powerful for any person, especially a layperson, to encounter directly. As an afterthought, Gregory offered to send her *brandea*, a box of cloths that had come in contact with the saint, or the filings from the chains of Peter.

In this context, images of miracles were not necessarily confined to a catacomb wall or a sarcophagus frontal.[7] Material culture effected miracles, transmitting the power of Christ through his emissaries, the saints. Just as Peter was endowed with the staff in fourth-century relief sculpture, marking his authority as the Christian Moses, the relics of the saints and their miraculous healings also marked the authority of Christ's church. Moreover, relics could hurt transgressors and were a way to assert episcopal authority and control.[8] In Gregory's Tours, healings usually consisted of confession, forgiveness, and reconciliation and were public events. In an era when relics proliferated, towns competed over whose relics were most efficacious, and Gregory promoted Martin at the expense of any rival communities. While many people were

5. See *Life of Gregory*, (PG 46.941D-944A).

6. See Gregory the Great, *Ep.* 4.30 (*NPNF* 2.12.155-156; CCSL 140.248-50); and Dennis Trout, "Damasus and the Invention of Early Christian Rome," *Journal of Medieval and Early Modern Studies* 33, no. 3 (2003): 528. He claims at the end of his letter that the ease of removing the filings is due in part to the faith or worthiness of the supplicant. Sometimes the filings come off quickly, but if Constantina is not worthy, it may take a while.

7. Miracle images do continue. There was a group of ivories produced in Italy just after 400, featuring the healings and miracles of Christ including the Carrand diptych. Also note the fifth-century Andrews diptych depicted in Jensen, *Understanding Early Christian Art*, fig. 48, and images of Santa Sabina (Figures 44–45) from 432–435 CE. See Kessler, "Scenes from the Acts of the Apostles," *Gesta*, vol. 18, no. 1 (November 1977-Februrary 1978), 112 for further reading on the ivories.

8. See Van Dam, *Saints and Their Miracles*, 89–91. Gregory notes those afflicted for not observing saints' days (192).

purportedly cured of their ailments, the miracles reflected "care" more than "cure." Miracles of the saints did not restore a suffering life to perfection; that would come in the future life. Instead, miracles offered opportunities for a brief respite in an already embittered existence while fostering faith in Christ. Moreover, healing miracles were events that the entire public could observe and reap their spiritual benefit. The images of Christ the Miracle Worker dissipated in this context, but healings and miracles were still on the forefront of most believers' minds.

THE SIGNIFICANCE OF CHRIST THE MIRACLE WORKER

The significance of Christ the Miracle Worker in early Christian art is demonstrated by the multiple appearances this image makes in catacomb art and relief sculpture, as well as the manifold references in texts and sermons of the church fathers. Life, death, and life after death are all motifs in Christian funerary art. Images of Adam and Eve, Jonah, Daniel, and even Orpheus and Hercules indicate an interest in the life beyond in catacomb wall paintings and relief sculpture. Images of Christ function in a similar manner. The image of Christ the Miracle Worker reveals an interest in the pertinent themes of rebirth and resurrection; they also exhibit a specific intention in the portrayal of Christ.

Miracles held special value in fourth-century congregations. Augustine's changing attitude toward the present reality of miracles demonstrated their popularity in the minds of his followers. The image of Christ the Miracle Worker comforted the Christian believers who desired some hope for physical cure and comfort in a context where healing methods were consistently entwined with religion and the supernatural. The preached image of Christ the healer and worker of miracles parallels the popularity of the portrayal of Christ in art, as well as foreshadowing the age of the relics of the saints. Christian art reflects the popularity and desire of early Christians to witness Jesus as the supreme worker of miracles.

However, the staff that Jesus utilizes in the performance of his healings and miracles illustrates a specific connection to Moses. In the catacomb art, the raising of Lazarus with the staff is often juxtaposed with Moses striking the rock, suggesting a parallel between the wonders of Moses and the wonders of Christ. In the relief sculpture, Christ utilizes his staff, while Moses is replaced with the figure of Peter. Peter inherits the wonder-working staff in a deliberate attempt to cast Peter as the New Moses and patriarch of the emerging Christian church.

Before Constantine, when Christianity was in its initial development, representing Christ as a superior healer and miracle worker, greater than Asclepius, Moses, or Apollonius, is understandable. Later, during the fourth and fifth centuries, when Christianity is more established, a decrease would seem more likely. However, the material evidence, specifically relief sculpture, reveals a large number of portrayals of Christ the Miracle Worker during this period. The image of Christ the Miracle Worker greatly proliferated during an age of Christian acceptance, rather than in the earlier age of Christian persecution.

The nascent church did not desire any recidivism in its members. Christians were tempted with lingering cults and heresies as well as partaking in familiar customs and feasts of their neighbors.[9] Church leaders could not allow any small fracture in their congregations to turn into a wider chasm, and they combated any opponents by focusing on their chosen deity in Christ. The textual references to Christ the healer and miracle worker in the works of Ambrose and Augustine imply this attitude.

The evidence shows that the image of Christ the Miracle Worker remained popular in the fourth and fifth centuries, when the visibility of Christ's rivals was fading. An additional explanation to the image's frequent appearance lies in the platform visual art provided. Visual art represented an effective frame to present the importance and superiority of Christianity to educated elite and uneducated commoner alike. Even images woven into textile fabrics and worn by wealthy congregants became an effective medium to promote the miracles of Jesus. The fifth-century bishop of Pontus, Asterius of Amasea, richly depicted the luxurious garments that some of the rich in his congregation chose to wear: "[Rich and religious men and women] having picked out the story of the Gospels, have handed it over to the weavers—I mean our Christ together with all his disciples, and each one of the miracles the way it is related. You may see the wedding of Galilee with the water jars, the paralytic carrying his bed on his shoulders, the blind man healed by means of clay, the woman with an issue of blood seizing Christ's hem, the sinful woman falling at the feet of Jesus, Lazarus coming back to life from his tomb."[10] The Victoria and Albert Museum in London preserves a fifth-century textile illustrating the same miracles Asterius describes.[11] His remarks list nearly every image captured in the scenes of Christ

9. Consider John Chrysostom's sermons against the Judaizers in Antioch, although he certainly was not the first patristic author to vociferously argue for strong boundaries between Christians and Jews. Melito, Justin, and other authors of the second century are most interested in creating a Christian self-identity. Tertullian ardently excoriated his listeners to abandon Jewish lustration practices as well as what he deemed other heretical rituals. *On Baptism* 15. More recently, see Daniel Boyarin, *Borderlines: The Partition of Judaeo-Christianity* (Philadelphia: University of Pennsylvania Press, 2004).

10. Asterius of Amasea, *Homily I: On the Rich Man and Poor Lazarus*, in *Homilies I–XIV*, text, introduction, and notes by C. Datema (Leiden: Brill, 1970).

in the catacombs and relief sculpture. Asterius's congregants were wealthy enough to commission such garments and found the scenes of healing and miracles important enough to wear. In an age of Christian acceptance, viewers wanted to visually see and physically "wear" the miracles of Jesus.

Like the image of an enthroned Jesus, the images of Jesus performing miracles can easily be interpreted as triumphal images. However, the images of Christ the Miracle Worker appear to reflect the polyvalent function of early Christian art. Jesus could appear superior yet comforting, powerful yet pastoral, and as in the Gospel of John's Jesus, heavily divine yet human.

The material culture of post-Constantinian Christianity illustrates that early Christian piety largely consisted of sincere devotion to the miracles of Christ. Thus, early Christians surrounded themselves with this emphasis on miracles in their visual language, especially in funerary art. The images themselves provide a platform and an opportunity to examine how early Christians conceived this person called Christ. While the viewpoints arguing that *post-pacem* Christian art was purely influenced by the imperial cult will persist, the art of this period should continue to be discussed and evaluated by art historians and scholars of the early church. We would be wise to follow the advice of the historian Peter Brown and not "doze off again in the comfortable embrace of received wisdom." We should dedicate ourselves to continue the conversation and at least consider that early Christians did not recognize Jesus purely as an emperor, a magician, a philosopher, or a miracle worker akin to Moses.[12] Instead, the early Christians understood Christ the way the art renders him: as the inimitable Word of God made flesh.

11. For the textile, see Thomas Mathews, *The Clash of Gods* (Princeton, NJ: Princeton University Press, 1993), 59, and pl. 40.

12. Peter Brown, review of *The Clash of Gods: A Reinterpretation of Early Christian Art*, by Thomas Mathews, *Art Bulletin* 77 (1995): 499–502. For a recent piece representing the orthodox argument on the enthroned Jesus, see Johannes Deckers, "Constantine the Great and Early Christian Art," in *Picturing the Bible: The Earliest Christian Art*, ed. Jeffrey Spier (New Haven, CT: Yale University Press, 2007), 107.

Appendix of Images

Figure 1. This icon of Jesus is the oldest featuring Christ Pantocrator (Almighty), as Jesus holds a gospel book and has his other hand in the gesture of speech pronouncing judgment. Sixth century, St. Catherine's Monastery, Sinai (Photo: WikiMedia Commons)

Figure 2. This scene showing the healed paralytic, next to an image of Jesus' baptism, does not include an image of Christ. Rather, the solitary figure of the healed man is shown holding his pallet above his head in a manner that becomes emblematic of the healing act of Christ. Early third century, Catacomb of Callistus, Rome (Photo: Josef Wilpert, Die Malereien der Katakomben Roms, Freiburg im Breisgau, 1903)

Figure 3. This wall painting features several scriptural scenes, clockwise from the top left: Moses striking the rock, Jesus dividing loaves, the visitation of the magi, figures praying, Noah, the raising of Lazarus, Job, the healing of the paralytic, Tobias, and Daniel flanked by two lions. Fourth century, Catacomb under the Vigna Massimo, Rome (Photo: Wilpert)

Figure 4. Jesus healing the paralytic appears on the left side of the frontal. In the center, Jesus touches his miracle-working staff to wine jars, indicating the Cana miracle. Peter is striking the rock at the far left. Mid-fourth century, Museo Pio Cristiano, Vatican Museums (Photo: Author)

Figure 5. Jesus touches the paralytic's mat, featured in the center of this frontal, while the Cana miracle is portrayed at the far right. Peter is striking the rock at the far left. Mid-fourth century, Museo Pio Cristiano, Vatican Museums (Photo: Author)

Figure 6. The Bethesda Sarcophagus, featuring the healing of the paralytic in the center and a reclining figure resembling Jonah/Endymion. Late fourth century to early fifth century, Museo Pio Cristiano, Vatican Museums (Photo: Author)

Figure 7. The healing of the paralytic appears on the lower register to the right of the scene of Daniel with the lions. Mid-fourth century, Museo Pio Cristiano, Vatican Museums (Photo: Author)

Figure 8. On the lower right register, Jesus heals a seated paralytic, deviating from the motif of the paralytic carrying his mat. On the top register, Jesus uses his miracle-working staff to touch an inert body on the ground, evoking his power to raise the dead. 330–350 CE, Museo Pio Cristiano, Vatican Museums (Photo: Author)

Figure 9. On the top register to the left of the shell featuring the patrons, Jesus heals a seated paralytic. Mid-fourth century, Musée de l'Arles et de la Provence Antiques, Arles, France (Photo: Robin M. Jensen; used with permission)

Figure 10. Jesus heals the woman with the issue of blood. In this scene, the woman touches Jesus by grasping the hem of his garment, rather than Jesus touching the woman. Late third century, Catacomb of Peter and Marcellinus, Rome (Photo: International Catacomb Society)

Figure 11. This column sarcophagus features Jesus touching the woman with the issue of blood. Mid-fourth century, Museo Pio Cristiano, Vatican Museums (Photo: Author)

Figure 12. Moses strikes water from the rock, and Jesus heals the woman with the issue of blood, seemingly touching the woman as she gestures toward the hem of his robe. Late fourth century, Museo Pio Cristiano, Vatican Museums (Photo: Author)

Figure 13. On the top register at the far left, Jesus raises Lazarus. The woman next to him is Lazarus's sister (Mary or Martha), rather than the woman with the issue of blood. Mid-fourth century, Museo Pio Cristiano, Vatican Museums (Photo: Author)

Figure 14. Jesus heals a diminutive blind person in the central scene. Mid-fourth century, Museo Pio Cristiano, Vatican Museums (Photo: Author)

Figure 15. Jesus is depicted touching the eyes of the blind man. Mid-fourth century, Musée de l'Arles et de la Provence Antiques, Arles, France (Photo: Robin M. Jensen; used with permission)

Figure 16. This is a statuary representation of the god Asclepius, who is typically featured holding a serpent-entwined staff and wearing a himation baring his chest. Third century, Capitoline Museums, Rome (Photo: Author)

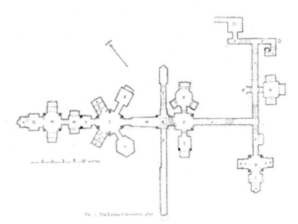

Figure 17. This Roman catacomb features paintings of both Christian and non-Christian figures, including Hercules and Jesus. Mid-fourth century, Plan of the Via Latina Catacomb (Photo: International Catacomb Society)

Figure 18. This catacomb painting features Hercules rescuing King Admetus's wife, Alcestis. The mythical three-headed dog Cerberus the guards the underworld is also included, recalling the Hercules cycle of stories. Mid-fourth century, Via Latina Catacomb, Rome (Photo: WikiMedia Commons)

Figure 19. This wall painting features Christ as Orpheus. The lyre and the dress are typical of Orpheus depictions in antiquity. Fourth century, Catacomb of Peter and Marcellinus, Rome (Photo: WikiMedia Commons)

Figure 20. At the far right, Jesus touches a body at his feet with the staff, likely evoking Jesus as Ezekiel in the Valley of the Dry Bones. Mid-fourth century, Museo Pio Cristiano, Vatican Museums (Photo: Author)

Figure 21. On the far left, Jesus pulls a figure up from a bed. The figure is likely Jairus's daughter, recalling Luke's gospel: "But [Jesus] said, but he said, "Do not weep; for she is not dead but sleeping." (Luke 8:52 NRSV). Mid-fourth century, Museo Pio Cristiano, Vatican Museums (Photo: Author)

Figure 22. The Brescia Casket, featuring carved scenes of the miracles of Jesus. Jesus heals the woman with the issue of blood on the left frontal, and on the left side pulls a figure up from a bed. Late fourth century, Museo di Santa Giulia at San Salvatore, Brescia, Italy (Photo: WikiMedia Commons)

Figure 23. On the far left, Jesus uses his staff to touch a body on the ground, beckoning the man to life. The heads and two other nude figures depict other resurrected figures, intended to recall Ezekiel in the Valley of the Dry Bones, with Jesus as Ezekiel. Mid-fourth century, Museo Pio Cristiano, Vatican Museums (Photo: Author)

Figure 24. A fresco in the synagogue at Dura exhibits the passage of Ezekiel in the Valley of the Dry Bones (Ezekiel 37). Heads, arms, and other body parts at the feet of the standing prophet are in the process of coming to renewed life. Mid-third century, Dura-Europos synagogue, Syria (Photo: WikiMedia Commons)

Figure 25. The raising of Lazarus is featured at the far right of this sarcophagus frontal. Lazarus is mummified in his burial wrappings, with his facial features not easily discernible, while Mary or Martha is at Jesus' feet. Mid-fourth century, Museo Pio Cristiano, Vatican Museums (Photo: Author)

Figure 26. In this catacomb representation, Lazarus is standing instead of mummified, fully restored to life, making this example of the scene unique. Third century, Catacomb of Callistus, Rome (Photo: Wilpert)

Figure 27. Jesus raises Lazarus on the far left side with Mary or Martha at his feet and a diminutive nude youth on the right side. Peter is arrested directly next to the raising of Lazarus scene. Mid-fourth century, Museo Pio Cristiano, Vatican Museums (Photo: Author)

Figure 28. In this representation of the raising of Lazarus, the resurrected figure is mummified, showing a progression in representation since the Callistus example. Early to mid-third century, Catacomb of Priscilla, Rome (Photo: Wilpert)

Figure 29. This chamber, known as the "Red Cubiculum," features the raising of Lazarus on the upper left side. Jesus physically touches the wrapped Lazarus with his staff. Opposite this scene, Moses strikes water from the rock. Mid-third century, Catacomb of Domitilla, Rome (Photo: International Catacomb Society)

Figure 30. Below a representation of Moses receiving the Law, Jesus touches the head of Lazarus with his miracle-working staff. Late fourth century, Via Latina Catacomb, Rome (Photo: International Catacomb Society)

Figure 31. Christ is depicted with a band of followers and is touching the aediculum of Lazarus, but there is no body to be found within it. The lack of a mummified Lazarus may be evidence that the Lazarus scene was not the original representation. Late fourth century, Via Latina Catacomb, Rome (Photo: International Catacomb Society)

Figure 32. On this ceiling painting, the raising of Lazarus is depicted on the right, and Moses striking the rock is featured on the left. Late third century, Catacomb of Peter and Marcellinus (Photo: International Catacomb Society)

Figure 33. Moses utilizes his miracle-working staff as he leads the Israelites across the Red Sea. In this image, the Egyptians are in chaos on the left, and the Israelites are fleeing Egypt on the right. Mid-fourth century, Cubiculum O, Via Latina Catacomb, Rome (Photo: International Catacomb Society)

Figure 34. In this unique fragment, Jesus is featured healing and preaching in dress and guise similar to those of the healing god Asclepius. Late third or early fourth century, Museo Nazionale delle Terme, Rome (Photo: Robin M. Jensen; used with permission)

Figure 35a. The scene on the far right is perhaps one of the earliest catacomb representations of Moses striking the rock. Early to mid-third century, Catacomb of Callistus, Rome (Photo: Wilpert)

Figure 35b. In a much clearer image, Moses strikes the rock while an Israelite gathers the released water. Late third century, Catacomb of Callistus, Rome (Photo: International Catacomb Society)

Figure 36. In a painting on an arched doorway, the image of Noah separates the flanking images of the division of the loaves and the Cana miracle. Late third century, Catacomb of Peter and Marcellinus, Rome (Photo: Wilpert)

Figure 37. This depiction of the miracle at Cana is flanked by scenes of Christ being baptized and Moses striking the rock. Similarly to images that show Jesus dividing the loaves, Jesus is portrayed touching the jars of wine with his staff. Late third century, Catacomb of Peter and Marcellinus, Rome (Photo: Wilpert)

Figure 38. In the center, Jesus is depicted blessing loaves with baskets at his feet. Representations of the division of the loaves usually do not depict a miracle-working tool. Mid-fourth century, Museo Pio Cristiano, Vatican Museums (Photo: Author)

Figure 39. This sarcophagus exhibits the proclivity of early Christian funerary art to portray miracles. Peter strikes the rock; Jesus divides loaves, changes water to wine, heals the blind man and raises Lazarus. 330–340 ce, Sarcophagus of Marcus Claudianus, Museo Nazionale Romano, Rome (Photo: Author)

Figure 40. Jesus is seated above the heavens, handing the law to Peter and Paul. This motif, which became known as the traditio legis, is popular in post-Constantinian Christian art. 359 ce, Sarcophagus of Junius Bassus, Vatican Museums (Photo: Author)

Figure 41. On the far right of this double-register sarcophagus, Jesus uses a staff to raise Lazarus from the dead, and directly below, Peter uses the staff to release water from a rock. 330–350 ce, Museo Pio Cristiano, Vatican Museums (Photo: Author)

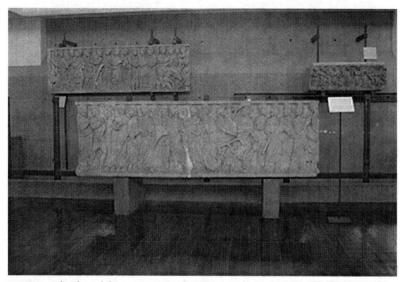

Figure 42. This frontal features Jesus performing miracles with the staff, while on the far left, Peter strikes the rock with the staff. Late fourth century, Museo Pio Cristiano, Vatican Museums (Photo: Author)

Figure 43. This wooden panel features Moses utilizing the staff, possibly recalling the Exodus story of a contest with pharaoh's magicians. 432 ce, Santa Sabina, Rome (Photo : Author)

Figure 44. This panel, diagonally above the Moses panel, features Jesus performing miracles with his staff, including raising Lazarus, dividing loaves, and turning water into wine at Cana. 432 ce, Santa Sabina, Rome (Photo : Author)

Figure 45. The figure on the far left is a depiction of a philosopher, seated and studying. Mid-fourth century, Museo Pio Cristiano, Vatican Museums (Photo: Author)

Figure 46. Jesus is seated among his disciples, teaching and pointing to his open scroll. This image is akin to representations of philosophers. Fourth century, Musée de l'Arles et de la Provence Antiques, Arles, France (Photo: Robin M. Jensen; used with permission)

Figure 47. The left side of this sarcophagus frontal features Peter's arrest and Peter striking the rock. Late fourth century, Museo Pio Cristiano, Vatican Museums (Photo: Author)

*Figure 48. This fragment features Peter's arrest and the striking of the rock. Mid-
to late fourth century, Museo Pio Cristiano, Vatican Museums (Photo: Author)*

Bibliography

Achelis, Hans. *Die Katacomben von Neapol*. Leipzig: Karl W. Hiersemann, 1936.

Acta Apostolorum Apocrypha, vol. 1 and 2. Edited by Richard Lipsius. Hildesheim: G. Olms, 1959.

The Acts of the Christian Martyrs. Translated by Herbert Musurillo. Oxford: Clarendon, 1972.

Aelius Aristides. *The Complete Works*. Translated by Charles Behr. Leiden: Brill, 1981.

Ambrose. *De Helia et Ieiunio*. Translated by Sister Mary Joseph Aloysius Buck. Washington, DC: Catholic University of America Press, 1929.

Amundsen, Darrel W. *Medicine, Society, and Faith in the Ancient and Medieval Worlds*. Baltimore: Johns Hopkins University Press, 1996.

The Ante-Nicene Fathers. Edited by Alexander Roberts and James Donaldson. 10 vols. Peabody, MA: Hendrickson, 1994.

The Apocryphal New Testament. Translated by M. R. James. Oxford: Clarendon, 1924.

Arbesmann, Rudolf. "The Concept of 'Christus Medicus' in St. Augustine," *Traditio* 10 (1954): 1–28.

Arnobius of Sicca. *The Case against the Pagans*. Translated and annotated by George E. McCracken. Westminster, MD: Newman, 1949.

Athanasius. *On the Incarnation*. Translated by A Religious of C.S.M.V. Crestwood, NY: St. Vladimir's Seminary Press, 2003.

Athanassiadi-Fowden, Polymnia. *Julian and Hellenism: An Intellectual Biography*. Oxford: Clarendon, 1981.

Avalos, Hector. *Health Care and the Rise of Christianity*. Peabody, MA: Hendrickson, 1999. Augustine. *City of God*. Translated by Henry Bettenson. New York: Penguin, 1972.

———. *Confessions.* Translated by Henry Chadwick. Oxford: Oxford University Press, 1991.

———. *Earlier Writings*. Translated by John H.S. Burleigh. Philadelphia: Westminster, 1953.

————. *Exposition of the Psalms.* Translated by Maria Boulding. *The Works of St. Augustine: A Translation for the 21st Century.* Edited by John E. Rotelle. Hyde Park, NY: New City Press, 2002.

————. *Letters.* Translated by R. Teske. *The Works of St. Augustine: A Translation for the 21st Century.* Edited by John E. Rotelle. Hyde Park, NY: New City Press, 2003.

————. *Sermons.* Translated by Edmund Hill. *The Works of St. Augustine: A Translation for the 21st Century.* Edited by John E. Rotelle. Hyde Park, NY: New City Press, 1990–.

————. *Retractations.* Translation by Sister Mary Inez Bogan. Fathers of the Church. Washington, DC: Catholic University of America Press, 1968.

Aune, David. "Heracles and Christ: Heracles Imagery in the Christology of Early Christianity." In *Greeks, Romans, and Christians,* edited by David L. Balch, Everett Ferguson, and Wayne Meeks. Minneapolis: Fortress Press, 1990.

Babcock, William S. "Image and Culture: An Approach to the Christianization of the Roman Empire" *Perkins Journal* 81, no. 3 (July 1988): 4–6.

————. "MacMullen on Conversion: A Response." *Second Century* 5.2 (1985/1986): 82–89.

————. "Sin and Punishment: The Early Augustine on Evil." In *Augustine: Presbyter, Factus Sum.* New York: Peter Lang, 1993.

Barrett-Lennard, R. J. S. *Christian Healing after the New Testament: Some Approaches to Illness in the Second, Third, and Fourth Centuries.* Lanham, MD: University Press of American, 1994.

Baynes, Norman H. "Idolatry and the Early Church." In *Byzantine Studies and Other Essays,* 116–239. London: Athlone, 1955.

Beckwith, John. *Early Christian and Byzantine Art.* London: Penguin, 1970.

Belting, Hans. *Likeness and Presence: A History of the Image before the Era of Art.* Chicago: University of Chicago Press, 1994.

Benko, Stephen, and John J. O'Rourke, eds. *The Catacombs and the Colosseum: The Roman Empire as the Setting of Primitive Christianity.* Valley Forge, PA: Judson, 1971.

Benoit, F. *Sarcophages paleochréttiens d'Arles et de Marseille.* Paris, 1954.

Berg, Beverly. "Alcestis and Hercules in the Catacomb of Via Latina." *VChr* 48, no. 3 (September 1994): 219–34.

Besnier, Maurice. *Les catacombes de Rome.* Paris: Leroux, 1909.

Betz, Hans Dieter, ed. *The Greek Magical Papyri in Translation, Including the Demotic Spells.* Chicago: University of Chicago Press, 1986.

Bevan, Edwyn. *Holy Images: An Inquiry into Idolatry and Image-Worship in Ancient Paganism and in Christianity.* London: George Allen and Unwin, 1940.

Bigham, Steven. *Early Christian Attitudes towards Images.* Rollinsford, NH: Orthodox Research Institute, 2004.

Bisconti, Fabrizio. *Temi di iconografia paleocristiana, cure e introduzione.* Citta del Vaticano: Pontificio Istituto di archeologia cristiana, 2000. (Sussidi allo studio della antichita cristiana, 13).

Bookidis, Nancy. "The Sanctuary of Demeter and Kore on Acrocorinth, Preliminary Report III." *Hesperia* 38, no. 3 (July 1969): 297–310.

———, and Ronald S. Stroud. "The Sanctuary of Demeter and Kore at Acrocorinth." In *Corinth*, vol. 18, pt. 3. Princeton, NJ: American School of Classical Studies at Athens, 1997.

Bovini, Giuseppe. *I sarcofagi paleocristiani; determinazione della loro cronologia mediante l'analisi dei ritratti.* Città del Vaticano: Società amici catacombe presso Pontificio Istituto di archeologia cristiana, Roma, 1949.

———, and Brandenburg H. *Repertorium der christlich-antiken Sarcophage.* I. Edited by F. W. Deichmann. Wiesbaden: F. Steiner, 1976.

Bovon, François. "Miracles, magie, et guérison dans les Actes apocryphes des apôtres," in *Journal of Early Christian Studies* 3 (1995): 245–59.

Bowersock, G. W. *Julian the Apostate.* Cambridge, MA: Harvard University Press, 1978.

Boyarin, Daniel. *Borderlines: The Partition of Judaeo-Christianity.* Philadelphia: University of Pennsylvania Press, 2004.

Brandenburg, Hugo. *Ancient Churches of Rome from the Fourth to the Seventh Century.* Turnhout, Belg.: Brepols, 2005.

Breckenridge, James D. *Likeness: A Conceptual History of Ancient Portraiture.* Evanston, IL: Northwestern University Press, 1968.

Brenk, Beat. *Spätankike und Frühes Christentum.* Frankfurt, 1977.

Brenk, F. E. *In Mist Paralleled: Religious Themes in Plutarch's Moralia and Lives.* Brill: Leiden, 1977.

Brookes, Ian. "The Death of Chiron: Ovid, *Fasti* 5.379-414." *The Classical Quarterly* 44, no. 2 (1994): 444–50.

Brown, Peter. *Augustine of Hippo.* Berkeley: University of California Press, 1967.

———. "The Clash of Gods: A Reinterpretation of Early Christian Art, a Review," *Art Bulletin* 77 (1995): 499–502.

———. *The Cult of the Saints: Its Rise and Function in Latin Christianity*. Chicago: University of Chicago Press, 1981.

———. *The Making of Late Antiquity*. Cambridge, MA: Harvard University Press, 1978.

Brown, Peter. *Religion and Society in the Age of Augustine*. London: Faber and Faber, 1972.

———. *The World of Late Antiquity, AD 150–750*. New York: Harcourt Brace Jovanovich, 1971.

Brox, N. "Magie und Aberglaube an den Anfängen des Christentums." *Trierer theologische Zeitschrift* 83 (1974): 157–80.

Bultmann, Rudolf. *The History of the Synoptic Tradition*. Translated by John Marsh. Revised edition. New York: Harper and Row, 1968.

Burns, J. Patout. *Cyprian the Bishop*. London/New York: Routledge, 2002.

Butterworth, G. W. "Clement of Alexandria and Art." *Journal of Theological Studies* 17 (1916): 68–76.

Cicero. *De Natura Deorum*. Translation by H. Rackham. Loeb Classical Library. New York: G. P. Putnam, 1933.

Clark, Elizabeth. *The Origenist Controversy: The Cultural Construction of an Early Christian Debate*. Princeton, NJ: Princeton University Press, 1992.

Clark-Soles, Jaime. *Death and Afterlife in the New Testament*. New York: T. & T. Clark, 2006.

Compton, Michael T. "The Association of Hygieia with Asklepios in Graeco-Roman Asklepieion Medicine" *Journal of the History of Medicine and Allied Sciences* 57, no. 3 (2002): 312–29.

———. "The Union of Religion and Health in Ancient Asklepiea." *Journal of Religion and Health* 37, no. 4 (Winter 1998): 301–12.

Cotter, Wendy. *Miracles in Greco-Roman Antiquity*. New York: Routledge, 1999.

Crossan, John Dominic. *Jesus: A Revolutionary Biography*. San Francisco: HarperSanFrancisco, 1994.

Cutler, Anthony. "Ezekiel and the Politics of Resurrection." In *Dumbarton Oaks Papers* 46. Washington, DC: Dumbarton Oaks Research Library and Collection, 1992.

D'Ambra, Eve. *Roman Art in Context*. Englewood Cliffs, NJ: Prentice Hall, 1993.

Davies, J. G. *The Architectural Setting of Baptism*. London: Barrie and Rockliff, 1962.

———. *The Origin and Development of Early Christian Church Architecture.* London: SCM, 1952.

De Bruyne, L. "L'imposition des mains dans l'art chrétien ancien." In *Rivista di Archeologia Cristiana*, 20, 1–4. Rome: Pontificio Istituto di Archeologia Cristiana.

Deonna, W. *De Télesphore au "moine bourru": Dieux, genies, et demons encapuchonnés.* Brussels, 1955.

De Waele, F. J. M. *The Magic Staff or Rod in Greco-Italian Antiquity.* The Hague, 1927.

Deckers, Johannes. "Constantine the Great and Early Christian Art." In *Picturing the Bible: The Earliest Christian Art.* Edited by Jeffrey Spier. New Haven: Yale University Press, 2007.

Deichmann, F. W., ed. *Repertorium der christlich-antiken Sarkophage.* Vols. 1–3. Wiesbaden: F. Steiner, 1967.

———. "Zur Frage der Gesamtschau der frühchristlichen und frühbyzantinischen Kunst." *Byzantinische Zeitschrift* 63 (1970).

———, and Theodor Klauser. *Frühchristliche Sarkophage in Bild und Wort,* Olten: Urs Graf-Verlag, 1966.

Deubner, Otfried. *Das Asklepeion von Pergamon.* Berlin: Verlag für Kunstwissenschaft, 1938.

De Villiers, Pieter G. R., and E. Germiquet. "*Religio* and *Superstitio* in Early Christianity and Graeco-Roman Society: Christian Perspectives on Paganism." *Acta Patristica et Byzantina* 9 (1998): 52–69.

Dibelius, Martin. *From Tradition to Gospel.* Translated by Bertram Lee Wolf. Second edition. New York: Scribner, 1965.

Dickie, Matthew W. *Magic and Magicians in the Greco-Roman World.* New York: Routledge, 2003.

Dinkler, Erich. *Christus und Asklepios.* Heidelberg: Carl Winter, 1980.

———. *Der Einzug in Jerusalem.* Opladen: Westdeutscher Verlag, 1970.

Dio Cassius. *Roman History.* Translated by Earnest Carey. Loeb Classical Library. Cambridge, MA: Harvard University Press, 1914–27.

Dorigo, Wladimiro. *Pittura tardoromana.* Milan, 1966.

Dulaey, Martine. "Le symbole de la baguette dans l'art paleochrétien." *Revue des études augustiniennes*, 19, 1–2 (1973): 3–38.

Dumeige, Gervais. "Le Christ Médecin." *Rivista di Archeologia Cristiana*, no. 1–4 (1972): 115–41.

Edelstein, Emma J. and Ludwig Edelstein. *Asclepius: A Collection and Interpretation of the Testimonies.* Vols. I and II. Baltimore: Johns Hopkins Press, 1945.

Edwards, Mark, ed. *Neoplatonic Saints: The Lives of Plotinus and Proclus by their Students.* Liverpool: Liverpool University Press, 2000.

Elizondo, Virgil, and Sean Freyne, eds. *Pilgrimage.* Maryknoll, NY: Orbis, 1996.

Elsner, Jás. *Imperial Rome and Christian Triumph: The Art of the Roman Empire AD 100–450.* Oxford/New York: Oxford University Press, 1998.

———. *Art and Text in Roman Culture.* Cambridge: Cambridge University Press, 1996.

———. *Art and the Roman Viewer: The Transformation of Art from the Pagan World to Christianity.* Cambridge: Cambridge University Press, 1995.

———, and Ian Rutherford, eds. *Pilgrimage in Graeco-Roman and Early Christian Antiquity: Seeing the Gods.* New York: Oxford University Press, 2005.

Eusebius. *Ecclesiastical History.* Translated by J. E. L. Oulton. Loeb Classical Library. Cambridge, MA: Harvard University Press, 1926–32.

Farnell, Lewis Richard. *Greek Hero Cults and Ideas of Immortality.* Oxford: Clarendon, 1921.

Ferrua, A. *Le Pitture della Nuova Catacombs di Via Latina.* Città del Vaticano, 1960.

———. "Una nuova regione in SS. Marcellino e Pietro." *Rivista di Archeologia Cristiana* no. 44, 1–4. Rome: Pontificio Istituto di Archeologia Cristiana, 1968.

———. *The Unknown Catacomb: A Unique Discovery of Early Christian Art.* Florence: Geddes and Grosset, 1990.

Farnell, L. R. *Greek Hero Cults and Ideas of Immortality.* Gifford Lectures, 1920. Oxford: Clarendon, 1921.

Fasola, Umberto. *Le Catacombe di S. Gennaro a Capodimonte.* Rome: Editalia, 1975.

Fichtner, Gerhard. "Christus als Arzt: Ursprünge und Wirkungen eines Motivs." *Frühmittelalterliche Studien* 16 (1982): 1–17.

Fink, Josef. *Bildfrommigkeit und Bekenntnis: Das Alte Testament, Herakles und die Herrlichkeit Christi an der Via Latina in Rom.* Cologne, 1978.

Finney, Paul Corby. "Antecedents of Byzantine Iconoclasm: Christian Evidence before Constantine." In *The Image and the Word*, edited by J. Gutmann, 27–47. Missoula, MT: Scholars, 1977.

———. "Did Gnostics Make Pictures?" In *The Rediscovery of Gnosticism*, edited by B. Layton, 434–54. *Numen Suppl.* 41.1, Leiden, 1980.

————. "Do You Think God Is a Magician?" in *Akten Des Symposiums Früchristliche Sarkophage*, Marburg: Deutches Archäologisches Institut (1999): 99–108.

————. "Gnosticism and the Origins of Early Christian Art." *CIAC. Atti* 9, no. 1 (1978): 391–405.

————. "Idols in Second and Third Century Apology." *Studia Patristica* 17, pt. 2 (1982): 684–87.

————. *The Invisible God: The Earliest Christians on Art.* New York: Oxford University Press, 1994.

————. *The Oldest Surviving Literary and Archaeological Evidence for Christian Attitudes toward Visual Arts.* Cambridge, MA: Harvard University Press, 1973.

Fox, Robin Lane. *Pagans and Christians.* San Francisco: Harper and Row, 1986.

Frede, Michael. "Origen's Treatise *Against Celsus.*" In *Apologetics in the Roman Empire: Pagans, Jews and Christians,* edited by Mark Edwards, Martin Goodman, and Simon Price. Oxford: Oxford University Press, 1999.

Freedberg, David. *The Power of Images.* Chicago: University of Chicago Press, 1989.

Frend, W. H. C. *Martyrdom and Persecution in the Early Church: A Study of a Conflict from the Maccabees to Donatus.* Grand Rapids, MI: Baker, 1981.

————. *Religion Popular and Unpopular in the Early Christian Centuries.* London: Variorum Reprints, 1976.

Frings, H. J. *Medizin und Arzt bei den griechischen Kirchenvätern bis Chrysostomos.* Bonn, 1959.

Gager, John G. *The Origins of Anti-Semitism: Attitudes Towards Judaism in Pagan and Christian Antiquity.* New York: Oxford University Press, 1983.

————. *Moses in Greco-Roman Paganism.* Nashville: Abingdon, 1972.

Gallagher, Eugene V. *Divine Man or Magician? Celsus and Origen on Jesus.* SBL Dissertation Series. Chico, CA: Scholars, 1982.

Gaventa, Beverly. *The Acts of the Apostles.* Nashville: Abingdon, 2003.

Gero, Stephen. "The True Image of Christ: Eusebius' Letter to Constantia Reconsidered." *Journal of Theological Studies* 32 (1981): 460–70.

Goodenough, E. R. "Catacomb Art." *JBL* 81, no. 2. (June 1962): 113–42.

————. *Jewish Symbols in the Greco-Roman Period.* Vol. I. New York: Pantheon, 1953–68.

————. *The Theology of Justin Martyr.* Jena: Frommann, 1923.

Gough, Michael. *The Origins of Early Christian Art.* London: Thames and Hudson, 1973.

Grabar, André. *The Beginnings of Christian Art, 200–395.* Thames and Hudson, 1966.

———. *Christian Iconography: A Study of its Origins.* Princeton, NJ: Princeton University Press, 1968.

Graf, Fritz. "Excluding the Charming: The Development of the Greek Concept of Magic." In *Ancient Magic and Ritual Power,* edited by Marvin W. Meyer and Paul Mirecki, 29–42. Leiden: Brill, 2001.

———. "How to Cope with a Difficult Life: A View of Ancient Magic." In *Envisioning Magic: A Princeton Seminar and Symposium,* edited by Peter Schäfer and Hans G. Kippenberg, 93–114. Leiden: Brill, 1997.

———. *Magic in the Ancient World.* Translated by Franklin Philip. Cambridge, MA: Harvard University Press, 1997.

Grant, Robert M. "The Chronology of the Greek Apologists." *Vigiliae Christianae* 9 (1955): 25–34.

———. *Greek Apologists of the Second Century.* Philadelphia: Westminster, 1988.

———. *Paul in the Roman World: The Conflict at Corinth.* Louisville: Westminster John Knox, 2001.

Gray, Patrick. "Athenian Curiosity: Acts 17:21." *Novum Testamentum* 47, no. 2 (April 2005): 109–16.

Gregory, Andrew. *The Reception of Luke and Acts in the Period before Irenaeus.* Tübingen: Mohr Siebeck, 2003.

Gregory of Nyssa. *St. Gregory Thaumaturgus: Life and Works.* Translated by Michael Slusser Fathers of the Church. Washington, DC: The Catholic University of America Press, 1998.

Gutmann, J. "Early Synagogue and Jewish Catacomb Art and Its Relation to Christian Art," *Aufstieg und Niedergang der römischen Welt* II.21.2 (1984): 1313–42.

———. "The Second Commandment and the Image in Judaism," *Hebrew Union College Annual* 32 (1961): 161–174.

Habicht, Christian. *Die Inschriften des Asklepeions.* Vol. 8, Part 3. Berlin: De Gruyter, 1969.

Hanson, J. W. "Dreams and Visions in the Graeco-Roman World and Early Christianity." *Aufstieg und Niedergang der römischen Welt* II.23.2 (1980): 1395–1427.

Hargis, Jeffrey. *Against the Christians: The Rise of Early Anti-Christian Polemic.* New York: Peter Lang, 1999.

Harnack, Adolf von. *Medizinisches aus der ältesten Kirchengeschichte.* Leipzig: 1892.

———. *Militia Christi: The Christian Religion and the Military in the First Three Centuries.* Translated and introduced by David McInnes Gracie. Philadelphia: Fortress Press, 1981.

———. *Die Mission und Ausbreitung des Christentums in den Ersten Drei Jahrhunderten.* Translated and edited by James Moffatt. New York: G. P. Putnam, 1908.

Hart, G. D. *Asclepius the God of Medicine.* London: Royal Society of Medicine Press, 2000.

Henderson, Ian H. "Apuleius of Madauros" in *The Historical Jesus in Context.* Edited by Amy-Jill Levine, Dale C. Allison Jr., and John Dominic Crossan: 193–205. Princeton, NJ: Princeton University Press, 2006.

Herzog, R. *Die Wunderheilungen von Epidauros.* Leipzig: Dieterich'sche Verlagsbuchhandlung, 1931.

Hill, Andrew E. "The Temple of Asclepius: An Alternative Source for Paul's Body Theology." *Journal of Biblical Literature* 99 (Spring 1980): 437–39.

Historia Augusta. *Life of Severus Alexander.* Translated by David Magie. Loeb Classical Library. Cambridge, MA: Harvard University Press, 1924.

Hoffmann, R. Joseph. *Celsus On True Doctrine.* New York: Oxford University Press, 1987.

———. *Julian's Against the Galileans.* Amherst, NY: Prometheus, 2004.

———. *Porphyry's Against the Christians: The Literary Remains.* Amherst, NY: Prometheus, 1994.

Holfmann, Adolf. "The Roman Remodeling of the Asklepieion." In *Pergamon: Citadel of the Gods,* edited by Helmut Koester, 41–61. Harrisburg, PA: Trinity Press International, 1998.

Hollander, E. *Askülap und Venus: Eine Kultur- und Sittengeschichte im Spiegel des Artzes.* Berlin, 1928.

Honecker, Martin. "Christus Medicus." *Kerygma und Dogma* 31, O-D (1985): 307–23.

Hausmann, Ulrich. *Kunst und Heiltum: Untersuchungen zu den griechischen Asklepiosreliefs.* Potsdam, 1948.

Jaeger, Wolfgang. *Die Heilung des Blinden in der Kunst.* Konstanz: 1960.

Jefferson, Lee M. "Is This Man a Physician, a Philosopher, or a God?: Revisiting the 'Anatomy Lesson' Catacomb Painting." *Sewanee Theological Review* 56, no. 2 (March 2013): 169–95.

———. "Perspectives on the Nude Youth in Fourth-Century Sarcophagi Representations of the Raising of Lazarus." *Studia Patristica* 59 (2013): 77–88.

————. "Picturing Theology: A Primer on Early Christian Art." *Religion Compass* 4, no. 7 (July 2010): 410–25.

————. "The Staff of Jesus in Early Christian Art." *Religion and the Arts* 14, no. 3 (2010): 221–51.

————. "Superstition and the Significance of the Image of Christ Performing Miracles in Early Christian Art," 15–20. *Studia Patristica* vols. XLIV–XLIX. Leuven: Peeters, 2010.

Jensen, Robin M. *Baptismal Imagery in Early Christianity: Ritual, Visual and Theological Dimensions.* Grand Rapids, MI: Baker Academic, 2012.

————. "The Economy of the Trinity at the Creation of Adam and Eve." *Journal of Early Christian Studies* 7, no. 4 (1999): 527–46.

————. "The Emperor Cult and Christian Iconography." In *Rome and* Religion, 153–71. Atlanta: SBL, 2011.

————. *Face to Face: Portraits of the Divine in Early Christianity.* Minneapolis: Fortress Press, 2005.

————. "Moses Imagery in Jewish and Christian Art: Problems of Continuity and Particularity." *Society of Biblical Literature Seminar Papers* (1992): 389–418.

————. *The Substance of Things Seen: Art, Faith, and the Christian Community.* Grand Rapids, MI: Eerdmans, 2004.

————. *Understanding Early Christian Art.* New York: Routledge, 2000.

John of Damascus. *Selected Writings.* Translated by Frederic H. Chase Jr. Fathers of the Church. Washington, DC: Catholic University of America Press, 1958.

Josi, Enrico. "Découverte d'une série de peintures dans un hypogée de la voie Latine." *Comptes rendus de l'Academie des Inscriptions et Belles-Lettres* (1956): 275–79.

Justin Martyr. *The First and Second Apologies.* Translated by Leslie William Barnard. Ancient Christian Writers. New York: Paulist, 1997.

————. *Dialogue.* Translated by Thomas B. Falls. Washington, DC: Catholic University of America Press, 2003.

Karivieri, Arja. "The Christianization of an Ancient Pilgrimage Site: A Case Study of the Athenian Asklepion." In *Akten des XII Internationalen Kongresses für Christliche Archäologie*, 898–905. Vol. 2. Munster, Ger.: Aschendorff, 1995.

Kee, Howard Clark. *Good News to the Ends of the Earth: The Theology of Acts.* Philadelphia: Trinity Press International, 1990.

————. *Medicine, Miracle, and Magic in New Testament Times.* New York: Cambridge University Press, 1986.

———. *Miracle in the Early Christian World*. New Haven: Yale University Press, 1983.

Keenan, Mary Emily. "Augustine and the Medical Profession." *Transactions and Proceedings of the American Philological Association* vol. 67 (1936): 168–90.

Keim, Theodor. *Celsus Wahres Wort*. Zurich, 1873.

Kelhoffer, James A. *Miracle and Mission: The Authentication of Missionaries and Their Message in the Longer Ending of Mark*. Tübingen: Mohr Siebeck, 2000.

Kelly, David Martin. *Seeing the Face of God: A Thematic Exploration of the Vision of God in the Spirituality of St. Augustine*. Ann Arbor, MI: UMI Dissertation Services, 2003.

Kerényi, C. *Asklepios: Archetypal Images of the Physician's Existence*. New York: Pantheon, 1959.

Kessler, Herbert L. "Scenes from the Acts of the Apostles on Some Early Christian Ivories." *Gesta* 18, no. 1 (November 1977–Februrary 1978): 109–19.

———. *Seeing Medieval Art*. Orchard Park, NY: Broadview, 2004.

———. *Spiritual Seeing: Picturing God's Invisibility in Medieval Art*. Philadelphia: University of Pennsylvania Press, 2000.

———, and Kurt Weitzmann. *The Frescoes of the Dura Synagogue and Christian Art*. Washington, DC: Dumbarton Oaks Research Library and Collection, 1990.

———, and Gerhard Wolf, eds. *The Holy Face and the Paradox of Representation*. Bologna: Nuova Alfa, 1998.

Keuls, E. *Plato and Greek Painting*. Leiden: Brill, 1978.

Kitzinger, Ernst. *The Art of Byzantium and the Medieval West: Selected Studies*. Bloomington: Indiana University Press, 1976.

———. "The Cult of Images before Iconoclasm." *Dumbarton Oaks Papers* no. 8 (1954): 85–150.

Kleiner, Diana E. E. *Roman Imperial Funerary Altars with Portraits*. Rome: G. Breitschneider, 1987.

———. *Roman Sculpture*. New Haven: Yale University Press, 1992.

Klinger, Jerzy. "Bethesda and the Universality of the Logos." *St. Vladimir's Theological Quarterly* 27, no. 3 (1983): 169–85.

Knipp, David. *"Christus Medicus" in Der Frühchristlichen Sarkophagskulptur: Ikonographische Studien Der Sepulkralkunst Des Späten Vierten Jahrhunderts*. Leiden: Brill, 1998.

Koch, G., and H. Sichtermann. *Römische Sarkophage* (Handbuch der Archäologie). Munich, 1982.

Kollmann, Bernd. *Jesus und die Christen als Wundertäter: Studien zu Magie, Medizin und Schamanismus in Antike und Christentum.* Göttingen: Vandenhoeck and Ruprecht, 1996.

Koortbojian, Michael. *Myth, Meaning and Memory on Roman Sarcophagi.* Berkeley: University of California Press, 1995.

Kraye, Jill. "Hermetica: The Greek 'Corpus Hermeticum' and the Latin 'Asclepius'." *Journal of the History of Philosophy* 34, issue 4 (October 1996): 608–11.

Kuhn, Walther. *Frühchristliche Kunst aus Rom.* Essen: Villa Hügel, 1962.

Kümmel, W. G. *The New Testament: The History of Investigation of its Problems,* Translated by S. McLean Gilmour and Howard Clark Kee. London: SCM, 1973.

Ladner, Gerhart B. *Handbuch der früchristlichen Symbolik.* Stuttgart und Zürich: 1992.

Lampe, G. W. H. *Essays on Typology.* Naperville, IL: A. R. Allenson, 1957.

Lang, Mabel. *Cure and Cult in Ancient Corinth: A Guide to the Asklepieion.* Princeton, NJ: American School of Classical Studies at Athens, 1977.

Lawrence, Marion. *The Sarcophagi of Ravenna.* New York: College Art Association of America, 1945.

Libanius. *Selected Works.* Translated by A.F. Norman. Loeb Classical Library. Cambridge, MA: Harvard University Press, 1987.

LiDonnici, L. R. *The Epidaurian Miracle Inscriptions: Text, Translation, and Commentary.* Atlanta: Scholars, 1995.

Lowden, John. *Early Christian and Byzantine Art.* New York: Phaidon, 1997.

Lucian. Translated by A. M. Harmon. Loeb Classical Library. Cambridge, MA: Harvard University Press, 1936.

Lüdemann, Gerd. *Early Christianity according to the Traditions in Acts.* Minneapolis: Fortress Press, 1987.

MacMullen, Ramsay. *Christianity and Paganism in the Fourth to Eighth Centuries.* New Haven: Yale University Press, 1997.

———. *Christianizing the Roman Empire (A.D. 100–400).* New Haven: Yale University Press, 1984.

———. "Conversion: A Historian's View." *Second Century* 5, no. 2 (1985/1986): 67–81.

———, ed. *Paganism and Christianity, 100–425 C.E.: A Sourcebook.* Minneapolis: Fortress Press, 1992.

Mackie, Gillian Vallance. *Early Christian Chapels in the West: Decoration, Function, and Patronage.* Toronto: University of Toronto Press, 2003.

Maguire, Henry, and Eunice Dauterman Maguire. *Art and Holy Powers in the Early Christian House.* Chicago: University of Illinois Press, 1989.

Malbon, Elizabeth Struthers. *The Iconography of the Sarcophagus of Junius Bassus.* Princeton, NJ: Princeton University Press, 1990.

Malley, William J. *Hellenism and Christianity: The Conflict Between Hellenic and Christian Wisdom in the Contra Galileos of Julian the Apostate and the Contra Julianum of St. Cyril of Alexandria.* Rome: Università Gregoriana Editrice, 1978.

Mango, Cyril. *The Art of the Byzantine Empire 312–1453.* Toronto: University of Toronto Press, 1986.

Marcus Aurelius, *Meditations.* Translated by Georgy Long. Amherst, NY: Prometheus, 1991.

Markus, Robert. *Christianity in the Roman World.* London: Thames and Hudson, 1974.

———. *The End of Ancient Christianity.* Cambridge: Cambridge University Press, 1990.

Mathews, Thomas. *The Clash of Gods.* Princeton, NJ: Princeton University Press, 1993.

McCasland, S. Vernon. "The Asklepios Cult in Palestine." *Journal of Biblical Literature* 58, no. 3 (1939): 221–27.

McGinn, Thomas A. J. *Prostitution, Sexuality, and the Law in Ancient Rome.* New York: Oxford University Press, 1998.

McLynn, Neil B. *Ambrose of Milan: Church and Court in a Christian Capital.* Berkeley: University of California Press, 1994.

Merideth, Anne Elizabeth. *Illness and Healing in the Early Christian East.* Ann Arbor, MI: UMI Dissertation Services, 1999.

Miller, Patricia Cox. *Dreams in Late Antiquity: Studies in the Imagination of a Culture.* Princeton, NJ: Princeton University Press, 1994.

Milne, J. Grafton. "The *Kline* of Sarapis." *Journal of Egyptian Archaeology* 11, no. 1/2 (April 1925): 6–9.

Moellering, H. Armin. "*Deisidaimonia*: A Footnote to Acts 17:22." *Concordia Theological Monthly* 34 (1963): 466–71.

———. *Plutarch on Superstition.* Boston: Christopher, 1962.

Momigliano, Arnaldo, ed. *The Conflict between Paganism and Christianity in the Fourth Century.* Oxford: Clarendon, 1963.

———. *On Pagans, Jews, and Christians.* Middletown, CT: Wesleyan University Press, 1987.

Morey, C. R. *Christian Art.* New York: W. W. Norton, 1935.

Muir, Steven C. "Touched By a God: Aelius Aristides, Religious Healings, and Asclepius Cults." In *Society of Biblical Literature Seminar Papers.* Vol. 34. Atlanta: Scholars, 1995.

Murray, Mary Charles. "Art and the Early Church." *Journal of Theological Studies* 2 (1977): 303–45.

———. "The Christian Orpheus." *Cahiers Archéologiques* 23 (1974): 19–27.

———. *Rebirth and Afterlife: A Study of the Transmutation of Some Pagan Imagery in Early Christian Funerary Art.* Oxford: BAR International Series, 1981.

Neusner, Jacob, ed. *Religion, Science, and Magic: In Concert and in Conflict.* New York: Oxford University Press, 1989.

Nock, A. D. *Conversion: The Old and the New in Religion from Alexander the Great to Augustine of Hippo.* Oxford: Oxford University Press, 1933.

Nutton, Vivian. *Ancient Medicine.* New York: Routledge, 2004.

———. "From Galen to Alexander, Aspects of Medicine and Medical Practice in Late Antiquity," in *Dumbarton Oaks Papers* 38, Washington, DC: Dumbarton Oaks Research Library and Collection, 1985.

———. "Murders and Miracles: Lay Attitudes towards Medicine in Classical Antiquity," in *Patients and Practitioners: Lay Perceptions of Medicine in Pre-Industrial Society.* Edited by Roy Porter: 23–53. New York: Cambridge University Press, 1985.

Origen. *Contra Celsum.* Translated by Henry Chadwick. Cambridge: Cambridge University Press, 1965.

———. *Homilies on Joshua.* Translated by Barbara J. Bruce. Fathers of the Church. Washington, DC: Catholic University of America Press, 2002.

———. *Homilies on Levitius 1-16.* Translated by Gary Wayne Barkley. Fathers of the Church. Washington DC: Catholic University of America Press, 1990.

Ovid. *Metamorphoses.* Translated by A.D. Melville. With an introduction and notes by E.J. Kenney. Oxford: Oxford University Press, 1987.

Paton, W. R., trans. *The Greek Anthology.* Loeb Classical Library. New York: Putnam, 1916–18.

Pausanias. *Description of Greece.* Translated by W. H. S. Jones. Loeb Classical Library. Cambridge, MA: Harvard University Press, 1918.

Pease, Arthur Stanley. "Medical Allusions in the Works of St. Jerome." *Harvard Studies in Classical Philology* 25 (1914): 73–86.

Pettis, Jeffrey. "Earth, Dream, and Healing: The Integration of *Materia* and Psyche in the Ancient World." *Journal of Religion and Health* 45, no. 1 (April 2006): 113–29.

———. *The Sleeper's Dream: Asclepius Ritual and Early Christian Discourse*. Ann Arbor, MI: UMI Dissertation Services, 2004.

Philostratus. *Life of Apollonius*. Translated by F. C. Conybeare. Loeb Classical Library. Cambridge, MA: Harvard University Press, 1989.

Phillips, Charles Roberts. "Religious Fraud in the Roman Empire: Alexander and Others." *SBL Seminar Papers* 22 (1983): 333–35.

Pilch, John J. "Sickness and Healing in Luke–Acts." In *The Social World of Luke–Acts*, edited by Jerome H. Neyrey. Peabody, MA: Hendrickson, 1991.

Plotinus. *Enneads*. Translated by A. H. Armstrong. Loeb Classical Library. Cambridge, MA: Harvard University Press, 1966.

Plutarch. *Moralia*. Translated by Frank Cole Babbitt. Loeb Classical Library. Cambridge, MA: Harvard University Press, 1927– .

Porterfield, Amanda. *Healing in the History of Christianity*. New York: Oxford University Press, 2005.

Prudentius. Translated by H. J. Thompson. Loeb Classical Library. Cambridge, MA: Harvard University Press, 1949.

Remus, Harold. *Pagan-Christian Conflict over Miracle in the Second Century*. Cambridge, MA: Philadelphia Patristic Foundation, 1983.

Richardson, Peter. *Building Jewish in the Roman East*. Waco, TX: Baylor University Press, 2004.

Richmond, I. A. *Archaeology, and the After-Life in Pagan and Christian Imagery*. London: Oxford University Press, 1950.

Riess, Ernst. "On Ancient Superstition." In *Transactions of the American Philological Association*, 40–55. Vol. 26. (1869–1896) vol. 26 (1895). Baltimore: John Hopkins University Press.

Roebuck, Carl. "The Asklepieion and Lerna." In *Corinth*. Vol. 14. Princeton, NJ: American School of Classical Studies at Athens, 1951.

Roller, T. *Les catacombs de Rome: histoire de l'art et des croyances religieuses pendant les premiers siècles du Christianisme*. Paris, 1881.

Rose, Charles Brian. *Dynastic Commemoration and Imperial Portraiture in the Julio-Claudian Period*. Cambridge: Cambridge University Press, 1997.

Rosenthal, Franz. "An Ancient Commentary on the Hippocratic Oath." *Bulletin of the History of Medicine* 30 (1956): 52–87.

Rüttimann, René Josef. *Asclepius and Jesus: The Form, Character and Status of the Asclepius Cult in the Second Century CE and its Influence on Early* Christianity. Ann Arbor, MI: UMI Dissertation Services, 1987.

Salzman, Michele R. "'Superstitio' in the Codex Theodosianus and the Persecution of the Pagans." *Vigliae Christianae* 41, no. 2 (June 1987): 172–88.

Saradi-Mendelovici, Helen. "Christian Attitudes toward Pagan Monuments in Late Antiquity and Their Legacy in Later Byzantine Centuries." *Dumbarton Oaks Paper* 44 (1990): 47–61.

Scarborough, John. *Roman Medicine*. Ithaca, NY: Cornell University Press, 1969.

Schaff, Philip, ed. *Select Library of Nicene and Post-Nicene Fathers of the Christian Church*, Series 1. 1886–1889, 14 vols. Peabody, MA: Hendrickson, 1994.

———, ed. *Select Library of Nicene and Post-Nicene Fathers of the Christian Church*, Series 2. 1890–1900, 14 vols. Peabody, MA: Hendrickson, 1994.

Schauenburg, K. "Porträts auf römischen Sarkophagen," 153–59. In *EIKONES: Festschrift für Hans Jucker*. Basle: 1980.

Schlam, C. *Cupid and Psyche: Apuleius and the Monuments*. University Park, PA: 1976.

Schneemelcher, Wilhelm, ed. *New Testament Apocrypha*. London: SCM, 1963–65.

Schüssler Fiorenza, Elizabeth, ed. *Aspects of Religious Propaganda in Judaism and Early Christianity*. Notre Dame, IN: University of Notre Dame Press, 1976.

Sichtermann, H., and G. Koch. *Griechische Mythen auf römischen Sarkophagen*. Tübingen: 1975.

Smith, Jonathan Z. "Trading Places." In *Ancient Magic and Ritual Power*, edited by Marvin W. Meyer and Paul Mirecki. Leiden: Brill, 2001.

Smith, Morton. *Jesus the Magician*. San Francisco: Harper & Row, 1978.

———. "Superstitio." *Society of Biblical Literature Seminar Papers* 20, (1981): 349–5.

———. "De Superstitione." In *Plutarch's Theological Writings and Early Christian Literature,* edited by Hans Dieter Betz. Leiden: Brill, 1975.

Smith, Rowland. *Julian's Gods: Religion and Philosophy in the Thought and Action of Julian the Apostate*. London: Routledge, 1995.

Snyder, Graydon F. *Ante Pacem: Archaeological Evidence of Church Life Before Constantine*. Macon, GA: Mercer University Press, 2003.

Spier, Jeffrey, ed. *Picturing the Bible: The Earliest Christian Art*. New Haven: Yale University Press, 2007.

Stancliffe, Clare. *St. Martin and His Hagiographer: History and Miracle in Sulpicius Severus*. New York: Oxford University Press, 1983.

Staniforth, Maxwell, trans. *Early Christian Writings: The Apostolic Fathers*. London: Penguin, 1968.

Stevenson, James. *The Catacombs: Rediscovered Monuments of Early Christianity*. London: Thames and Hudson, 1978.

Sumption, Jonathan. *Pilgrimage: An Image of Medieval Religion*. London: Faber and Faber, 1975.

Swain, Simon. "Defending Hellenism: Philostratus, In Honour of Apollonius." In *Apologetics in the Roman Empire: Pagans, Jews and Christians*, edited by Mark Edwards, Martin Goodman, and Simon Price, 157–196. Oxford: Oxford University Press, 1999.

Swift, Louis J. "Arnobius and Lactantius: Two Views of the Pagan Poets," *Transactions and Proceedings of the American Philological Association* 96 (1965): 439–48.

Tertullian. *Apology*. Translated by Gerald Rendall. Loeb Classical Library. Cambridge, MA: 1931.

———. *On the Shows*. Translated by T. R. Glover. Loeb Classical Library. Cambridge, MA, 1931.

TeSelle, Eugene. *Augustine the Theologian*. New York: Herder and Herder, 1970.

———. "Porphyry and Augustine." *Augustinian Studies* 5 (1974): 113–47.

Theissen, Gerd. *The Miracle Stories of the Early Christian Tradition*. Translated by Francis McDonagh. Philadelphia: Fortress Press, 1974.

Thomas, Christine M. *The Acts of Peter, Gospel Literature, and the Ancient Novel: Rewriting the Past*. New York: Oxford University Press, 2003.

Thorndike, Lynn. *A History of Magic and Experimental Science*. Vol. 1. New York: Macmillan, 1923–58.

Tkacz, Catherine Brown. *The Key to the Brescia Casket: Typology and the Early Christian Imagination*. Paris: University of Notre Dame Press; Institut d'Etudes Augustiennes, 2001.

Tronzo, William. *The Via Latina Catacomb: Imitation and Discontinuity in Fourth-Century Roman Painting*. University Park: Pennsylvania State University Press, 1986.

Trout, Dennis. "Damasus and the Invention of Early Christian Rome." *Journal of Medieval and Early Modern Studies* 33, no. 3 (2003): 517–36.

Twelftree, Graham H. *Jesus the Exorcist*. Tübingen: Mohr Siebeck, 1993.

Van Dam, Raymond. "Hagiography and History: The Life of Gregory Thaumaturgus." *Classical Antiquity* 1/2 (1982): 274–308.

———. *Saints and Their Miracles in Late Antique Gaul*. Princeton, NJ: Princeton University Press, 1993.

Van den Hoek, A., and J. J. Herrmann. "Celsus' Competing Heroes: Jonah, Daniel, and their Rivals." In *Poussières de christianisme et de judaïsme antiques*, edited by Albert Frey and Remi Gounelle, 307–39. Lausanne: Éditions du Zèbre, 2007.

Van Straten, F. T. "Gifts for the Gods." In *Faith, Hope and Worship: Aspects of Religious Mentality in the Ancient World*. Leiden: Brill, 1981.

Vermès, Géza. *Jesus the Jew*. London: Collins, 1973.

Vikan, Gary. "Art, Medicine, and Magic in Early Byzantium." In *Dumbarton Oaks Papers*. Vol. 38. Washington, DC: Dumbarton Oaks Research Library and Collection, 1985.

———. *Sacred Images and Sacred Power in Byzantium*. Burlington, VT: Ashgate, 2003.

Volbach, W. F. *Early Christian Mosaics: From the Fourth to the Seventh Centuries*. New York: Oxford University Press, 1946.

———. *Frühchristliche Kunst*. München: 1958.

Von Simson, Otto. *Sacred Fortress: Byzantine Art and Statecraft in Ravenna*. Chicago: University of Chicago Press, 1948.

Walzer, Richard. *Galen on Jews and Christians*. London: Oxford University Press, 1949.

Weiss, Charles Gray. *Literary Turns: The Representation of Conversion in Aelius Aristides' Hieroi Logoi and Apuleius' Metamorphoses*. Ann Arbor, MI: UMI Dissertation Services, 1998.

Weitzmann, Kurt. *The Icon: Holy Images—Sixth to Fourteenth Century*. New York: George Braziller, 1978.

Wharton, Annabel Jane. "The Baptistery of the Holy Sepulcher in Jerusalem and the Politics of Sacred Landscape." In *Dumbarton Oaks Papers*. Vol. 46. Washington, DC: Dumbarton Oaks Center for Byzantine Studies, 1992.

———. *Refiguring the Post-Classical City: Dura Europos, Jerash, Jerusalem, and Ravenna*. New York: Cambridge University Press, 1995.

White, L. Michael. "Adolf Harnack and the 'Expansion' of Early Christianity: A Reappraisal of Social History." *Second Century* 5, no. 2 (1985/1986): 97–127.

Wilken, Robert Louis. *The Christians As the Romans Saw Them*. New Haven: Yale University Press, 2003.

———. *The Spirit of Early Christian Thought*. New Haven: Yale University Press, 2003.

Willoughby, Edwin Eliott. "The Role of Hercules in the Resurrection of Alcestis." *The Classical Journal* 22, no. 5 (February 1927): 380–82.

Wilpert, Josef. *Die Malereien der Katakomben Roms*. Freiburg im Breisgau, 1903.

———. *I Sarcophagi cristiani antichi*. Rome: Pontificio istituto di archaeologica cristiana, 1929.

Wilson, Stephen G. *Leaving the Fold: Apostates and Defectors in Antiquity.* Minneapolis: Fortress Press, 2004.

Witherington, Ben. *The Acts of the Apostles, Vol. III.* Grand Rapids, MI: Eerdmans, 1998.

Wickkiser, Bronwen Lara. *The Appeal of Asklepios and the Politics of Healing in the Greco-Roman World.* Ann Arbor, MI: UMI Dissertation Services, 2003.

Wolmarans, Johannes. "Asclepius of Epidaurus and Jesus of Nazareth." *Acta Patristica et Byzantina* 7 (1996): 117–27.

Wright, William Cave, trans. *Julian.* Loeb Classical Library. Cambridge, MA: Harvard University Press, 1923.

Zanker, Paul. *The Mask of Socrates.* Berkeley: University of California Press, 1995.

———. *The Power of Images in the Age of Augustus.* Ann Arbor, MI: University of Michigan Press, 1988.

Index